Instant Pot Cookbook for Beginners

550 Easy, Healthy and Delicious Recipes That'll Save You So Much Time

Dave Pine

Table of contents

Introduction

Cooking might be a difficult task these days. We don't have enough time, we don't have the knowledge or the right tools. All these can stop today! You can forget about spending long hours in the kitchen, about using pans and pots. You only need one simple kitchen appliance: the instant pot.

The instant pot is such an original tool that allows you to cook great and tasty dishes in a matter of minutes. You can cook succulents, flavored and textured meals for all your loved ones and the best thing is that you don't need to be an expert in the kitchen. You just have to follow the directions and of course, to get the right ingredients.

The instant pot has so many fans all over the world and it has become such a useful tool.
The recipes collection we bring to you today is meant to help you get used to your instant pot. This cooking guide shows you how to cook the best instant pot breakfast recipes, side dishes, soups, stews, appetizers, poultry dishes, meat and seafood ones but also pasta recipes, veggie ones and of course desserts.

The instant pot will become your new best friend in the kitchen! It will show you that cooking can be so much fun and a lot easier than you thought.

So, what are you still waiting for? You have to get your hands on a copy of this great instant pot cooking guide right away. Start cooking with your new instant pot today and enjoy some of the best dishes ever.
Have fun cooking and enjoy this amazing culinary trip you are about to start!

Instant Pot Breakfast Recipes
Squash Porridge
Preparation time: 10 minutes *Cooking time:* 15 minutes *Servings:* 2

Ingredients:
- 3 tablespoons sunflower seeds
- 2 tablespoons coconut, shredded
- 1 teaspoon ginger powder
- ½ teaspoon cinnamon powder
- ½ cup coconut water
- 1 tablespoons chia seeds
- 1 cup squash, cooked, peeled and blended
- 1 tablespoon coconut oil, melted
- 1/3 cup water
- 2 teaspoons raw honey

Directions:
Set the instant pot on Sauté mode, add the oil, heat it up, add the seeds, coconut, ginger, cinnamon, chia and the squash and sauté for 5 minutes. Add the rest of the ingredients, toss, put the lid on and cook on High for 10 minutes. Release the pressure naturally for 10 minutes, divide the porridge into bowls and serve.

Nutrition: calories 331, fat 17.7, fiber 8.7, carbs 43.1, protein 7

Barley Bowls
Preparation time: 10 minutes *Cooking time:* 25 minutes *Servings:* 4

Ingredients:
- 1 tablespoon olive oil
- 1 cup pearl barley
- ¼ cup red onion, chopped
- 2 cups veggie stock
- 2 cups water
- 4 ounces baby kale
- 4 ounces turkey ham, chopped
- 4 eggs, hard boiled, peeled and halved
- A pinch of salt and black pepper

Directions:
Set the instant pot on Sauté mode, add the oil, heat it up, add the onion and the barley and sauté for 5 minutes. Add the rest of the ingredients except the eggs, toss, put the lid on and cook on High for 20 minutes. Release the pressure naturally for 10 minutes, divide the barley mix into bowls, top each serving with 2 egg halves and serve for breakfast.

Nutrition: calories 217, fat 10, fiber 5, carbs 15, protein 14

Quiche Lorraine

Preparation time: *10 minutes* **Cooking time:** *30 minutes* **Servings:** *4*

Ingredients:
- 2 cups Swiss cheese, shredded
- 8 bacon slices, chopped
- 1 yellow onion, chopped
- 8 eggs, whisked
- ½ teaspoon nutmeg, ground
- 1 and ½ cups heavy cream
- A pinch of salt and black pepper
- 1 cup water
- 1 tablespoon chives, chopped
- Cooking spray

Directions:
Set the instant pot on Sauté mode, add the bacon, stir and cook for 5 minutes. Add the onion, stir, sauté for 3 minutes more and transfer everything to a bowl. Grease a round baking pan with the cooking spray and arrange the bacon, eggs and half of the cheese inside. Add the eggs mixed with nutmeg, salt, pepper and the chives and sprinkle the remaining cheese on top. Put the water in the instant pot, add the trivet inside, add the pan into the machine, put the lid on and cook on High for 22 minutes. Release the pressure naturally for 10 minutes, slice the quiche, divide between plates and serve.

Nutrition: calories 223, fat 12, fiber 5, carbs 15, protein 5

Apple Oats

Preparation time: *10 minutes* **Cooking time:** *10 minutes* **Servings:** *4*

Ingredients:
- 4 cups water
- 2 cups steel cut oats
- 2 teaspoons raw honey
- 2 teaspoons cinnamon powder
- 2 apples, cored and cubed
- ¼ teaspoon nutmeg, ground

Directions:
In your instant pot, combine the oats with the water, the honey and the other ingredients, toss, put the lid on and cook on High for 10 minutes.
Release the pressure naturally for 10 minutes, divide the oats into bowls and serve for breakfast.

Nutrition: calories 371, fat 12, fiber 2, carbs 5, protein 5

Veggie and Eggs Burritos

Preparation time: *10 minutes* **Cooking time:** *30 minutes* **Servings:** *4*

Ingredients:
- 8 eggs, whisked
- ½ cup half and half
- A pinch of salt and black pepper
- ½ teaspoon garlic powder
- 2 tablespoons chives, chopped
- ¼ cup yellow onion, chopped
- 1 cup ham, chopped
- 1 cup cheddar cheese, shredded
- ½ cup red bell pepper, chopped
- 4 tortillas
- ½ cup water

Directions:
In a bowl, combine the eggs with the half and half, salt, pepper and the other ingredients except the tortillas and the water, whisk well and pour into a pan that fits the instant pot Put the water in the instant pot, add the trivet inside, add the pan with the eggs mix, cover it with tin foil, put the lid on and cook on High for 30 minutes Release the pressure naturally for 10 minutes, divide the eggs mix on each tortilla, wrap and serve for breakfast.

Nutrition: calories 367, fat 13, fiber 3, carbs 15, protein 12

Spinach Congee

Preparation time: *5 minutes* **Cooking time:** *15 minutes* **Servings:** *6*

Ingredients:
- 1 cup jasmine rice
- 2 chicken breasts, skinless, boneless and cubed
- 6 cups chicken stock
- A pinch of salt and black pepper
- 2 teaspoons ginger, grated
- 4 cups baby spinach
- 2 green onions, chopped
- 2 teaspoons sesame oil

Directions:
In your instant pot, combine the rice with the stock, the chicken and the other ingredients, toss, put the lid on and cook on High for 15 minutes. Release the pressure fast for 5 minutes, divide the congee into bowls and serve for breakfast.

Nutrition: calories 253, fat 4.9, fiber 2, carbs 26.4, protein 23.6

Baked Beans Bowls

Preparation time: 10 minutes **Cooking time:** *25 minutes* **Servings:** *4*

Ingredients:

- 1 and ½ cups cannellini beans, rinsed and drained
- 1 cup water
- 2 tablespoons olive oil
- 2 ounce shiitake mushrooms, sliced
- 1 yellow onion, chopped
- ½ red chili, minced
- A pinch of salt and black pepper
- 2 garlic cloves, minced
- 1 carrot, peeled and cubed
- 12 ounces canned tomato passata
- 1 tablespoon ketchup
- 1 tablespoon soy sauce
- 2 tablespoons brown sugar
- 1 teaspoon smoked paprika
- ½ teaspoon sweet paprika
- ½ teaspoon allspice, ground
- 2 bay leaves

Directions:

Set the instant pot on Sauté mode, add the oil, heat it up, add the mushrooms, onion, chili, garlic and the carrot and sauté for 5 minutes. Add the beans and the other ingredients, toss, put the lid on and cook on High for 20 minutes. Release the pressure naturally for 10 minutes, divide the beans into bowls and serve.

Nutrition: calories 342, fat 12, fiber 5, carbs 16, protein 15

Quinoa Bowls

Preparation time: 10 minutes **Cooking time:** *12 minutes* **Servings:** *6*

Ingredients:

- 1 and ½ cups quinoa
- 14 ounces coconut milk
- ¼ teaspoon maple syrup
- 1 teaspoon cinnamon powder
- 1 and ½ cups water
- 2 teaspoons vanilla extract
- 1 tablespoon coconut flakes
- ½ cup blackberries

Directions:

In the instant pot, combine the quinoa with the coconut milk, the maple syrup and the other ingredients, toss, put the lid on and cook on Low for 12 minutes. Release the pressure naturally for 10 minutes, divide the mix into bowls and serve.

Nutrition: calories 197, fat 2, fiber 3, carbs 36, protein 6

Tempeh Bowls

Preparation time: *10 minutes* ***Cooking time:*** *10 minutes* ***Servings:*** *4*

Ingredients:
- 29 ounces baby potatoes, peeled and cut into quarters
- 2 cups water
- 2 tablespoons maple syrup
- 1 teaspoon sriracha sauce
- 9 ounces tempeh, cubed
- 4 cups kale, chopped
- 2 tablespoons nutritional yeast
- 1 teaspoon garlic, minced
- 1 teaspoon smoked paprika
- A pinch of salt and black pepper

Directions:
Put the water in the instant pot, and add the trivet inside. Spread the potatoes on the bottom of a pan that fits the instant pot, add the maple syrup, sriracha sauce and the other ingredients, put the pan in the instant pot, put the lid on and cook on High for 10 minutes. Release the pressure naturally for 10 minutes, divide the tempeh bowls into bowls and serve for breakfast.

Nutrition: calories 438, fat 13, fiber 9, carbs 64, protein 26

Simple Buckwheat Porridge

Preparation time: *10 minutes* ***Cooking time:*** *15 minutes* ***Servings:*** *4*

Ingredients:
- 3 cups rice milk
- 1 cup buckwheat
- ¼ cup raisins
- 1 banana, peeled and sliced
- ½ teaspoon vanilla extract
- 1 teaspoon cinnamon powder
- 1 tablespoon walnuts, chopped

Directions:
In your instant pot, combine the buckwheat with the rice milk and the other ingredients, toss, put the lid on and cook on High for 15 minutes. Release the pressure naturally for 10 minutes, divide the buckwheat mix into bowls and serve.

Nutrition: calories 224, fat 12, fiber 5, carbs 15, protein 5

Eggs and Italian Sauce
Preparation time: *10 minutes* ***Cooking time:*** *12 minutes* ***Servings:*** *6*

Ingredients:
- 2 garlic cloves, minced
- 1 tablespoon coconut oil, melted
- 1 teaspoon chili powder
- 1 yellow onion, chopped
- 1 red bell pepper, chopped
- ½ teaspoon sweet paprika
- A pinch of salt and black pepper
- ½ teaspoon cumin, ground
- 1 and ½ cups marinara sauce
- 6 eggs
- 1 tablespoon parsley, chopped

Directions:
Set the instant pot on Sauté mode, add the oil, heat it up, add the onion, garlic, bell pepper, paprika, cumin, chili powder, salt and pepper and sauté for 5 minutes. Add the marinara sauce and sauté everything for 5 minutes more. Crack the eggs into the instant pot, put the lid on and cook everything on High for 2 minutes. Release the pressure naturally for 10 minutes, divide the eggs and sauce between plates, sprinkle the parsley on top and serve for breakfast.

Nutrition: calories 300, fat 12, fiber 6, carbs 16, protein 6

Sweet Potato Bowls
Preparation time: *10 minutes* ***Cooking time:*** *15 minutes* ***Servings:*** *2*

Ingredients:
- 2 sweet potatoes, peeled and cubed
- 4 eggs, whisked
- 1 avocado, peeled, pitted and cubed
- 1 tablespoon olive oil
- 2 spring onions, chopped
- A pinch of salt and black pepper
- 1 tablespoon cilantro, chopped

Directions:
Set the instant pot on Sauté mode, add the oil, heat it up, add the spring onions and the potatoes and sauté for 5 minutes. Add the eggs and the other ingredients, toss the mix, put the lid on and cook on High for 10 minutes. Release the pressure naturally fro 10 minutes, divide the mix into bowls and serve.

Nutrition: calories 424, fat 23, fiber 12, carbs 42, protein 15

Cinnamon Oatmeal

Preparation time: *5 minutes* **Cooking time:** *5 minutes* **Servings:** *4*

Ingredients:

- 4 cups cauliflower rice
- 2 cups almond milk
- 2 teaspoons cinnamon powder
- 4 tablespoons coconut sugar
- 1 teaspoon vanilla extract
- ½ teaspoon nutmeg
- 2 tablespoons tapioca starch
- 1 cup walnuts, chopped

Directions:

In your instant pot, combine the cauliflower rice with the milk and the other ingredients, toss, put the lid on and cook on High for 5 minutes. Release the pressure fast for 5 minutes, divide the oatmeal into bowls and serve for breakfast.

Nutrition: calories 305, fat 19, fiber 5, carbs 29, protein 8

Veggie and Sausage Casserole

Preparation time: *10 minutes* **Cooking time:** *15 minutes* **Servings:** *4*

Ingredients:

- 1 tablespoon olive oil
- ½ cup yellow onion, chopped
- ½ cup red bell pepper, chopped
- ½ pound pork sausage, chopped
- 2 garlic cloves, minced
- 6 eggs, whisked
- 1 sweet potato, peeled and cubed
- ½ teaspoon chili powder
- A pinch of salt and black pepper
- 1 cup water
- 1 tablespoon ghee, melted

Directions:

Set the instant pot on Sauté mode, add the oil, heat it up, add the onion, bell pepper, sausage, garlic, potato and chili powder, sauté for 5 minutes and transfer to a bowl. Add the eggs, salt and pepper over the veggie and sausage mix, and whisk the whole mixture. Grease a baking pan that fits the air fryer with the ghee and pour the eggs mix inside. Clean the instant pot, add the water, put the trivet inside, put the casserole into the machine, put the lid on and cook on High for 10 minutes. Release the pressure naturally for 10 minutes, divide the mix between plates and serve for breakfast.

Nutrition: calories 356, fat 29, fiber 2, carbs 3, protein 18

Potato and Peppers Bowls

Preparation time: *10 minutes* **Cooking time:** *25 minutes* **Servings:** *4*

Ingredients:
- 4 potatoes, peeled and cubed
- 1 cup veggie stock
- 2 tablespoons coconut oil, melted
- 1 tablespoon nutritional yeast
- 1 teaspoon onion powder
- 2 teaspoons garlic powder
- ¼ teaspoon sweet paprika
- A pinch of salt and black pepper
- 1 yellow onion, chopped
- 1 green bell pepper, chopped

Directions:
Set the instant pot on Sauté mode, add the oil, heat it up, add the onion, garlic and the potatoes and sauté for 5 minutes. Add the stock and the other ingredients, toss, put the lid on and cook on High for 20 minutes. Release the pressure naturally for 10 minutes, divide the mix into bowls and serve.

Nutrition: calories 203, fat 12, fiber 4, carbs 15, protein 4

Quinoa Bowls

Preparation time: *10 minutes* **Cooking time:** *1 minute* **Servings:** *6*

Ingredients:
- 1 and ½ cups quinoa
- 14 ounces coconut milk
- 1 and ½ cups water
- 2 tablespoons coconut sugar
- 2 teaspoons vanilla extract
- 1 teaspoon cinnamon powder
- 2 apples, cored and cubed

Directions:
In your instant pot, combine all the ingredients except the apples, toss, put the lid on and cook on High for 1 minute. Release the pressure naturally for 10 minutes, stir the quinoa, divide into bowls, sprinkle the apples on top and serve.

Nutrition: calories 200, fat 8, fiber 5, carbs 6, protein 10

Mushroom Bowls

*Preparation time: 10 minutes **Cooking time:** 25 minutes **Servings:** 4*

Ingredients:
- 1 cup coconut milk
- 10 eggs, whisked
- ½ cup cheddar cheese, grated
- A pinch of salt and black pepper
- 1 pound white mushrooms, sliced
- 2 cups spinach, chopped
- 1 cup shallots, chopped
- 2 tablespoons chives, chopped
- 1 tablespoon olive oil

Directions:
Set the instant pot on Sauté mode, add the oil, heat it up, add the shallots and the mushrooms and sauté for 10 minutes stirring often. Add the eggs mixed with the milk and the other ingredients except the chives, stir a bit, put the lid on and cook on High for 15 minutes. Release the pressure naturally for 10 minutes, divide the mix into bowls, sprinkle the chives on top and serve.

Nutrition: calories 200, fat 12, fiber 6, carbs 7, protein 9

Blackberries and Pears Bowls

*Preparation time: 5 minutes **Cooking time:** 15 minutes **Servings:** 4*

Ingredients:
- 1 and ½ cups almond milk
- ¼ cup coconut sugar
- 2 eggs, whisked
- 1 cup pears, cored and cubed
- 1 tablespoon walnuts, chopped
- 1 cup blackberries
- Cooking spray

Directions:
Grease the instant pot with the cooking spray and combine the berries with the pears and the other ingredients inside. Toss everything, put the lid on, cook on High for 15 minutes, release the pressure fast for 5 minutes, divide the mix into bowls and serve for breakfast.

Nutrition: calories 170, fat 10, fiber 4, carbs 7, protein 9

Creamy Eggs and Shallots

Preparation time: 10 minutes *Cooking time:* 15 minutes *Servings:* 4

Ingredients:

- 1 tablespoon olive oil
- ½ cup shallots, chopped
- 8 eggs, whisked
- 2 tablespoons chives, chopped
- 1 teaspoon chili powder
- 1 teaspoon cumin, ground
- 4 tablespoons heavy cream
- A pinch of salt and black pepper
- 1 cup water

Directions:

Set the instant pot on Sauté mode, add the oil, heat it up, add the shallots, chili powder and cumin, sauté for 5 minutes stirring often and transfer to a bowl. Add the eggs and the other ingredients except the water, whisk everything well and divide into 4 ramekins. Clean the instant pot, put the water inside, add the trivet inside, add the ramekins in the pot, put the lid on and cook on High for 10 minutes. Release the pressure naturally for 10 minutes and serve the eggs for breakfast.

Nutrition: calories 181, fat 11, fiber 2, carbs 6, protein 9

Cherry Muffins

Preparation time: 10 minutes *Cooking time:* 12 minutes *Servings:* 4

Ingredients:

- 2 eggs, whisked
- 1 and ½ cups almond milk
- 3 tablespoons coconut oil, melted
- 2 teaspoons vanilla extract
- 1 tablespoon cinnamon powder
- 1 cup almond flour
- ½ teaspoon baking soda
- 1 cup cherries, pitted and halved
- 1 cup water
- Cooking spray

Directions:

In a bowl, combine the eggs with the milk, the oil and the other ingredients except the water and the cooking spray, whisk well and divide into a muffin tin Add the water to the instant pot, put the racket in the pot, put the muffin tins inside, put the lid on and cook on High for 12 minutes. Release the pressure naturally for 10 minutes, divide the muffins between plates and serve for breakfast.

Nutrition: calories 188, fat 11, fiber 6, carbs 9, protein 7

Salsa Bowls

Preparation time: 10 minutes **Cooking time:** *20 minutes* **Servings:** *4*

Ingredients:

- 2 tablespoons olive oil
- 8 eggs, whisked
- A pinch of salt and black pepper
- ½ pound pork stew meat, ground
- ½ cup mild salsa
- ½ cup sour cream
- 1 avocado, peeled, pitted and cubed
- 1 tomato, cubed
- 1 zucchini, cubed
- ¼ cup green onions, chopped
- 1 tablespoon chives, chopped

Directions:

Set the instant pot on Sauté mode, add the oil, heat it up, add the green onions, stir and cook for 5 minutes. Add the meat and brown for 5 minutes more. Add the rest of the ingredients, toss, put the lid on and cook on High for 10 minutes. Release the pressure naturally for 10 minutes, divide the mix into bowls and serve for breakfast.

Nutrition: calories 200, fat 8, fiber 5, carbs 7, protein 11

Kale Eggs

Preparation time: 10 minutes **Cooking time:** *15 minutes* **Servings:** *4*

Ingredients:

- 2 tablespoons avocado oil
- ½ pound kale, torn
- 8 eggs, whisked
- 1 red onion, chopped
- 1 teaspoon sweet paprika
- 1 teaspoon chili powder
- A pinch of salt and black pepper
- ¼ cup heavy cream
- 2 tablespoons cheddar cheese, shredded

Directions:

Set the instant pot on Sauté mode, add the oil, heat it up, add the onion, paprika and chili powder and sauté for 5 minutes. Add the eggs and the other ingredients except the cheese, and stir. Sprinkle the cheese on top, put the lid on, and cook on High for 10 minutes. Release the pressure for 10 minutes, divide the mix between plates and serve for breakfast.

Nutrition: calories 200, fat 12, fiber 5, carbs 6, protein 8

Beans and Spinach Porridge

Preparation time: 10 minutes Cooking time: 20 minutes Servings: 4

Ingredients:
- ¼ cup black eye beans
- ¼ cup red beans
- ½ cup baby spinach
- 2 tablespoons olive oil
- 1 red onion, chopped
- ¼ cup tomato passata
- 2 cups veggie stock
- A pinch of salt and black pepper
- 1 teaspoon rosemary, dried
- 1 teaspoon cumin, ground
- 1 tablespoon cilantro, chopped

Directions:
Set the instant pot on Sauté mode, add the oil, heat it up, add the onion, rosemary and cumin and sauté for 5 minutes Add the beans and the other ingredients, toss, put the lid on and cook on High for 15 minutes Release the pressure naturally for 10 minutes, stir the porridge, divide into bowls and serve.

Nutrition: calories 180, fat 8, fiber 5, carbs 8, protein 6

Coconut Cocoa Oatmeal

Preparation time: 5 minutes Cooking time: 10 minutes Servings: 4

Ingredients:
- 2 tablespoons cocoa powder
- 2 cups coconut milk
- ½ cup heavy cream
- 1 cup coconut, unsweetened and shredded
- 1 teaspoon vanilla extract
- 2 tablespoons brown sugar

Directions:
In your instant pot, combine the coconut milk with the cream, the cocoa and the other ingredients, toss, put the lid on and cook on High for 10 minutes. Release the pressure fast for 5 minutes, divide the mix into bowls and serve for breakfast.

Nutrition: calories 173, fat 5, fiber 2, carbs 5, protein 5

Banana Coconut Mix

Preparation time: 10 minutes Cooking time: 10 minutes Servings: 4

Ingredients:
- 2 cups coconut milk
- 1/3 cup coconut, unsweetened and flaked
- 2 bananas, peeled and sliced
- ½ teaspoon coconut sugar
- ¼ teaspoon vanilla extract

Directions:
In your instant pot, combine the coconut with the coconut milk and the other ingredients, toss, put the lid on and cook on High for 10 minutes. Release the pressure naturally for 10 minutes, divide into bowls and serve for breakfast.

Nutrition: calories 167, fat 8, fiber 4, carbs 6, protein 10

Fruity Rice Pudding

Preparation time: 10 minutes Cooking time: 20 minutes Servings: 4

Ingredients:
- 2 cups white rice
- 4 cups coconut milk
- 1 tablespoon cinnamon powder
- 3 tablespoons brown sugar
- 1 apple, cored and cubed
- 1 pear, cored and cubed
- 1 mango, peeled and cubed
- 1 teaspoon vanilla extract

Directions:
In your instant pot, combine the rice with the milk, the cinnamon and the other ingredients, toss, put the lid on and cook on High for 20 minutes. Release the pressure naturally for 10 minutes, divide the pudding into bowls and serve for breakfast.

Nutrition: calories 180, fat 11, fiber 2, carbs 4, protein 7

Veggie Pudding

Preparation time: *10 minutes* ***Cooking time:*** *25 minutes* ***Servings:*** *8*

Ingredients:
- 1 cup water
- Cooking spray
- 2 tablespoons olive oil
- 1 cup red onion, chopped
- 1 cup white mushrooms, sliced
- 8 eggs, whisked
- 1 cup heavy cream
- ½ teaspoon rosemary, dried
- 1 teaspoon cumin, ground
- 1 teaspoon chili powder
- ½ teaspoon mustard powder
- Salt and black pepper to the taste
- 1 cup cheddar cheese, grated

Directions:
Set your instant pot on Sauté mode, add the oil, heat it up, add the onion and the mushrooms and sauté for 5 minutes. Add the rosemary, cumin, chili powder and the mustard powder, stir and cook for 5 minutes more. Transfer this to a bowl, add the eggs, cream, salt and pepper, whisk everything, transfer this to a baking pan greased with cooking spray and sprinkle the cheese on top. Put the water in the instant pot, add the trivet inside, put the baking pan into the pot, put the lid on and cook on High for 15 minutes. Release the pressure naturally for 10 minutes, divide the pudding between plates and serve for breakfast.

Nutrition: calories 201, fat 11, fiber 2, carbs 5, protein 10

Coffee and Mango Oatmeal

Preparation time: *10 minutes* ***Cooking time:*** *15 minutes* ***Servings:*** *4*

Ingredients:
- 3 cups almond milk
- 1 cup steel cut oats
- 2 tablespoons brown sugar
- ¼ cup brewed coffee
- 1 mango, peeled and cubed
- 2 teaspoons vanilla extract

Directions:
In your instant pot, combine the milk with the oats, the coffee and the other ingredients, toss, put the lid on and cook on High for 15 minutes. Release the pressure naturally for 10 minutes, divide the oatmeal into bowls and serve.

Nutrition: calories 200, fat 8, fiber 2, carbs 7, protein 10

Orange and Dates Salad

Preparation time: 5 minutes *Cooking time:* 5 minutes *Servings:* 4

Ingredients:
- 1 cup heavy cream
- 1 cup steel cut oats
- 1 cup orange juice
- 1 cup oranges, peeled and cut into segments
- 2 tablespoons brown sugar
- 1 cup dates, chopped
- 2 tablespoons pecans, chopped
- ¼ teaspoon vanilla extract

Directions:
In your instant pot, combine the oats with the orange juice, the cream and the other ingredients, toss, put the lid on and cook on High for 5 minutes. Release the pressure fast for 5 minutes, divide the mix into bowls and serve for breakfast.

Nutrition: calories 190, fat 4, fiber 2, carbs 8, protein 10

Zucchini Omelet

Preparation time: 10 minutes *Cooking time:* 20 minutes *Servings:* 4

Ingredients:
- 8 eggs, whisked
- A pinch of salt and black pepper
- ½ cup heavy cream
- 1 cup zucchinis, chopped
- 1 red onion, chopped
- ½ teaspoon chili powder
- 2 tablespoons olive oil
- 3 tablespoons cheddar cheese, shredded

Directions:
Set the instant pot on Sauté mode, add the oil, heat it up, add the onion and the chili powder and sauté for 5 minutes. Add the eggs and the other ingredients, toss and spread well, put the lid on and cook on High for 15 minutes. Release the pressure naturally for 10 minutes, divide the omelet between plates and serve.

Nutrition: calories 211, fat 12, fiber 5, carbs 6, protein 10

Avocado and Mango Yogurt

Preparation time: 5 minutes Cooking time: 10 minutes Servings: 4

Ingredients:
- 2 cups Greek yogurt
- 1 avocado, peeled, pitted and mashed
- 1 mango, peeled and cubed
- 2 teaspoons raw honey
- 1 tablespoon vanilla extract

Directions:
In your instant pot, combine the yogurt with the avocado and the other ingredients, stir, put the lid on and cook on Low for 10 minutes. Release the pressure fast for 5 minutes, divide into fruity yogurt into bowls and serve for breakfast.

Nutrition: calories 152, fat 4, fiber 3, carbs 6, protein 9

Figs and Avocado Bowls

Preparation time: 5 minutes Cooking time: 5 minutes Servings: 4

Ingredients:
- 1 cup figs, halved
- 1 cup avocado, peeled, pitted and cubed
- 3 teaspoons raw honey
- 2 cups heavy cream
- ½ teaspoon vanilla extract
- 1 cup coconut milk

Directions:
In your instant pot, combine the figs with the avocado, the honey and the other ingredients, toss, put the lid on and cook on Low for 5 minutes. Release the pressure fast for 5 minutes, divide into bowls and serve for breakfast.

Nutrition: calories 161, fat 7, fiber 3, carbs 5, protein 5

Black Tea Oatmeal

Preparation time: 10 minutes Cooking time: 15 minutes Servings: 4

Ingredients:
- 1 cup millet
- 2 tablespoons black tea powder
- 2 tablespoons brown sugar
- 2 cups almond milk
- ½ teaspoon ginger, grated
- ½ teaspoon vanilla extract

Directions:
In your instant pot, combine the millet with the green tea, the milk and the other ingredients, toss, put the lid on and cook on High for 15 minutes. Release the pressure naturally for 10 minutes, stir the mix, divide it into bowls and serve for breakfast.

Nutrition: calories 170, fat 6, fiber 4, carbs 8, protein 10

Rice Carrot Pudding

Preparation time: 10 minutes Cooking time: 15 minutes Servings: 4

Ingredients:
- 1 cup white rice
- 3 cups coconut milk
- 3 tablespoons brown sugar
- 1 teaspoon vanilla extract
- 1 teaspoon nutmeg, ground
- 1 cup carrots, grated

Directions:
In your instant pot, combine the rice with the milk, the sugar and the other ingredients, stir, put the lid on and cook on High for 15 minutes. Release the pressure naturally for 10 minutes, stir the pudding, divide into bowls and serve for breakfast.

Nutrition: calories 180, fat 5, fiber 5, carbs 7, protein 6

Lime Orange Bowls

Preparation time: *5 minutes* ***Cooking time:*** *5 minutes* ***Servings:*** *4*

Ingredients:
- 1 cup orange, peeled and cut into segments
- 2 tablespoons brown sugar
- 1 tablespoon orange juice
- 1 tablespoon orange zest, grated
- 1 cup coconut milk

Directions:
In your instant pot, combine the orange with the sugar and the other ingredients, put the lid on and cook on High for 5 minutes. Release the pressure fast for 5 minutes, divide everything into bowls and serve for breakfast.

Nutrition: calories 172, fat 5, fiber 4, carbs 7, protein 6

Creamy Broccoli Medley

Preparation time: *10 minutes* ***Cooking time:*** *15 minutes* ***Servings:*** *4*

Ingredients:
- 1 pound broccoli florets
- 2 tablespoons avocado oil
- 1 red onion, chopped
- 1 teaspoon turmeric powder
- ½ teaspoon smoked paprika
- 2 cups heavy cream
- 1 tablespoon ginger, grated
- 2 garlic cloves, minced
- 1 tablespoon chives, chopped

Directions:
Set the instant pot on Sauté mode, add the oil, heat it up, add the onion, turmeric, paprika, ginger and the garlic and sauté for 5 minutes. Add the broccoli and the other ingredients, toss, put the lid on and cook on High for 10 minutes. Release the pressure naturally for 10 minutes, divide into bowls and serve for breakfast.

Nutrition: calories 190, fat 7, fiber 2, carbs 5, protein 7

Olives and Rice Bowls

*Preparation time: 10 minutes **Cooking time:** 20 minutes **Servings:** 4*

Ingredients:
- 1 cup brown rice
- 2 cups chicken stock
- 1 yellow onion, chopped
- 1 tablespoon olive oil
- 1 cup kalamata olives, pitted and cubed
- 2 tablespoons mild salsa
- 1 tablespoon basil, chopped
- A pinch of salt and black pepper

Directions:
Set the instant pot on Sauté mode, add the oil, heat the it up, add the onion and sauté for 2 minutes. Add the rice and fry it for 3 minutes more. Add the rest of the ingredients, toss, put the lid on and cook on High for 15 minutes. Release the pressure naturally for 10 minutes, divide the mix into bowls and serve for breakfast.

Nutrition: calories 193, fat 6, fiber 3, carbs 6, protein 6

Warm Tomato Salad

*Preparation time: 10 minutes **Cooking time:** 12 minutes **Servings:** 4*

Ingredients:
- 1 pound cherry tomatoes, halved
- 1 avocado, peeled, pitted and cubed
- 1 cucumber, cubed
- 2 tablespoons avocado oil
- 1 tablespoon pine nuts, toasted
- 1 garlic clove, minced
- ½ teaspoon chili powder
- 1 red onion, chopped
- 1 tablespoon chives, chopped
- 2 tablespoons balsamic vinegar
- 2 tablespoons basil, chopped
- A pinch of salt and black pepper

Directions:
Set the instant pot on Sauté mode, add the oil, heat it up, add the garlic and the onion and sauté for 2 minutes. Add the tomatoes, avocado and the other ingredients, toss, put the lid on and cook on High for 10 minutes. Release the pressure naturally for 10 minutes, divide the salad into bowls and serve for breakfast.

Nutrition: calories 200, fat 12, fiber 2, carbs 5, protein 9

Potato and Eggs Salad

Preparation time: 10 minutes *Cooking time:* 15 minutes *Servings:* 4

Ingredients:
- 1 pound baby potatoes, peeled and halved
- 2 spring onions, chopped
- 4 eggs, hard boiled, peeled and cut into wedges
- 1 tablespoon rosemary, chopped
- 2 tablespoons olive oil
- 2 tablespoons balsamic vinegar
- A pinch of salt and black pepper
- 1 cup chicken stock

Directions:
In the instant pot, combine the potatoes with the stock, salt and pepper, toss, put the lid on and cook on High for 15 minutes. Release the pressure naturally for 10 minutes, transfer the potatoes to a bowl, add the spring onions, the eggs and the rest of the ingredients, toss and serve for breakfast.

Nutrition: calories 221, fat 6, fiber 4, carbs 7, protein 10

Berries Salad

Preparation time: 5 minutes *Cooking time:* 5 minutes *Servings:* 4

Ingredients:
- ½ cup heavy cream
- 3 teaspoons raw honey
- 1 cup blueberries
- 1 cup blackberries
- 1 cup strawberries, halved
- 1 avocado, peeled, pitted and cubed
- 1 teaspoon vanilla extract

Directions:
In your instant pot, combine the berries with the avocado and the other ingredients, toss, put the lid on and cook on High for 5 minutes. Release the pressure fast for 5 minutes, divide the mix into bowls and serve for breakfast.

Nutrition: calories 190, fat 7, fiber 4, carbs 7, protein 5

Walnuts Pudding

*Preparation time: 10 minutes **Cooking time:** 20 minutes **Servings:** 4*

Ingredients:
- 1 cup brown rice
- 2 cups almond milk
- ½ cup heavy cream
- 2 teaspoons vanilla extract
- ¼ cup walnuts, toasted and chopped
- 2 tablespoons brown sugar

Directions:
In your instant pot, combine the rice with the milk, the cream and the other ingredients, put the lid on and cook on High for 20 minutes. Release the pressure naturally for 10 minutes, stir the mix, divide into bowls and serve for breakfast,

Nutrition: calories 192, fat 6, fiber 3, carbs 6, protein 9

Buckwheat and Nuts Bowls

*Preparation time: 10 minutes **Cooking time:** 15 minutes **Servings:** 4*

Ingredients:
- 1 cup buckwheat
- 2 cups coconut milk
- 1 cup heavy cream
- 1 tablespoon walnuts, chopped
- 1 tablespoon almonds, chopped
- 2 tablespoons brown sugar
- 1 teaspoon cinnamon powder

Directions:
In your instant pot, combine the buckwheat with the cream and the other ingredients, toss, put the lid on and cook on High for 15 minutes. Release the pressure naturally for 10 minutes, toss, divide the mix into bowls and serve for breakfast.

Nutrition: calories 198, fat 7, fiber 5, carbs 7, protein 8

Cauliflower Frittata

Preparation time: 10 minutes *Cooking time:* 20 minutes *Servings:* 4

Ingredients:

- 1 cup cauliflower florets, chopped
- 1 red onion, chopped
- 1 teaspoon turmeric powder
- 1 teaspoon chili powder
- 1 tablespoon avocado oil
- 8 eggs, whisked
- ½ cup heavy cream
- A pinch of salt and black pepper
- 1 tablespoon chives, chopped
- 1 teaspoon hot paprika

Directions:

Set your instant pot on sauté mode, add the oil, heat it up, add the onion, turmeric, paprika and chili powder and sauté for 5 minutes. Add the eggs and the rest of the ingredients, toss, spread well into the pot, put the lid on and cook on High for 15 minutes. Release the pressure naturally for 10 minutes, divide the frittata between plates and serve.

Nutrition: calories 201, fat 9, fiber 4, carbs 7, protein 10

Basil Sausage Mix

Preparation time: 10 minutes *Cooking time:* 20 minutes *Servings:* 4

Ingredients:

- 2 tablespoons olive oil
- 1 yellow onion, chopped
- 2 garlic cloves, minced
- 1 pound sausage, chopped
- 1 cup cherry tomatoes, halved
- 1 zucchini, cubed
- A pinch of salt and black pepper
- 1 teaspoon cumin, ground
- 1 teaspoon fennel seeds, crushed
- 1 tablespoon basil, chopped
- ¼ cup chicken stock

Directions:

Set your instant pot on sauté mode, add the oil, heat it up, add the onion, and the garlic and sauté for 5 minutes. Add the sausage and brown for 5 minutes more. Add the rest of the ingredients, toss, put the lid on and cook on High for 10 minutes. Release the pressure naturally for 10 minutes, divide everything into bowls and serve.

Nutrition: calories 222, fat 13, fiber 4, carbs 7, protein 10

Bread Pudding

Preparation time: 10 minutes **Cooking time:** *25 minutes* **Servings:** *4*
Ingredients:
- 2 cups almond milk
- 3 eggs, whisked
- ½ cup coconut sugar
- 1 tablespoon orange juice
- Zest of 1 orange, grated
- Zest of 1 lime, grated
- 1 teaspoon nutmeg, ground
- 1 teaspoon vanilla extract
- 1 loaf bread, cubed
- 1 cup water

Directions:
In a pan that fits the instant pot, combine the milk with the bread, the eggs and the other ingredients except the water and toss gently. Put the water in the instant pot, put the trivet inside, add the pan in the pot, put the lid on and cook on High for 25 minutes. Release the pressure naturally, divide the mix into bowls and serve for breakfast.

Nutrition: calories 200, fat 7, fiber 5, carbs 7, protein 10

Broccoli Spread

Preparation time: 10 minutes **Cooking time:** *20 minutes* **Servings:** *4*
Ingredients:
- 1 cup heavy cream
- 2 cups broccoli florets
- 1 yellow onion, chopped
- 2 tablespoons olive oil
- A pinch of salt and black pepper
- 2 teaspoons sweet paprika
- 1 tablespoon lime juice
- 1 tablespoon tahini paste
- 1 tablespoon chives, chopped

Directions:
Set the instant pot on Sauté mode, add the oil, heat it up, add the onion and the paprika and sauté for 5 minutes. Add the broccoli and the other ingredients except the chives, toss, put the lid on and cook on High for 15 minutes. Release the pressure naturally for 10 minutes, transfer the mix to a blender, pulse well, divide into bowls, sprinkle the chives on top and serve for breakfast.

Nutrition: calories 200, fat 7, fiber 3, carbs 7, protein 10

Mushroom Salad

*Preparation time: 10 minutes **Cooking time:** 15 minutes **Servings:** 4*

Ingredients:
- 1 yellow onion, chopped
- 2 tablespoons olive oil
- 2 garlic cloves, minced
- 1 tablespoon rosemary, chopped
- 1 pound white mushrooms, halved
- 1 cup cherry tomatoes, halved
- 1 cup eggplant, roughly cubed
- 2 tablespoons lime juice
- Salt and black pepper to the taste

Directions:
Set your instant pot on sauté mode, add the oil, heat it up, add the onion, garlic and the mushrooms and sauté for 5 minutes. Add the rest of the ingredients, toss, put the lid on and cook on High for 15 minutes. Release the pressure naturally for 10 minutes, divide the mix into bowls and serve.

Nutrition: calories 221, fat 11, fiber 5, carbs 7, protein 8

Pomegranate Rice

*Preparation time: 10 minutes **Cooking time:** 25 minutes **Servings:** 4*

Ingredients:
- 1 cup brown rice
- ½ cup pomegranate seeds
- 2 cups almond milk
- 1 teaspoon vanilla extract
- 1 teaspoon cinnamon powder

Directions:
In your instant pot, combine the rice with the milk and the other ingredients, toss, put the lid on and cook on High for 25 minutes. Release the pressure naturally for 10 minutes, divide the rice mix into bowls and serve.

Nutrition: calories 180, fat 4, fiber 3, carbs 7, protein 10

Grapes Salad

Preparation time: 5 minutes *Cooking time:* 5 minutes *Servings:* 4

Ingredients:
- 1 cup grapes
- 1 avocado, peeled, pitted and cubed
- 1 mango, peeled and cubed
- 1 banana, peeled and sliced
- 2 teaspoons cinnamon powder
- 1 and ½ cups heavy cream

Directions:
In your instant pot, combine the grapes with the avocado, the mango and the other ingredients, toss, put the pressure lid on and cook on High for 5 minutes. Release the pressure fast for 5 minutes, divide the salad bowls and serve for breakfast.

Nutrition: calories 181, fat 11, fiber 4, carbs 7, protein 9

Nuts Bowls

Preparation time: 5 minutes *Cooking time:* 12 minutes *Servings:* 4

Ingredients:
- 1 cup quinoa
- ½ cup brown rice
- 4 cups almond milk
- ¼ cup walnuts, chopped
- ¼ cup pecans, chopped
- ¼ cup almonds, chopped
- 1 teaspoon nutmeg, ground
- 1 teaspoon vanilla extract
- 1 teaspoon cinnamon powder

Directions:
In your instant pot, combine the quinoa with the rice, the milk and the other ingredients, toss, put the lid on and cook on High for 12 minutes. Release the pressure fast for 5 minutes, stir the mix, divide into bowls and serve.

Nutrition: calories 200, fat 8, fiber 5, carbs 7, protein 9

Rice Salad

Preparation time: 10 minutes Cooking time: 20 minutes Servings: 4

Ingredients:
- 4 cups chicken stock
- 2 cups black rice
- ½ cup cherry tomatoes, halved
- 1 red onion, chopped
- ½ cup green beans, trimmed and halved
- 2 tablespoons olive oil
- A pinch of salt and black pepper
- 1 cup brown mushrooms, sliced
- 2 tablespoons parsley, chopped

Directions:
Set the instant pot on Sauté mode, add the oil, heat it up, add the onion and the mushrooms and sauté for 5 minutes. Add the rice and the remaining ingredients, toss, put the lid on and cook on High for 15 minutes. Release the pressure naturally for 10 minutes, divide the rice mix into bowls and serve for breakfast.

Nutrition: calories 181, fat 7, fiber 6, carbs 8, protein 11

Chickpeas Spread

Preparation time: 10 minutes Cooking time: 20 minutes Servings: 4

Ingredients:
- 1 cup canned chickpeas, drained and rinsed
- 1 and ½ cups veggie stock
- A pinch of salt and black pepper
- 1 teaspoon turmeric powder
- 1 teaspoon chili powder
- 1 tablespoon olive oil
- 1 tablespoon tahini paste
- 1 tablespoon lime juice
- 1 tablespoon chives, chopped

Directions:
In your instant pot, combine the chickpeas with the stock, salt, pepper, turmeric and chili powder, stir, put the lid on and cook on High for 20 minutes. Release the pressure naturally for 10 minutes, transfer the mix to a blender, add the rest of the ingredients, pulse well, divide into bowls and serve as a spread.

Nutrition: calories 171, fat 8, fiber 4, carbs 6, protein 8

Lentils Salad

*Preparation time: 5 minutes **Cooking time:** 20 minutes **Servings:** 4*

Ingredients:
- 2 cups canned lentils, drained and rinsed
- 2 tablespoons olive oil
- ¼ cup chicken stock
- 1 red onion, chopped
- 4 garlic cloves, minced
- 2 tablespoons lime juice
- 1 cup zucchinis, cubed
- 1 cup cherry tomatoes, halved
- ¼ teaspoon cumin, ground
- A pinch of salt and black pepper
- 1 tablespoon avocado oil
- ½ teaspoon sweet paprika
- ¼ cup chives, chopped

Directions:
Set the instant pot on Sauté mode, add the oil, heat it up, add the onion and the garlic and sauté for 5 minutes. Add the rest of the ingredients except the chives, toss, put the lid on and cook on High for 15 minutes. Release the pressure fast for 5 minutes, divide the salad into bowls and serve for breakfast.
Nutrition: calories 200, fat 12, fiber 3, carbs 5, protein 9

Tomato and Pork Bowls

*Preparation time: 10 minutes **Cooking time:** 20 minutes **Servings:** 4*

Ingredients:
- 1 cup cherry tomatoes, halved
- 1 pound pork stew meat, cubed
- 2 tablespoons olive oil
- 1 red onion, chopped
- 1 teaspoon rosemary, dried
- 1 teaspoon cumin, ground
- 1 teaspoon chili powder
- ½ cup beef stock
- A pinch of salt and black pepper
- 1 tablespoon oregano, chopped
- 1 tablespoon chives, chopped

Directions:
Set the instant pot on Sauté mode, add the onion and the meat and brown for 5 minutes. Add the tomatoes and the other ingredients, toss, put the lid on and cook on High for 15 minutes. Release the pressure naturally for 10 minutes, divide the mix into bowls and serve for breakfast.
Nutrition: calories 273, fat 13, fiber 3, carbs 6, protein 14

Sweet Potato and Nuts Mix

*Preparation time: 10 minutes **Cooking time:** 15 minutes **Servings:** 4*

Ingredients:
- 1 cup heavy cream
- 1 teaspoon nutmeg, ground
- 1 tablespoon almonds, chopped
- 1 tablespoon walnuts, chopped
- 1 tablespoon pecans, chopped
- 2 tablespoons brown sugar
- 4 sweet potatoes, peeled and cut into wedges

Directions:
In your instant pot, mix the sweet potatoes with the cream and the other ingredients, put the lid on and cook on High for 15 minutes. Release the pressure naturally for 10 minutes, divide the mix into bowls and serve for breakfast.

Nutrition: calories 200, fat 12, fiber 4, carbs 7, protein 8

Squash Salad

*Preparation time: 10 minutes **Cooking time:** 15 minutes **Servings:** 4*

Ingredients:
- 1 pound squash, peeled and roughly cubed
- 2 scallions, chopped
- 1 tablespoon avocado oil
- 1 tablespoon pumpkin seeds
- 1 tablespoon sunflower seeds
- ¼ cup veggie stock
- 2 tomatoes, cut into wedges
- ½ cup black olives, pitted and halved
- A pinch of salt and black pepper

Directions:
Set the instant pot on Sauté mode, add the oil, heat it up, add the scallions and the seeds and cook for 2 minutes. Add the squash and the other ingredients, toss, put the lid on and cook on High for 13 minutes. Release the pressure naturally for 10 minutes, divide the mix into bowls and serve.

Nutrition: calories 171, fat 11, fiber 5, carbs 9, protein 5

Cauliflower and Eggs Salad

Preparation time: 10 minutes *Cooking time:* 14 minutes *Servings:* 4

Ingredients:
- 2 cups cauliflower florets
- 4 eggs, hard boiled, peeled and cubed
- 1 and ½ cups water
- ½ cup heavy cream
- 2 tablespoons mayonnaise
- 4 scallions, chopped
- 1 tablespoon balsamic vinegar
- 2 tablespoons parsley, chopped
- Salt and black pepper to the taste

Directions:
Put the water in your instant pot, add steamer basket, add the broccoli florets inside, put the lid on and cook on High for 14 minutes. Release the pressure naturally for 10 minutes, transfer the broccoli to a bowl, add the eggs, cream and the other rest of the ingredients, toss and serve for breakfast.

Nutrition: calories 200, fat 11, fiber 4, carbs 7, protein 9

Potato and Sausage Mix

Preparation time: 10 minutes *Cooking time:* 20 minutes *Servings:* 4

Ingredients:
- 4 gold potatoes, peeled and roughly cubed
- ½ pound pork sausage, roughly chopped
- ½ cup tomato passata
- 1 red onion, chopped
- 2 tablespoons olive oil
- 2 teaspoons Italian seasoning
- 1 teaspoon sage, chopped
- 1 teaspoon rosemary, chopped
- 1 teaspoon hot paprika
- 1 teaspoon basil, chopped
- 1 tablespoon parsley, chopped
- A pinch of salt and black pepper

Directions:
Set the instant pot on Sauté mode, add the oil, heat it up, add the onion and the sausage and brown for 5 minutes. Add the potatoes and the other ingredients, toss, put the lid on and cook on High for 15 minutes. Release the pressure naturally for 10 minutes, divide the mix between plates, and serve for breakfast.

Nutrition: calories 161, fat 7, fiber 4, carbs 8, protein 11

Kale Salad

Preparation time: 10 minutes Cooking time: 15 minutes Servings: 4
Ingredients:
- 1 pound kale leaves, roughly chopped
- 1 leek, sliced
- 1 red onion, chopped
- 2 tablespoons olive oil
- 1 cup cherry tomatoes, halved
- 1 cup zucchini, cubed
- 1 teaspoon sweet paprika
- ½ cup tomato sauce
- A pinch of salt and black pepper
- 1 tablespoon balsamic vinegar
- 2 tablespoons cilantro, chopped

Directions:
Set the instant pot on Sauté mode, add the oil, heat it up, add the onion and the leeks and sauté for 5 minutes. Add the kale and the other ingredients, toss, put the lid on and cook on High for 15 minutes. Release the pressure naturally for 10 minutes, divide the salad into bowls and serve for breakfast.
Nutrition: calories 200, fat 9, fiber 5, carbs 7, protein 10

Basil Tomato Scramble

Preparation time: 10 minutes Cooking time: 15 minutes Servings: 4
Ingredients:
- 2 scallions, chopped
- 1 tablespoon avocado oil
- 3 garlic cloves, minced
- ¼ cup heavy cream
- 1 cup cherry tomatoes, halved
- 1 teaspoon chili powder
- 8 eggs, whisked
- 1 tablespoon Italian seasoning
- Salt and black pepper to the taste
- 1 tablespoon basil, chopped

Directions:
Set your instant pot on Sauté mode, add oil, heat it up, add the scallions and the garlic and sauté for 5 minutes. Add the rest of the ingredients except the basil, toss well, put the lid on and cook on High for 10 minutes. Release the pressure naturally for 10 minutes, divide the scramble between plates and serve with the basil sprinkled on top.
Nutrition: calories 188, fat 11, fiber 6, carbs 7, protein 9

Instant Pot Side Dish Recipes

Baked Potatoes

Preparation time: *10 minutes* ***Cooking time:*** *12 minutes* ***Servings:*** *2*

Ingredients:
- 2 potatoes, scrubbed
- A pinch of salt and black pepper
- 1 teaspoon chili powder
- 1 teaspoon rosemary, dried
- 1 tablespoon olive oil
- 1 cup water

Directions:
Put the water in the instant pot, add the steamer basket inside, put the potatoes in the pot, prick them with a fork, put the lid on and cook on High for 12 minutes. Release the pressure naturally for 10 minutes, divide the potatoes between plates, cut them in halves, drizzle the oil all over, also add the remaining ingredients on each potato half and serve as a side dish.

Nutrition: calories 149, fat 5, fiber 3, carbs 33, protein 4

Creamy Corn

Preparation time: *10 minutes* ***Cooking time:*** *10 minutes* ***Servings:*** *8*

Ingredients:
- 8 ounces cream cheese, cubed
- 32 ounces fresh corn
- ½ cup butter, melted
- ½ cup heavy cream
- ½ cup milk
- A pinch of salt and black pepper
- 1 tablespoon olive oil
- 1 tablespoon brown sugar

Directions:
In your instant pot, combine the cream cheese with the corn, the milk and the other ingredients, toss, put the lid on and cook on Low for 10 minutes. Release the pressure naturally for 10 minutes, divide the mix between plates and serve as a side dish.

Nutrition: calories 293, fat 19, fiber 2, carbs 28, protein 6

Spiced Cauliflower

*Preparation time: 10 minutes **Cooking time:** 10 minutes **Servings:** 4*

Ingredients:
- 1 cauliflower head, florets separated
- 1 yellow onion, chopped
- 2 tablespoons olive oil
- ½ teaspoon ginger powder
- 1 cup water
- 4 tablespoons cilantro, chopped
- 1 teaspoon cumin seeds
- ½ teaspoon turmeric powder
- 1 tablespoon cumin powder
- 1 tablespoon coriander powder
- ½ teaspoon garam masala
- ½ teaspoon chili powder
- A pinch of salt and black pepper

Directions:
Set the instant pot on Sauté mode, add the oil, heat it up, add the onion, ginger, and cumin seeds, stir and sauté for 2 minutes. Add the cauliflower, water, turmeric and the other ingredients except the cilantro, toss, put the lid on and cook on High for 8 minutes. Release the pressure naturally for 10 minutes, divide the mix between plates and serve as a side dish.

Nutrition: calories 168, fat 12, fiber 6, carbs 14, protein 5

Green Beans Mix

*Preparation time: 10 minutes **Cooking time:** 15 minutes **Servings:** 6*

Ingredients:
- 4 bacon slices, chopped
- 1 cup yellow onion, chopped
- ¼ cup water
- 6 cups green beans, trimmed and halved
- A pinch of salt and black pepper
- 1 teaspoon chili powder

Directions:
In your instant pot, combine the green beans with the bacon and the other ingredients, toss, put the lid on and cook on High for 15 minutes. Release the pressure naturally for 10 minutes, divide the mix between plates and serve.

Nutrition: calories 122, fat 7, fiber 3, carbs 10, protein 4

Broccoli Mash

Preparation time: *10 minutes* ***Cooking time:*** *10 minutes* ***Servings:*** *4*

Ingredients:
- 1 tablespoon butter, soft
- 1 pound broccoli florets
- 2 garlic cloves, minced
- ½ cup water
- A pinch of salt and black pepper
- 4 ounces cream cheese
- ½ teaspoon red pepper flakes, crushed

Directions:
Set the instant pot on Sauté mode, add the butter, melt it, add the garlic and cook for 1 minute. Add the broccoli and the other ingredients, toss, put the lid on and cook on High for 9 minutes. Release the pressure naturally for 10 minutes, mash the mix using a potato masher, whisk, divide between plates and serve.
Nutrition: calories 166, fat 13, fiber 3, carbs 9.6, protein 5

Beans Dal

Preparation time: *10 minutes* ***Cooking time:*** *30 minutes* ***Servings:*** *4*

Ingredients:
- 1 cup gram dal
- ¼ cup kidney beans
- 1 tablespoon olive oil
- 1 bay leaf
- 1 teaspoon cumin seeds
- 1 yellow onion, chopped
- 1 tablespoon ginger, grated
- 2 garlic cloves, minced
- 2 tablespoons cilantro, chopped
- 1 teaspoon red chili powder
- ½ teaspoon turmeric powder
- 2 tomatoes, crushed
- 2 teaspoons coriander powder
- Salt and black pepper to the taste
- 5 cups water

Directions:
Set the instant pot on Sauté mode, add the oil, heat it up, add the cumin sees, onion, ginger, and garlic and sauté for 5 minutes. Add the gram dal, the beans and the other ingredients, toss, put the lid on and cook on High for 25 minutes. Release the pressure naturally for 10 minutes, divide the mix between plates and serve as a side dish.
Nutrition: calories 256, fat 14, fiber 5, carbs 15, protein 5

Spaghetti Squash

Preparation time: *5 minutes* ***Cooking time:*** *7 minutes* ***Servings:*** *4*

Ingredients:
- 1 spaghetti squash, halved lengthwise
- 1 cup water
- 1 tablespoon ghee, melted
- A pinch of salt and black pepper
- 1 teaspoon red pepper flakes, crushed

Directions:
Put the water in the instant pot, add the steamer basket, place the squash halves inside, put the lid on and cook on High for 7 minutes. Release the pressure fast for 5 minutes, use a fork to loosen the squash strands, transfer them to a bowl, add the remaining ingredients, toss, divide between plates and serve as a side dish.

Nutrition: calories 230, fat 12, fiber 4, carbs 8, protein 5

Butter Carrots Mix

Preparation time: *10 minutes* ***Cooking time:*** *10 minutes* ***Servings:*** *6*

Ingredients:
- 1 cup water
- ¼ cup butter, soft
- 2 pounds carrots, peeled and cut into chunks
- 2 tablespoons honey
- A pinch of salt and black pepper
- 1 tablespoon parsley, chopped

Directions:
In your instant pot, combine the carrots with the water, salt and pepper, put the lid on and cook on High for 10 minutes. Release the pressure naturally for 10 minutes, transfer the carrots to a bowl, add the butter and the remaining ingredients, toss, divide between plates and serve as a side dish.

Nutrition: calories 152, fat 4, fiber 4, carbs 12, protein 5.3

Fast Polenta

Preparation time: *5 minutes* **Cooking time:** *15 minutes* **Servings:** *6*
Ingredients:
- 1 cup polenta
- 2 tablespoons butter, soft
- 4 cups chicken stock
- ½ cup cheddar cheese, shredded
- ¼ cup half and half
- A pinch of salt and white pepper

Directions:
Set the instant pot on Sauté mode, add the stock and the polenta and whisk well. Put the lid on and cook on High for 15 minutes. Release the pressure fast for 5 minutes, add the remaining ingredients, whisk, divide between plates and serve as a side dish.
Nutrition: calories 170, fat 6, fiber 3, carbs 22, protein 5

Veggie Korma

Preparation time: *10 minutes* **Cooking time:** *15 minutes* **Servings:** *8*
Ingredients:
- 3 tablespoons olive oil
- 1 cup cauliflower florets
- 1 cup red onion, chopped
- 1 cup zucchini, cubed
- 1 cup red bell pepper, cubed
- 2 radishes, sliced
- 8 French beans, chopped
- 1 plantain, peeled and cubed
- ½ cup green peas
- 1 carrot, sliced
- ½ cup coconut milk
- 1 sweet potato, peeled and cubed
- ½ cup water
- 2 cups canned chickpeas, drained
- ½ cup coconut milk
- 1 teaspoon red pepper powder
- 1 teaspoon turmeric powder
- 1 teaspoon curry powder
- 1 bay leaf
- A pinch of salt and black pepper
- 1 tablespoon coriander, chopped

Directions:
Set the instant pot on Sauté mode, add the oil, heat it up, add the onion, pepper powder, turmeric, curry powder and bay leaf and sauté for 2 minutes. Add the cauliflower florets, zucchinis, bell peppers and the other ingredients, toss, put the lid on and cook on High for 13 minutes. Release the pressure naturally for 10 minutes, divide the mix between plates and serve as a side dish,
Nutrition: calories 220, fat 15, fiber 4, carbs 18, protein 4

Teriyaki Rice

Preparation time: *10 minutes* **Cooking time:** *20 minutes* **Servings:** *4*

Ingredients:
- 1 tablespoon sesame oil
- 4 garlic cloves, minced
- 1 yellow onion, chopped
- 2 carrots, shredded
- 2 celery ribs, chopped
- 2 red bell peppers, chopped
- 2 cups brown rice
- 2 cups water
- ½ cup coconut aminos
- ¼ cup rice vinegar
- ¼ cup maple syrup
- 1 cup peas
- A pinch of salt and black pepper

Directions:
Set the instant pot on Sauté mode, add the oil, heat it up, add the onion and the garlic and sauté for 2 minutes. Add the carrots, celery and the other ingredients, toss, put the lid on and cook on High for 18 minutes. Release the pressure naturally for 10 minutes, divide the mix between plates and serve.

Nutrition: calories 525, fat 6.9, fiber 8.2, carbs 104, protein 10.5

Mushroom Rice

Preparation time: *10 minutes* **Cooking time:** *12 minutes* **Servings:** *8*

Ingredients:
- 1 pound mushrooms, sliced
- 1 tablespoon avocado oil
- 1 and ½ cups Arborio rice
- 2 shallots, chopped
- 4 cups veggie stock
- ½ cup white wine
- A pinch of salt and black pepper
- 3 tablespoons butter
- 1 tablespoon parsley, chopped
- ½ cup parmesan, grated

Directions:
Set the instant pot on Sauté mode, add the oil, heat it up, add the shallots and the mushrooms and sauté for 2 minutes. Add the rice ad the other ingredients, toss, put the lid on and cook on High for 10 minutes. Release the pressure naturally for 10 minutes, divide the mix between plates and serve.

Nutrition: calories 260, fat 9, fiber 1, carbs 34, protein 6

Potato Side Salad

Preparation time: *10 minutes* ***Cooking time:*** *20 minutes* ***Servings:*** *4*

Ingredients:
- 1 pound baby potatoes, peeled and quartered
- A pinch of salt and black pepper
- 3 tablespoons olive oil
- 1 cup chicken stock
- 1 cup edamame, steamed and shelled
- 1 tablespoon ginger, grated

Directions:
In your instant pot, combine the potatoes with the stock, and the other ingredients, toss, put the lid on and cook on High for 20 minutes. Release the pressure naturally for 10 minutes, divide the mix between plates and serve as a side salad.

Nutrition: calories 246, fat 5.4, fiber 3.4, carbs 12, protein 4.5

Zucchini and Eggplant Medley

Preparation time: *10 minutes* ***Cooking time:*** *12 minutes* ***Servings:*** *4*

Ingredients:
- 1 zucchini, roughly cubed
- 1 eggplant, roughly cubed
- 1 red onion, chopped
- 1 tomato, cubed
- 2 tablespoons olive oil
- 2 garlic cloves, minced
- 1 tablespoon thyme, chopped
- A pinch of salt and black pepper
- 1 tablespoon balsamic vinegar
- 1 cup water

Directions:
In a baking pan that fits the instant pot, combine the zucchini with the eggplants, onion and the other ingredients except the water. Put the water in the instant pot, add the trivet inside, add the baking pan into the pot, put the lid on and cook on High for 12 minutes. Release the pressure naturally for 10 minutes, divide the mix between plates and serve.
Nutrition: calories 162, fat 12, fiber 3, carbs 5. protein 5

Garlic and Sage Asparagus
Preparation time: *5 minutes* **Cooking time:** *8 minutes* **Servings:** *4*

Ingredients:
- 2 tablespoons olive oil
- 3 garlic cloves, minced
- 2 tablespoons sage, chopped
- Salt and black pepper to the taste
- 2 teaspoons balsamic vinegar
- 1 pound asparagus, trimmed
- 1 cup water

Directions:

In a bowl, combine the asparagus with the oil, garlic and the other ingredients except the water and toss well Put the water in the instant pot, add the steamer basket, put the asparagus inside, put the lid on and cook on High for 8 minutes Release the pressure fast for 5 minutes, divide between plates and serve as a side dish.

Nutrition: calories 100, fat 10.5, fiber 1.2, carbs 2.3, protein 2.1

Dill Zucchini and Cucumber Mix

Preparation time: *5 minutes* **Cooking time:** *5 minutes* **Servings:** *4*

Ingredients:
- 2 cucumbers, roughly cubed
- 2 zucchinis, roughly cubed
- 2 tablespoons olive oil
- ½ cup veggie stock
- 1 yellow onion, chopped
- 2 garlic cloves, minced
- 1 teaspoon cumin, ground
- 1 teaspoon sweet paprika
- 2 tablespoons lime juice
- 1 tablespoon dill, chopped
- Salt and black pepper to the taste

Directions:

In the instant pot, combine the cucumbers with the zucchinis, the oil and the other ingredients, toss, put the lid on and cook on High for 5 minutes Release the pressure fast for 5 minutes, divide the mix between plates and serve as a side dish.

Nutrition: calories 123, fat 4.3, fiber 2.3, carbs 5.6, protein 2

Chili Eggplant Mix

Preparation time: *5 minutes* ***Cooking time:*** *12 minutes* ***Servings:*** *4*

Ingredients:
- 2 eggplants, roughly cubed
- ¼ cup veggie stock
- 2 garlic cloves, minced
- 1 red onion, chopped
- 2 green chilies, chopped
- 1 teaspoon chili powder
- 1 tablespoon olive oil
- Salt and black pepper to the taste
- 1 tablespoon lemon juice
- 3 tablespoons walnuts, chopped
- 1 tablespoon balsamic vinegar
- 1 teaspoon cilantro, chopped

Directions:
Set the instant pot on Sauté mode, add the oil, heat it up, add the garlic, onion and the chilies and sauté for 2 minutes. Add the eggplants and the other ingredients, toss, put the lid on and cook on High for 10 minutes. Release the pressure fast for 5 minutes, divide the mix between plates and serve.

Nutrition: calories 121, fat 2.3, fiber 2.0, carbs 6.7, protein 2.4

Zucchinis and Beet Salad

Preparation time: *10 minutes* ***Cooking time:*** *20 minutes* ***Servings:*** *4*

Ingredients:
- 4 beets, peeled and cut into wedges
- 2 zucchinis, roughly cubed
- 4 scallions, chopped
- 2 tablespoons olive oil
- Salt and black pepper to the taste
- ¼ cup lime juice
- 1/3 cup walnuts, chopped
- 1 tablespoons cilantro, chopped

Directions:
Set the instant pot on Sauté mode, add the oil, heat it up, add the scallions, stir and cook for 5 minutes. Add the beets, zucchinis and the other ingredients, toss, put the lid on and cook on High for 15 minutes. Release the pressure naturally for 10 minutes, divide the mix between plates and serve as a side salad.

Nutrition: calories 156, fat 4.2, fiber 3.4, carbs 6.5, protein 4

Balsamic Beets Mix

*Preparation time: 10 minutes **Cooking time:** 25 minutes **Servings:** 4*

Ingredients:
- 4 medium beets, peeled and cut into wedges
- 1/3 cup balsamic vinegar
- 1 teaspoon sweet paprika
- 1 teaspoon chili powder
- A pinch of salt and black pepper
- 1 garlic clove, minced
- ½ teaspoon rosemary, dried
- 1 tablespoon olive oil

Directions:
In your instant pot, combine the beets with the balsamic vinegar and the other ingredients, toss, put the lid on and cook on High for 25 minutes. Release the pressure naturally for 10 minutes, divide the mix between plates and serve.

Nutrition: calories 165, fat 3.4, fiber 4.5, carbs 11.3, protein 2.3

Cilantro Tomatoes Mix

*Preparation time: 10 minutes **Cooking time:** 12 minutes **Servings:** 4*

Ingredients:
- 1 pound cherry tomatoes, halved
- ¼ cup veggie stock
- A pinch of salt and black pepper
- 2 tablespoons olive oil
- 1 tablespoon pine nuts, toasted
- 1 tablespoon walnuts, chopped
- 4 scallions, chopped
- 2 tablespoons cilantro, chopped
- 2 tablespoons lemon juice

Directions:
In your instant pot, combine the cherry tomatoes with the oil, salt, pepper and the other ingredients, toss, put the lid on and cook on High for 12 minutes. Release the pressure naturally for 10 minutes, divide the mix between plates and serve as a side dish.

Nutrition: calories 200, fat 4.5, fiber 3.4, carbs 6.7, protein 4

Balsamic Zucchini and Tomato Mix

*Preparation time: 10 minutes **Cooking time:** 15 minutes **Servings:** 4*

Ingredients:
- 1/3 cup chicken stock
- 1 pound cherry tomatoes, halved
- 2 zucchinis, roughly cubed
- 2 tablespoons olive oil
- 1 red onion, chopped
- 2 tablespoons balsamic vinegar
- A pinch of salt and black pepper
- 1 tablespoon lime juice
- 1 tablespoon rosemary, chopped
- ¼ cup chives, chopped

Directions:
Set the instant pot on Sauté mode, add the oil, heat it up, add the onion and sauté for 5 minutes Add the tomatoes, zucchinis and the other ingredients, toss, put the lid on and cook on High for 10 minutes Release the pressure naturally for 10 minutes, divide the mix between plates and serve as a side dish.

Nutrition: calories 201, fat 4.5, fiber 3, carbs 5.4, protein 3

Parmesan Rice

*Preparation time: 10 minutes **Cooking time:** 25 minutes **Servings:** 4*

Ingredients:
- 1 tablespoon olive oil
- 1 yellow onion, chopped
- 2 cups black rice
- 4 cups chicken stock
- 1 tablespoon chives, chopped
- ½ tablespoon parmesan, grated
- Salt and black pepper to the taste

Directions:
Set the instant pot on Sauté mode, add the oil, heat it up, add the onion and sauté for 5 minutes. Add the rice and the other ingredients, toss, put the lid on and cook on High for 20 minutes. Release the pressure naturally for 10 minutes, divide the mix between plates and serve.

Nutrition: calories 210, fat 6.5, fiber 3.4, carbs 8.6, protein 3.4

Lemon Chickpeas

Preparation time: 10 minutes *Cooking time:* 20 minutes *Servings:* 4

Ingredients:
- 2 cups canned chickpeas, drained and rinsed
- 1 yellow onion, chopped
- 2 tablespoons olive oil
- Juice of 1 lemon
- Zest of 1 lemon, grated
- 1 cup chicken stock
- 1 teaspoon rosemary, dried
- 1 teaspoon cumin, ground
- 1 tablespoon parsley, chopped
- Salt and pepper to the taste

Directions:
Set the instant pot on Sauté mode, add the oil, heat it up, add the onion and sauté for 2 minutes. Add the chickpeas and the other ingredients, toss, put the lid on and cook on High for 18 minutes. Release the pressure naturally for 10 minutes, divide the mix between plates and serve as a side dish.

Nutrition: calories 199, fat 4.5, fiber 2.3, carbs 6.5, protein 3.3

Creamy Zucchini Mix

Preparation time: 10 minutes *Cooking time:* 15 minutes *Servings:* 4

Ingredients:
- 2 tablespoons olive oil
- 3 garlic clove, minced
- 1 pound zucchinis, roughly sliced
- 1 red onion, sliced
- Juice of 1 lime
- 2 tablespoons dill, chopped
- 1 cup heavy cream
- Salt and black pepper to the taste

Directions:
Set the instant pot on Sauté mode, add the oil, heat it up, add the garlic and the onion and sauté for 2 minutes. Add the zucchinis and the other ingredients, toss, put the lid on and cook on High for 13 minutes. Release the pressure naturally for 10 minutes, divide the mix between plates and serve.

Nutrition: calories 214, fat 5.6, fiber 3.4, carbs 6.5, protein 3.1

Paprika Cabbage Mix

Preparation time: 10 minutes Cooking time: 15 minutes Servings: 4

Ingredients:
- 1 yellow onion, chopped
- 1 green cabbage head, shredded
- ½ cup chicken stock
- 2 tablespoons olive oil
- 1 tablespoon balsamic vinegar
- 4 spring onions, chopped
- 1 tablespoon sweet paprika
- 1 tablespoon dill, chopped
- Salt and black pepper to the taste

Directions:
Set the instant pot on Sauté mode, add the oil, heat it up, add the onion and spring onions and sauté for 2 minutes. Add the cabbage and the other ingredients, toss, put the lid on and cook on High for 13 minutes. Release the pressure naturally for 10 minutes, divide the mix between plates and serve.

Nutrition: calories 199, fat 4.5, fiber 2.4, carbs 5.6, protein 2.2

Lime Mushroom Mix

Preparation time: 10 minutes Cooking time: 15 minutes Servings: 4

Ingredients:
- 1 pound white mushrooms, halved
- 1 cup veggie stock
- 2 tablespoons olive oil
- 1 yellow onion, chopped
- 2 garlic cloves, minced
- Juice and zest of 1 lime
- 1 tablespoon chives, chopped
- Salt and black pepper to the taste

Directions:
Set the instant pot on Sauté mode, add the oil, heat it up, add the onion and the garlic and sauté for 2 minutes. Add the mushrooms and the other ingredients, toss, put the lid on and cook on High for 13 minutes. Release the pressure naturally for 10 minutes, divide the mix between plates and serve as a side dish.

Nutrition: calories 222, fat 5.5, fiber 5.4, carbs 12.3, protein 5.6

Chives Potatoes

Preparation time: 10 minutes Cooking time: 20 minutes Servings: 4

Ingredients:
- 4 sweet potatoes, peeled and cut into wedges
- 4 scallions, chopped
- 1 tablespoon olive oil
- 1 teaspoon turmeric powder
- 1 teaspoon chili powder
- ½ cup veggie stock
- 1 teaspoon sweet paprika
- Salt and black pepper to the taste
- 2 tablespoons chives, chopped

Directions:
Set the instant pot on Sauté mode, add the oil, heat it up, add the scallions and sauté for 5 minutes. Add the potatoes, the turmeric and the other ingredients, toss, put the lid on and cook on High for 15 minutes.Release the pressure naturally for 10 minutes, divide the mix between plates and serve as a side dish.

Nutrition: calories 233, fat 8.7, fiber 4.5, carbs 14.4, protein 6.4

Bulgur and Spinach Mix

Preparation time: 10 minutes Cooking time: 20 minutes Servings: 4

Ingredients:
- 4 ounces bulgur
- 1 and ½ cup chicken stock
- 1 cup baby spinach
- 1 yellow onion, chopped
- 1 tablespoon olive oil
- 1 tablespoon mint, chopped
- 3 spring onions, chopped
- ½ teaspoon allspice, ground
- Juice of 1 lime
- 2 tablespoons cilantro, chopped

Directions:
Set the instant pot on Sauté mode, add the oil, heat it up, add the yellow onion and the allspice and sauté for 5 minutes. Add the bulgur, stock and the other ingredients, toss, put the lid on and cook on High for 15 minutes. Release the pressure naturally for 10 minutes, divide the mix between plates and serve.

Nutrition: calories 200, fat 6.7, fiber 3.4, carbs 15.4, protein 4.5

Cheesy Green Beans

Preparation time: 5 minutes **Cooking time:** 20 minutes **Servings:** 4

Ingredients:
- 2 tablespoons olive oil
- 2 garlic cloves, minced
- 1 pound green beans, trimmed and halved
- ½ cup goat cheese, shredded
- ½ teaspoon hot paprika
- ½ teaspoon chili powder
- ½ cup veggie stock
- 1 yellow onion, sliced
- 2 tablespoons chives, chopped

Directions:
Set the instant pot on Sauté mode, add the oil, heat it up, add the garlic and the onion and sauté for 5 minutes. Add the green beans and the other ingredients, toss, put the lid on and cook on High for 15 minutes. Release the pressure fast for 5 minutes, divide the mix between plates and serve as a side dish.

Nutrition: calories 188, fat 4, fiber 3, carbs 12.4, protein 4.4

Beans and Shallots Mix

Preparation time: 10 minutes **Cooking time:** 25 minutes **Servings:** 4

Ingredients:
- 1 tablespoon olive oil
- 1 cup shallots, chopped
- 2 celery stalks, chopped
- 2 garlic cloves, minced
- 1 cup canned black beans, rinsed and drained
- 1 cup canned red kidney beans, drained and rinsed
- 1 cup canned cannellini beans, drained and rinsed
- 2 cups chicken stock
- Salt and black pepper to the taste

Directions:
Set the instant pot on Sauté mode, add the oil, heat it up, add the shallots, celery and garlic and sauté for 5 minutes. Add the beans and the remaining ingredients, toss, put the lid on and cook on High for 20 minutes. Release the pressure naturally for 10 minutes, divide the mix between plates and serve.

Nutrition: calories 224, fat 8.4, fiber 3.4, carbs 15.3, protein 6.2

Lemon Millet Mix

Preparation time: *10 minutes* ***Cooking time:*** *20 minutes* ***Servings:*** *6*
Ingredients:
- 2 tablespoons olive oil
- 1 cup millet
- Zest of 1 lemon, grated
- Juice of 1 lemon
- 3 cups chicken stock
- 2 spring onions, chopped
- ½ cup cilantro, chopped
- 1 teaspoon chili paste
- 1 teaspoon turmeric powder
- Salt and black pepper to the taste

Directions:
Set the instant pot on Sauté mode, add the oil, heat it up, add the spring onions, chili paste and turmeric powder and sauté for 5 minutes. Add the millet and the other ingredients, toss, put the lid on and cook on High for 15 minutes. Release the pressure naturally for 10 minutes, divide the millet mix between plates and serve.
Nutrition: calories 222, fat 10.2, fiber 3.4, carbs 14.5, protein 2.4

Collard Green and Sprouts Mix

Preparation time: *10 minutes* ***Cooking time:*** *20 minutes* ***Servings:*** *4*
Ingredients:
- 1 pound Brussels sprouts, trimmed and halved
- 1 medium bunch collard greens, chopped
- 2 tablespoons almonds, chopped
- 4 scallions, chopped
- 2 tablespoons avocado oil
- 1 tablespoon pine nuts, toasted
- 2 tablespoons balsamic vinegar
- 1 cup chicken stock
- A pinch of salt and black pepper
- 1 tablespoon cilantro, chopped

Directions:
 Set the instant pot on Sauté mode, add the oil, heat it up, add the scallions, almonds and pine nuts and sauté for 5 minutes Add the sprouts, the greens and the other ingredients, toss, put the lid on and cook on High for 15 minutes Release the pressure naturally for 10 minutes, divide the mix between plates and serve.
Nutrition: calories 175, fat 3, fiber 3, carbs 5, protein 3

Cilantro Radish Mix

Preparation time: 10 minutes Cooking time: 10 minutes Servings: 4

Ingredients:
- 1 pound radishes, halved
- 2 tablespoons avocado oil
- 2 scallions, chopped
- 4 tablespoons cilantro, chopped
- 4 tablespoons Greek yogurt
- 1 teaspoons balsamic vinegar
- 2 tablespoons lime juice
- Salt and black pepper to the taste

Directions:
Set the instant pot on Sauté mode, add the oil, heat it up add the scallions and sauté for 2 minutes. Add the radishes, cilantro and the other ingredients, toss, put the lid on and cook on High for 8 minutes. Release the pressure naturally for 10 minutes, divide the mix between plates and serve.

Nutrition: calories 403, fat 30.5, fiber 10, carbs 23.5, protein 3.5

Radish and Beets Mix

Preparation time: 10 minutes Cooking time: 25 minutes Servings: 4

Ingredients:
- 1 pound beets, cooked, peeled and roughly cubed
- 2 cups radishes, halved
- 1 cup chicken stock
- 4 scallions, chopped
- 2 tablespoons olive oil
- 1 tablespoon lemon juice
- 2 tablespoons balsamic vinegar
- 3 small garlic cloves, minced
- 2 tablespoons parsley, chopped
- Salt and black pepper to the taste

Directions:
Set the instant pot on Sauté mode, add the oil, heat it up, add the scallions and sauté for 5 minutes. Add the beets and the other ingredients, toss, put the lid on and cook on High for 20 minutes. Release the pressure naturally for 10 minutes, divide the mix between plates and serve.

Nutrition: calories 268, fat 15.5, fiber 5.1, carbs 25.7, protein 9.6

Herbed Quinoa

Preparation time: 10 minutes *Cooking time:* 20 minutes *Servings:* 4

Ingredients:
- 2 cups quinoa
- 4 cups chicken stock
- 2 tablespoons olive oil
- 4 scallions, chopped
- A pinch of salt and black pepper
- 2 tablespoons chives, chopped
- 2 tablespoons basil, chopped
- 2 tablespoons oregano, chopped
- 1/3 cup parmesan, grated
- 2 green onions, chopped

Directions:
Set the instant pot on Sauté mode, add the oil, heat it up, add the scallions and sauté for 2 minutes. Add the quinoa, the stock and the other ingredients, toss, put the lid on and cook on High for 18 minutes. Release the pressure naturally for 10 minutes, divide the mix between plates and serve as a side dish.

Nutrition: calories 181, fat 3.4, fiber 3.2, carbs 8.6, protein 7.6

Pesto Rice Mix

Preparation time: 10 minutes *Cooking time:* 25 minutes *Servings:* 6

Ingredients:
- 1 red onion, chopped
- 1 cup Arborio rice
- 2 cups chicken stock
- 1 teaspoon sweet paprika
- 1 teaspoon cumin, ground
- 1 tablespoon olive oil
- 2 tablespoons basil pesto
- Salt and black pepper to the taste
- 1 tablespoon cilantro, chopped

Directions:
Set your instant pot on Sauté mode, add the oil, heat it up, add the onion and the pesto and sauté for 5 minute Add the rice and the remaining ingredients, toss, put the lid on and cook on High for 20 minutes. Release the pressure naturally for 10 minutes, divide the mix between plates and serve as a side dish.

Nutrition: calories 151, fat 7, fiber 6, carbs 9, protein 6

Leeks and Broccoli Mix

Preparation time: 10 minutes *Cooking time:* 20 minutes *Servings:* 4

Ingredients:
1. 3 leeks, sliced
2. 2 scallions, chopped
3. 1 pound broccoli florets
4. 2 garlic cloves, minced
5. 2 tablespoons olive oil
6. 1 cup chicken stock
7. A pinch of salt and black pepper
8. 1 teaspoon chili powder
9. 2 tablespoons cilantro, chopped

Directions:

Set your instant pot on Sauté mode, add oil, heat it up, add the scallions, garlic and leeks and sauté for 5 minutes. Add the broccoli and the rest of the ingredients, toss, put the lid on and cook on High for 15 minutes. Release the pressure naturally for 10 minutes, divide the mix between plates and serve as a side dish.

Nutrition: calories 171, fat 4, fiber 5, carbs 9, protein 6

Tomato and Radish Mix

Preparation time: 10 minutes *Cooking time:* 15 minutes *Servings:* 4

Ingredients:
1. 1 red onion, chopped
2. 1 tablespoon olive oil
3. 1 cup radishes, halved
4. 1 pound tomatoes, cut into wedges
5. 1 tablespoon chives, chopped
6. 1 cup veggie stock
7. 1 teaspoon nutmeg, ground
8. 1 teaspoon oregano, dried
9. A pinch of salt and black pepper
10. 2 tablespoons parsley, chopped

Directions:

Set your instant pot on Sauté mode, add the oil, heat it up, add the onion, nutmeg and oregano and sauté for 5 minutes Add the rest of the ingredients except the parsley and the chives, put the lid on and cook on High for 10 minutes. Release the pressure naturally for 10 minutes, divide the mix between plates, sprinkle the parsley and the chives on top and serve as a side dish.

Nutrition: calories 182, fat 6, fiber 3, carbs 6, protein 7

Cayenne Rice

*Preparation time: 10 minutes **Cooking time:** 25 minutes **Servings:** 4*

Ingredients:
- A pinch of salt and black pepper
- 1 teaspoon cayenne pepper
- 3 scallions, chopped
- 2 cups black rice
- 4 cups chicken stock
- ½ teaspoon turmeric powder
- ½ teaspoon allspice, ground
- 1 tablespoon avocado oil
- 1 tablespoon cilantro, chopped

Directions:
Set the instant pot on Sauté mode, add the oil, heat it up, add the scallions, turmeric and allspice and sauté for 5 minutes Add the rice, cayenne and the rest of the ingredients, put the lid on and cook on High for 20 minutes. Release the pressure naturally for 10 minutes, divide the mix between plates and serve as a side dish.

Nutrition: calories 162, fat 6, fiber 4, carbs 6, protein 8

Creamy Rice Mix

*Preparation time: 10 minutes **Cooking time:** 25 minutes **Servings:** 4*

Ingredients:
1. 2 cups wild rice
2. 4 cups chicken stock
3. 1 cup heavy cream
4. 2 garlic cloves, minced
5. 2 tablespoon olive oil
6. 1 yellow onion, chopped
7. 1 tablespoon cilantro, chopped
8. 2 tablespoons parmesan, grated

Directions:
Set your instant pot on Sauté mode, add the oil, heat it up, add the garlic and the onion and sauté for 5 minutes Add the rice, stock and the rest of the ingredients except the parmesan, put the lid on and cook on High for 20 minutes Release the pressure naturally for 10 minutes, add the parmesan, toss, divide between plates and serve as a side dish.

Nutrition: calories 200, fat 8, fiber 4, carbs 6, protein 7

Basil Tomato Mix

Preparation time: *5 minutes* ***Cooking time:*** *15 minutes* ***Servings:*** *4*

Ingredients:
1. 2 tablespoons olive oil
2. 1 yellow onion, chopped
3. ½ cup veggie stock
4. 1 pound cherry tomatoes, halved
5. ½ teaspoon nutmeg, ground
6. 2 tablespoons basil, chopped
7. ½ teaspoon ginger, grated

Directions:
Set your instant pot on Sauté mode, add the oil, heat it up, add onion and the ginger and sauté for 5 minutes Add the tomatoes and the rest of the ingredients, toss, put the lid on and cook on High for 10 minutes. Release the pressure fast for 5 minutes, divide the mix between plates and serve as a side dish.

Nutrition: calories 200, fat 7, fiber 4, carbs 7, protein 6

Cardamom Carrots

Preparation time: *5 minutes* ***Cooking time:*** *15 minutes* ***Servings:*** *4*

Ingredients:
1. 1 pound baby carrots, peeled
2. 1 cup chicken stock
3. ½ teaspoon ginger, grated
4. 2 tablespoons olive oil
5. 1 yellow onion, chopped
6. 1 teaspoon cardamom, ground
7. 1 teaspoon sweet paprika
8. 1 tablespoon chives, chopped
9. A pinch of salt and black pepper

Directions:
Set the instant pot on sauté mode, add the oil, heat it up, add the onion and ginger and sauté for 2 minutes Add the carrots and the remaining ingredients, put the lid on and cook on High for 13 minutes. Release the pressure fast for 5 minutes, divide the mix between plates and serve as a side dish.

Nutrition: calories 200, fat 8, fiber 4, carbs 6, protein 8

Potato Mash

Preparation time: 10 minutes *Cooking time:* 15 minutes *Servings:* 6

Ingredients:
- 2 garlic cloves, minced
- 2 tablespoons shallots, chopped
- 2 pounds potatoes, peeled and cubed
- A pinch of salt and black pepper
- ½ teaspoon rosemary, dried
- ½ teaspoon turmeric powder
- 2 cups water
- ¼ cup almond milk
- 1 tablespoon chives

Directions:
Add the water to the instant pot, add the steamer basket, put the potatoes in the basket, put the lid on and cook on High for 15 minutes. Release the pressure naturally for 10 minutes, transfer the potatoes to a bowl, mash them with a potato masher, add the garlic, shallots and the other ingredients, whisk, divide between plates and serve as a side dish.

Nutrition: calories 181, fat 7, fiber 3, carbs 6, protein 7

Rosemary Beets

Preparation time: 10 minutes *Cooking time:* 20 minutes *Servings:* 6

Ingredients:
- 2 tablespoons olive oil
- ½ teaspoon hot paprika
- 1 pound beets, peeled and roughly cubed
- 4 scallions, chopped
- 2 tablespoons rosemary, chopped
- 1 and ½ cups veggie stock
- A pinch of salt and black pepper

Directions:
Set your instant pot on Sauté mode, add the oil, heat it up, add the scallions and the paprika and sauté for 2 minutes. Add the beets and the rest of the ingredients, stir, put the lid on and cook on High for 18 minutes. Release the pressure naturally for 10 minutes, divide the mix between plates and serve as a side dish.

Nutrition: calories 184, fat 6, fiber 3, carbs 6, protein 6

Mint Brussels Sprouts

Preparation time: 10 minutes *Cooking time:* 20 minutes *Servings:* 4

Ingredients:
- 1 tablespoon balsamic vinegar
- 1 pound Brussels sprouts, trimmed and halved
- 1 red onion, chopped
- 2 tablespoons avocado oil
- 1 teaspoon lime juice
- A pinch of salt and black pepper
- 1 cup veggie stock
- 2 tablespoons mint leaves, chopped

Directions:
Set the instant pot on Sauté mode, add the oil, heat it up, add the onion and sauté for 5 minutes. Add the sprouts and the remaining ingredients, toss, put the lid on and cook on High for 15 minutes. Release the pressure naturally for 10 minutes, divide the mix between plates and serve as a side dish.

Nutrition: calories 200, fat 8, fiber 3, carbs 7, protein 8

Kale Rice

Preparation time: 10 minutes *Cooking time:* 25 minutes *Servings:* 4

Ingredients:
- 2 garlic cloves, minced
- 1 yellow onion, chopped
- 2 tablespoons olive oil
- 2 cups white rice
- 4 cups chicken stock
- 1 cup kale, torn
- ½ teaspoon cumin, ground
- A pinch of salt and black pepper
- 2 tablespoons lime zest, grated
- 1 tablespoon chives, chopped

Directions:
Set your instant pot on sauté mode, add the oil, heat it up, add the onion, garlic and cumin and sauté for 5 minutes Add the rice, stock and the other ingredients, toss, put the lid on and cook on High for 20 minutes. Release the pressure naturally for 10 minutes, divide the mix between plates and serve as a side dish.

Nutrition: calories 200, fat 7, fiber 4, carbs 6, protein 5

Cheesy Green Beans

Preparation time: 10 minutes *Cooking time:* 15 minutes *Servings:* 4

Ingredients:
- 1 tablespoon olive oil
- 1 pound green beans, trimmed and halved
- 2 garlic cloves, minced
- 1 cup chicken stock
- ½ cup parmesan, grated
- 1 tablespoon thyme, chopped
- A pinch of salt and black pepper

Directions:
Set your instant pot on Sauté mode, add the oil, heat up, add the garlic, stir and cook for 2 minutes. Add green beans and the rest of the ingredients, toss, put the lid on and cook on High for 13 minutes. Release the pressure naturally for 10 minutes, divide the mix between plates and serve as a side dish.

Nutrition: calories 185, fat 6, fiber 4, carbs 6, protein 8

Mozzarella Carrots Mix

Preparation time: 10 minutes *Cooking time:* 20 minutes *Servings:* 6

Ingredients:
- ¼ cup chicken stock
- 1 red onion, chopped
- 2 tablespoons olive oil
- 1 pound baby carrots, peeled
- A pinch of salt and black pepper
- 1 tablespoon cilantro, chopped
- 1 cup mozzarella cheese, shredded

Directions:
Set your instant pot on Sauté mode, add the oil, heat it up, add the onion, and sauté for 5 minutes Add the carrots and the other ingredients except the cheese, toss, put the lid on and cook on High for 15 minutes. Release the pressure naturally for 10 minutes, add the cheese, toss the mix, divide between plates and serve as side dish.

Nutrition: calories 200, fat 7, fiber 2, carbs 5, protein 6

Squash Mash

Preparation time: 10 minutes **Cooking time:** *20 minutes* **Servings:** *4*

Ingredients:
- 1 cup almond milk
- 1 pound butternut squash, peeled and cubed
- 1 teaspoon allspice, ground
- 1 teaspoon turmeric powder
- 1 teaspoon cumin, ground
- A pinch of salt and black pepper
- 2 tablespoons butter
- ½ teaspoon nutmeg, grated

Directions:
Combine the squash with the milk in the instant pot, put the lid on and cook on High for 20 minutes. Release the pressure naturally for 10 minutes, transfer the mix to a bowl, mash well with a potato masher, add the butter, turmeric and the other ingredients, whisk well, divide between plates and serve as a side dish.

Nutrition: calories 126, fat 4, fiber 5, carbs 8, protein 5

Cheesy Asparagus

Preparation time: 5 minutes **Cooking time:** *8 minutes* **Servings:** *4*

Ingredients:
- 1 pound asparagus, trimmed
- 1 cup parmesan, grated
- 2 tablespoons olive oil
- ½ cup chicken stock
- ½ teaspoon nutmeg, ground
- ¼ teaspoon allspice
- 2 tablespoons chives, chopped

Directions:
In your instant pot, combine the asparagus with the stock and the other ingredients except the parmesan, toss, put the lid on and cook on High for 8 minutes Release the pressure fast for 5 minutes, divide the asparagus between plates, sprinkle the cheese on top and serve as a side dish.

Nutrition: calories 175, fat 4, fiber 2, carbs 6, protein 8

Lime Artichokes

Preparation time: 5 minutes Cooking time: 15 minutes Servings: 4

Ingredients:
- 2 artichokes, trimmed and halved
- Juice of 1 lime
- 2 tablespoons olive oil
- 1 cup water
- A pinch of salt and black pepper
- ¼ teaspoon sweet paprika
- ¼ teaspoon basil, dried
- ½ teaspoon chili powder

Directions:
In a bowl, combine the artichokes with the lime juice and the other ingredients except the water and toss. Put the water in the instant pot, add the steamer basket inside, put the artichoke halves in the basket, put the lid on and cook on High for 15 minutes. Release the pressure fast for 5 minutes, divide the artichokes between plates and serve as a side dish.

Nutrition: calories 200, fat 5, fiber 3, carbs 6, protein 7

Tomato and Avocado Salad

Preparation time: 5 minutes Cooking time: 5 minutes Servings: 4

Ingredients:
- 1 pound cherry tomatoes, halved
- 2 avocados, peeled, pitted and cubed
- 2 spring onions, chopped
- 2 tablespoons olive oil
- A pinch of salt and black pepper
- 1 tablespoon cilantro, chopped
- 2 teaspoons balsamic vinegar

Directions:
In your instant pot, combine the tomatoes with the spring onions and the other ingredients, toss, put the lid on and cook on High for 5 minutes. Release the pressure fast for 5 minutes, divide the mix between plates and serve as a side salad.

Nutrition: calories 162, fat 6, fiber 2, carbs 6, protein 4

Tomato and Red Beans Mix

Preparation time: 10 minutes *Cooking time: 15 minutes* *Servings: 4*

Ingredients:
- 2 cups canned red kidney beans, drained and rinsed
- ½ pound cherry tomatoes, halved
- A pinch of salt and black pepper
- 2 tablespoons olive oil
- 1 teaspoon rosemary, dried
- 1 teaspoon chili powder
- 1 yellow onion, chopped
- 1 teaspoon thyme, dried
- 1 cup veggie stock
- 2 tablespoons chives, chopped
- 2 tablespoons cilantro, chopped

Directions:
Set your instant pot on Sauté mode, add the oil, heat it up, add the onion, rosemary, chili powder and the thyme, stir and sauté for 5 minutes. Add the beans, tomato and the rest of the ingredients except the cilantro, put the lid on and cook on High for 10 minutes. Release the pressure naturally for 10 minutes, divide the mix between plates and serve as a side dish.

Nutrition: calories 152, fat 4, fiber 2, carbs 6, protein 8

Cucumber and Avocado Salad

Preparation time: 5 minutes *Cooking time: 5 minutes* *Servings: 4*

Ingredients:
- ¼ cup veggie stock
- 2 cucumbers, sliced
- 2 avocados, peeled, pitted and roughly cubed
- 1 red onion, roughly chopped
- 2 tablespoons avocado oil
- A pinch of salt and black pepper
- 1 tablespoon dill, chopped

Directions:
In your instant pot, combine the cucumbers with the avocados and the other ingredients, put the lid on and cook on High for 5 minutes. Release the pressure fast for 5 minutes, divide the mix between plates and serve as a side salad.

Nutrition: calories 200, fat 8, fiber 4, carbs 7, protein 9

Masala Carrots

Preparation time: 10 minutes *Cooking time:* 15 minutes *Servings:* 4

Ingredients:
- 2 pounds baby carrots, peeled
- 3 tablespoons olive oil
- 1 red onion, chopped
- 2 garlic cloves, minced
- Salt and black pepper to the taste
- 1 cup veggie stock
- 1 teaspoon garam masala

Directions:
Set your instant pot on Sauté mode, add the oil, heat it up, add the onion and garlic and sauté for 2 minutes. Add the carrots and the rest of the ingredients, put the lid on and cook on High for 13 minutes. Release the pressure naturally for 10 minutes, divide the mix between plates and serve as a side dish.

Nutrition: calories 162, fat 4, fiber 4, carbs 9, protein 7

Turmeric Parsnips

Preparation time: 10 minutes *Cooking time:* 12 minutes *Servings:* 4

Ingredients:
- 1 pound parsnips, peeled and cut into sticks
- 2 tablespoons olive oil
- 1 teaspoon sweet paprika
- ½ teaspoon nutmeg, ground
- A pinch of salt and black pepper
- 1 cup veggie stock
- 1 teaspoon turmeric powder
- 1 tablespoon rosemary, chopped

Directions:
In your instant pot, combine the parsnips with the oil, paprika and the other ingredients except the rosemary, put the lid on and cook on High for 12 minutes. Release the pressure naturally for 10 minutes, divide the mix between plates and serve with the rosemary sprinkled on top.

Nutrition: calories 142, fat 2, fiber 4, carbs 9, protein 4

Creamy Cabbage

*Preparation time: 10 minutes **Cooking time:** 12 minutes **Servings:** 4*

Ingredients:
- 1 pound green cabbage, shredded
- 2 tablespoons olive oil
- 1 red onion, chopped
- 1 teaspoon Italian seasoning
- 1 teaspoon rosemary, dried
- 1 cup heavy cream
- ½ cup chicken stock
- Salt and black pepper to the taste
- 2 spring onions, chopped

Directions:
Set the instant pot on Sauté mode, add the oil, heat it up, add the onion, rosemary and Italian seasoning, stir and sauté for 2 minutes. Add the cabbage and the other ingredients, toss, put the lid on and cook on High for 10 minutes. Release the pressure naturally for 10 minutes, divide the mix between plates and serve as a side dish.

Nutrition: calories 142, fat 4, fiber 3, carbs 6, protein 10

Allspice Brussels Sprouts

*Preparation time: 10 minutes **Cooking time:** 15 minutes **Servings:** 4*

Ingredients:
- 1 pound Brussels sprouts, trimmed and halved
- 1 teaspoon allspice, ground
- 1 tablespoon avocado oil
- A pinch of salt and black pepper
- 1 cup veggie stock
- 1 tablespoon chives, chopped

Directions:
In your instant pot, combine the Brussels sprouts with the allspice and the other ingredients, toss, put the lid on and cook on High for 15 minutes. Release the pressure naturally for 10 minutes, divide the mix between plates and serve as a side dish.

Nutrition: calories 132, fat 4, fiber 3, carbs 6, protein 9

Eggplant Hash

Preparation time: 5 minutes **Cooking time:** 15 minutes **Servings:** 4

Ingredients:
- ½ cup chicken stock
- 1 pound eggplant, roughly cubed
- 2 tablespoons avocado oil
- 1 red onion, chopped
- ½ teaspoon basil, dried
- ½ teaspoon sweet paprika
- ½ teaspoon allspice, ground
- ½ teaspoon fennel seeds
- A pinch of salt and black pepper

Directions:
Set the instant pot on Sauté mode, add the oil, heat it up, add the onion, paprika, allspice and fennel and sauté for 5 minutes. Add the eggplant and the rest of the ingredients, put the lid on and cook on High for 10 minutes. Release the pressure fast for 5 minutes, divide the mix between plates and serve.

Nutrition: calories 142, fat 7, fiber 4, carbs 6, protein 8

Spinach and Carrots Mix

Preparation time: 10 minutes **Cooking time:** 15 minutes **Servings:** 4

Ingredients:
- ½ cup veggie stock
- 1 pound baby carrots, peeled
- ½ pound baby spinach
- 1 tablespoon olive oil
- ½ teaspoon nutmeg, ground
- ½ teaspoon allspice, ground
- 1 teaspoon dill, dried
- A pinch of salt and black pepper
- 2 tablespoons balsamic vinegar

Directions:
In your instant pot, combine the carrots with the spinach and the other ingredients, put the lid on and cook on High for 15 minutes. Release the pressure naturally for 10 minutes, divide the mix between plates and serve as a side dish.

Nutrition: calories 152, fat 7, fiber 2, carbs 7, protein 5

Orange Greens

Preparation time: 10 minutes Cooking time: 10 minutes Servings: 6
Ingredients:
1. 1 bunch collard greens
2. 1 cup red chard
3. 2 tablespoons olive oil
4. 1 red onion, chopped
5. A pinch of salt and black pepper
6. ¼ cup orange juice
7. 1 teaspoon orange zest, grated
8. 1 tablespoon cilantro, chopped

Directions:
Set the instant pot on Sauté mode, add the oil, heat it up, add the onion and orange zest and sauté for 2 minutes Add the collard greens and the other ingredients, toss, put the lid on and cook for 8 minutes Release the pressure naturally for 10 minutes, divide the mix between plates and serve.

Nutrition: calories 152, fat 4, fiber 3, carbs 4, protein 3

Broccoli Salad

Preparation time: 10 minutes Cooking time: 15 minutes Servings: 4
Ingredients:
- 1 pound broccoli florets
- 1 cup black olives, pitted and halved
- 1 cup cherry tomatoes, halved
- 1 red onion, chopped
- 2 garlic cloves, minced
- 1 teaspoon turmeric powder
- ½ teaspoon coriander, ground
- ½ teaspoon fennel seeds, crushed
- Salt and black pepper to the taste
- 2 tablespoons olive oil
- ½ cup chicken stock
- 1 tablespoon chives, chopped
- 1 teaspoon sweet paprika

Directions:
In your instant pot, combine the broccoli with the onion, garlic and the other ingredients, put the lid on and cook on High for 15 minutes. Release the pressure naturally for 10 minutes, divide the mix between plates and serve as a side salad.

Nutrition: calories 187, fat 7, fiber 3, carbs 5, protein 5

Olives and Tomato Mix

Preparation time: 10 minutes **Cooking time:** *15 minutes* **Servings:** *4*

Ingredients:
- 1 pound cherry tomatoes, halved
- 1 cup kalamata olives, pitted and halved
- ¼ cup veggie stock
- 2 tablespoon balsamic vinegar
- 2 tablespoons olive oil
- 2 tablespoons rosemary, chopped
- 2 tablespoons capers, drained
- A pinch of salt and black pepper

Directions:
In the instant pot, combine the tomatoes with the olives, the stock and the other ingredients, toss, put the lid on and cook on High for 15 minutes. Release the pressure naturally for 10 minutes, divide the mix between plates and serve.

Nutrition: calories 120, fat 4, fiber 3, carbs 8, protein 4

Creamy Spinach and Corn

Preparation time: 5 minutes **Cooking time:** *20 minutes* **Servings:** *4*

Ingredients:
- 2 cups baby spinach
- 2 cups fresh corn
- 1 red onion, chopped
- 2 tablespoons olive oil
- Juice of 1 lime
- 1 cup heavy cream
- A pinch of salt and black pepper
- ½ cup cream cheese, soft
- 2 tablespoons chives, chopped

Directions:
Set the instant pot on Sauté mode, add the oil, heat it up, add the onion and sauté for 5 minutes. Add the spinach, the corn and the other ingredients, toss, put the lid on and cook on High for 15 minutes. Release the pressure fast for 5 minutes, divide the mix between plates and serve.

Nutrition: calories 165, fat 4, fiber 3, carbs 7, protein 6

Mushroom and Tomato Mix

Preparation time: *10 minutes* **Cooking time:** *15 minutes* **Servings:** *4*

Ingredients:
- ½ pound baby Bella mushrooms, halved
- ½ pound cherry tomatoes, halved
- 2 tablespoons olive oil
- 4 scallions, chopped
- ½ cup chicken stock
- 1 teaspoon chili powder
- 1 tablespoon rosemary, chopped
- Salt and black pepper to the taste
- 1 tablespoon balsamic vinegar

Directions:
Set the instant pot on Sauté mode, add the oil, heat it up, add the scallions, mushrooms and chili powder, stir and sauté for 5 minutes. Add the tomatoes and the other ingredients, toss, put the lid on and cook on High for 10 minutes. Release the pressure naturally for 10 minutes, divide the mix between plates and serve.

Nutrition: calories 173, fat 5, fiber 2, carbs 5, protein 6

Zucchini Salad

Preparation time: *10 minutes* **Cooking time:** *15 minutes* **Servings:** *4*

Ingredients:
- ½ cup chicken stock
- 1 pound zucchinis, roughly sliced
- 2 tablespoons olive oil
- 4 scallions, chopped
- A pinch of salt and black pepper
- 2 teaspoon coriander, ground
- ½ teaspoon sweet paprika
- 3 tablespoons balsamic vinegar
- 2 tablespoons chives, chopped

Directions:
Set the instant pot on Sauté mode, add the oil, heat it up, add the scallions, coriander and paprika, stir and sauté for 5 minutes. Add the zucchinis and the other ingredients, toss, put the lid on and cook on High for 10 minutes. Release the pressure naturally for 10 minutes, divide the mix between plates and serve as a side dish.

Nutrition: calories 173, fat 8, fiber 2, carbs 6, protein 6

Cauliflower and Cabbage Mix

Preparation time: 10 minutes *Cooking time:* 15 minutes *Servings:* 4

Ingredients:
- 1 cup chicken stock
- 1 pound cauliflower florets
- 1 red cabbage head, shredded
- 1 tablespoon olive oil
- A pinch of salt and black pepper
- ¼ cup walnuts, chopped
- ½ teaspoon sweet paprika

Directions:
In your instant pot, combine the cauliflower florets with the cabbage and the other ingredients, toss, put the lid on and cook on High for 15 minutes. Release the pressure naturally for 10 minutes, divide the mix between plates and serve as a side dish.

Nutrition: calories 130, fat 5, fiber 3, carbs 6, protein 7

Pomegranate and Beans Mix

Preparation time: 10 minutes *Cooking time:* 12 minutes *Servings:* 4
Ingredients:
- 1 cup canned black beans, drained and rinsed
- 1 cup canned red kidney beans drained and rinsed
- ½ cup pomegranate seeds
- 1 tablespoon olive oil
- Juice of 1 orange
- 1 cup veggie stock
- 1 teaspoon chili powder
- 1 red chili pepper, chopped
- A pinch of salt and black pepper
- 2 tablespoons chives, chopped

Directions:
In your instant pot, combine the beans with the pomegranate seeds, the oil and the other ingredients, toss, put the lid and cook on High for 12 minutes. Release the pressure naturally for 10 minutes, divide the mix between plates and serve as a side dish.
Nutrition: calories 142, fat 4, fiber 2, carbs 4, protein 5

Dates Rice

Preparation time: 10 minutes *Cooking time:* 20 minutes *Servings:* 4

Ingredients:
- 2 cups chicken stock
- ¼ cup dates, chopped
- 1 and ½ cups cauliflower rice
- 1 teaspoon turmeric powder
- 1 teaspoon allspice, ground
- 4 garlic cloves, minced
- 1 teaspoon nutmeg, ground
- Salt and black pepper to the taste

Directions:

In your instant pot, combine the cauliflower rice with the stock and the other ingredients, toss, put the lid on and cook on High for 20 minutes. Release the pressure naturally for 10 minutes, divide the mix between plates and serve as a side dish.

Nutrition: calories 190, fat 6, fiber 2, carbs 6, protein 7

Chickpeas and Tomato Salad

Preparation time: 10 minutes *Cooking time:* 20 minutes *Servings:* 4

Ingredients:
- 2 cups canned chickpeas, drained and rinsed
- 1 pound cherry tomatoes, halved
- 1 cup chicken stock
- 1 tablespoon olive oil
- 1 red onion, sliced
- 1 red chili pepper, chopped
- ¼ teaspoon cumin, ground
- ½ teaspoon coriander, ground
- 2 tablespoons garlic, minced
- A pinch of salt and black pepper
- 1 tablespoon chives, chopped

Directions:

Set the instant pot on Sauté mode, add the oil, heat it up, add the onion, chili pepper, cumin, coriander and the garlic and sauté for 5 minutes Add the chickpeas and the rest of the ingredients except the chives, put the lid on and cook on High for 15 minutes Release the pressure naturally for 10 minutes, add the chives, toss, divide the mix between plates and serve.

Nutrition: calories 161, fat 6, fiber 5, carbs 7, protein 7

Instant Pot Soup Recipes
Chicken Soup
Preparation time: *10 minutes* ***Cooking time:*** *20 minutes* ***Servings:*** *6*

Ingredients:

- 1 yellow onion, chopped
- 2 tablespoons olive oil
- 2 celery stalks, chopped
- 2 carrots, peeled and cubed
- 2 teaspoons thyme, chopped
- 2 garlic cloves, minced
- 2 pounds chicken breasts, skinless, boneless and cubed
- A pinch of salt and black pepper
- 4 cups water
- 4 cups chicken stock
- A pinch of red pepper flakes
- Juice of ¼ lemon
- 2 tablespoons parsley, chopped

Directions:

Set the instant pot on Sauté mode, add the oil, heat it up, add the onion, celery, carrots and garlic and sauté for 10 minutes. Add the chicken and the other ingredients except the lemon juice and parsley, toss, put the lid on and cook on High for 10 minutes. Release the pressure naturally for 10 minutes, add the lemon juice and parsley, stir the soup, ladle into bowls and serve.

Nutrition: calories

Veggie Soup
Preparation time: *10 minutes* ***Cooking time:*** *20 minutes* ***Servings:*** *6*

Ingredients:

- 1 yellow onion, chopped
- 1 tablespoon olive oil
- 4 garlic cloves, minced
- 2 cups cabbage, shredded
- 1 tablespoon tomato passata
- 2 cups cauliflower florets
- 2 celery stalks, chopped
- 2 carrots, peeled and cubed
- 1 red bell pepper, chopped
- 1 zucchini, chopped
- 14 ounces canned kidney beans, drained and rinsed
- 14 ounces canned tomatoes, chopped
- 2 teaspoons Italian seasoning
- 4 cups veggie stock
- 1 teaspoon sweet paprika
- Salt and black pepper to the taste
- 1 tablespoon parsley, chopped

Directions:

Set the instant pot on Sauté mode, add the oil, heat it up, add the onion, garlic, celery, carrots and bell pepper and sauté for 5 minutes. Add the cabbage, tomato passata and the other ingredients except the parsley, toss, put the lid on and cook on High for 15 minutes. Release the pressure naturally for 10 minutes, add the parsley, stir the soup, ladle into bowls and serve.

Nutrition: calories

Tortilla Chicken Soup

Preparation time: *10 minutes* ***Cooking time:*** *30 minutes* ***Servings:*** *6*

Ingredients:

- 2 red bell peppers, chopped
- 2 tablespoons olive oil
- 1 yellow onion, chopped
- 1 teaspoon oregano, dried
- 2 garlic cloves, minced
- ½ teaspoon cumin, ground
- ½ teaspoon chili powder
- 2 pounds chicken breast, skinless, boneless and cubed
- Salt and black pepper to the taste
- 5 cups chicken stock
- 14 ounces canned tomatoes, chopped
- 14 ounces canned black beans, drained and rinsed
- 1 cup corn
- ¼ cup cilantro, chopped
- 4 corn tortillas, cut into strips
- 1 cup Monterey Jack cheese, shredded

Directions:

Set the instant pot on Sauté mode, add the oil, heat it up, add the onion, bell peppers, garlic, oregano, cumin and chili powder and sauté for 5 minutes. Add the meat and brown for 5 minutes more. Add the rest of the ingredients except the tortillas, cilantro and the cheese, stir, put the lid on and cook on High for 20 minutes. Release the pressure naturally for 10 minutes, divide the soup into bowls, top each serving with the cilantro, tortilla strips and the cheese and serve.
Nutrition: calories 353, fat 12.4, fiber 3.4, carbs 14, protein 5.4

Potato Soup

Preparation time: *10 minutes* ***Cooking time:*** *25 minutes* ***Servings:*** *4*

Ingredients:

- 1 yellow onion, chopped
- 2 tablespoons butter
- 2 garlic cloves, minced
- 6 potatoes, peeled and cubed
- 1 teaspoon thyme, chopped
- 1 cup milk
- 4 cups chicken stock
- 2 tablespoons cornstarch
- Salt and black pepper to the taste
- ½ cup heavy cream
- ¼ cup cheddar cheese, shredded

Directions:

Set the instant pot on Sauté mode, add the butter, melt it, add the onion, garlic and thyme and cook for 5 minutes. Add the potatoes and the stock, stir, put the lid on and cook on High for 10 minutes. Release the pressure naturally for 10 minutes, set the pot on Sauté mode again, add the milk combined with the cornstarch, cream, salt and pepper, stir and cook for 5 minutes more. Add the cheese, stir, cook the soup for another 5 minutes, divide the soup into bowls and serve.**Nutrition:** calories 300, fat 12, fiber 3, carbs 15, protein 5

Lentils Soup

Preparation time: *10 minutes* **Cooking time:** *30 minutes* **Servings:** *4*

Ingredients:

- 2 celery stalks, chopped
- 1 yellow onion, chopped
- 1 carrots, chopped
- 2 garlic cloves, minced
- 2 teaspoons thyme, chopped
- 2 cups green lentils
- 14 ounces canned tomatoes, chopped
- Salt and black pepper to the taste
- 1 teaspoon Italian seasoning
- 4 cups chicken stock
- 4 cups baby spinach

Directions:

In your instant pot, combine the celery with the onion, carrots, lentils and the other ingredients except the spinach, stir, put the lid on and cook on High for 25 minutes. Release the pressure naturally for 10 minutes, set the pot on Sauté mode again, add the spinach, cook the soup for 5 more minutes, ladle it into bowls and serve.**Nutrition:** calories 242, fat 12, fiber 3, carbs 15, protein 5

Split Pea Soup

Preparation time: *10 minutes* **Cooking time:** *30 minutes* **Servings:** *6*

Ingredients:

- 1 leek, sliced
- ¼ cup olive oil
- 3 carrots, sliced
- 1 yellow onion, chopped
- 3 garlic cloves, minced
- 2 celery stalks, chopped
- 1 and ½ cups split peas
- Salt and black pepper to the taste
- 4 ounces ham, chopped
- 4 cups chicken stock
- 1 tablespoon thyme, chopped
- 2 tablespoons lemon juice

Directions:

Set the instant pot on Sauté mode, add the oil, heat it up, add the leek, carrots, onion, garlic and celery, stir and sauté for 10 minutes. Add the peas and the other ingredients except the lemon juice, stir, put the lid on and cook on High for 20 minutes. Release the pressure naturally for 10 minutes, add the lemon juice, ladle the soup into bowls and serve.

Nutrition: calories 288, fat 12, fiber 4, carbs 16, protein 5

Italian Sausage Soup

Preparation time: 10 minutes **Cooking time:** *20 minutes* **Servings:** *6*

Ingredients:
- 1 tablespoon olive oil
- 1 yellow onion, chopped
- 2 garlic cloves, minced
- 1 pound Italian sausage, casings removed
- 3 gold potatoes, peeled and cubed
- ½ teaspoon oregano, dried
- 6 cups chicken stock
- Salt and black pepper to the taste
- ½ bunch kale, torn
- 1 cup half and half

Directions:
Set the instant pot on Sauté mode, add the oil, heat it up, add the onion, garlic and sausage and cook for 5 minutes. Add the potatoes and the other ingredients, toss, put the lid on and cook on High for 15 minutes. Release the pressure naturally for 10 minutes, ladle the soup into bowls and serve.

Nutrition: calories 344, fat 14, fiber 3.3, carbs 20.4, protein 5

Basil Tomato Soup

Preparation time: 10 minutes **Cooking time:** *1 hour* **Servings:** *6*

Ingredients:
- 4 pounds tomatoes, halved
- ¼ cup olive oil
- 2 tablespoons butter
- Salt and black pepper to the taste
- 6 garlic cloves, minced
- 2 cups yellow onion, chopped
- ¼ teaspoons red pepper flakes
- 1 teaspoon rosemary, chopped
- 1 teaspoon thyme, chopped
- 1 cup basil leaves
- 2 cups chicken stock

Directions:
Arrange the tomatoes on a baking sheet, add the oil, salt and pepper, toss and roast at 400 degrees F for 40 minutes. Set the instant pot on Sauté mode, add the butter, melt it, add the onion and the garlic and sauté for 5 minutes. Add the roasted tomatoes and the other ingredients except the basil, stir, put the lid on and cook on High for 15 minutes. Release the pressure naturally for 10 minutes, blend the soup using an immersion blender, add the basil, stir, divide into bowls and serve.

Nutrition: calories 245, fat 12, fiber 5. carbs 15, protein 5.6

Mushroom Cream Soup

*Preparation time: 10 minutes **Cooking time:** 25 minutes **Servings:** 4*

Ingredients:

- 1 tablespoon olive oil
- 1 carrots, chopped
- 1 celery stalk, chopped
- 1 yellow onion, chopped
- 4 garlic cloves, minced
- 8 ounces shiitake mushrooms, sliced
- 8 ounces cremini mushrooms, sliced
- 1 teaspoon thyme, dried
- Salt and black pepper to the taste
- 1 cup coconut milk
- 3 cups veggie stock

Directions:

Set the instant pot on Sauté mode, add the oil, heat it up, add the carrots, celery, onion and garlic and sauté for 5 minutes. Add the mushrooms and sauté for 5 minutes more. Add the rest of the ingredients except the coconut milk, stir, put the lid on and cook on High for 15 minutes. Release the pressure naturally for 10 minutes, transfer the soup to a blender, add the coconut milk, pulse well, divide into bowls and serve.

Nutrition: calories 108, fat 5.3, fiber 3.6, carbs 12.7, protein 4.8

Beef Soup

*Preparation time: 10 minutes **Cooking time:** 50 minutes **Servings:** 4*

Ingredients:

- 1 and ½ pounds beef stew meat, cubed
- 5 cups beef stock
- ½ teaspoon Italian seasoning
- 4 tablespoons Worcestershire sauce
- 1 teaspoon onion powder
- Salt and black pepper to the taste
- 2 teaspoons garlic powder
- 8 ounces mushrooms, sliced
- ½ cup sour cream
- 1/3 cup cold water
- ¼ cup cornstarch

Directions:

In your instant pot, combine the beef with the stock, the seasoning and the other ingredients except the cream, water and cornstarch, put the lid on and cook on High for 40 minutes. Release the pressure naturally for 10 minutes, add the water mixed with cornstarch and the cream, set the machine on Sauté mode again, cook the soup for 10 minutes more, divide into bowls and serve.

Nutrition: calories 400, fat 15, fiber 5, carbs 22, protein 14

Chili Chicken and Peppers Soup

Preparation time: 10 minutes **Cooking time:** *20 minutes* **Servings:** *4*

Ingredients:
- 2 tablespoons olive oil
- ¼ cup red onion, chopped
- 2 garlic cloves, minced
- 1 red bell pepper, chopped
- 1 green bell pepper, chopped
- 1 orange bell pepper, chopped
- 6 cups chicken stock
- 2 pounds chicken breasts, skinless, boneless and cubed
- 1 tablespoon chili powder
- 1 cup coconut cream
- 1 tablespoon parsley, chopped

Directions:

Set your instant pot on sauté mode, add the oil, heat it up, add the onion, garlic and bell peppers and sauté for 5 minutes. Add the chicken meat and cook for 5 minutes more. Add the rest of the ingredients except the parsley, stir, put the lid on and cook on High for 10 minutes. Release the pressure naturally for 10 minutes, divide into bowls and serve with the parsley sprinkled on top.

Nutrition: calories 273, fat 14, fiber 4, carbs 6, protein 18

Cauliflower Soup

Preparation time: 10 minutes **Cooking time:** *20 minutes* **Servings:** *4*

Ingredients:
- 1 yellow onion, chopped
- 1 tablespoon olive oil
- 3 garlic cloves, minced
- 1 pound cauliflower florets
- 3 cups veggie stock
- 1 teaspoon cumin, ground
- 1 teaspoon rosemary, dried
- 1 teaspoon basil, dried
- ½ cup heavy cream

Directions:

Set your instant pot on sauté mode, add the oil, heat it up, add the onion and garlic, stir and cook for 5 minutes. Add the cauliflower, stock and the rest of the ingredients except the cream, put the lid on and cook on High for 15 minutes. Release the pressure naturally for 10 minutes, add the cream, blend the soup using an immersion blender, divide into bowls and serve.

Nutrition: calories 271, fat 12, fiber 5, carbs 7, protein 9

Garlicky Beef Soup

*Preparation time: 10 minutes **Cooking time:** 30 minutes **Servings:** 4*

Ingredients:
- 2 pound beef stew meat, cubed
- 2 tablespoons olive oil
- 1 red onion, chopped
- 2 celery stalks, chopped
- 1 carrots, peeled and sliced
- A pinch of salt and black pepper
- 6 garlic cloves, minced
- 6 cups beef stock
- 1 tablespoon cilantro, chopped

Directions:
Set your instant pot on sauté mode, add the oil, heat it up, add the onion, celery and the carrots and sauté for 5 minutes Add the meat and brown for 5 minutes more. Add the rest of the ingredients, stir, put the lid on and cook on High for 20 minutes. Release the pressure naturally for 10 minutes, divide the soup into bowls and serve.

Nutrition: calories 283, fat 12, fiber 4, carbs 7, protein 10

Broccoli Soup

*Preparation time: 10 minutes **Cooking time:** 20 minutes **Servings:** 4*

Ingredients:
- 1 pound broccoli florets
- 1 red onion, chopped
- 1 tablespoon olive oil
- 3 garlic cloves, minced
- 4 cups veggie stock
- 1 cup heavy cream
- 1 teaspoon turmeric powder
- 2 tablespoons cilantro, chopped

Directions:
Set the instant pot, on Sauté mode, add the oil, heat it up, add the onion and the garlic and sauté for 5 minutes. Add the broccoli and the other ingredients, stir, put the lid on and cook on High for 15 minutes. Release the pressure naturally for 10 minutes, blend using an immersion blender, ladle into bowls and serve.

Nutrition: calories 201, fat 6, fiber 4, carbs 7, protein 10

Spinach Soup

Preparation time: 10 minutes *Cooking time:* 20 minutes *Servings:* 4

Ingredients:
- 1 tablespoon olive oil
- 1 yellow onion, chopped
- 1 carrots, peeled and sliced
- 3 cups baby spinach
- 4 garlic cloves, minced
- 1 teaspoon chili powder
- 1 teaspoon rosemary, dried
- 1 teaspoon turmeric powder
- 4 cups veggie stock
- 1 tablespoon cilantro, chopped

Directions:
Set your instant pot on sauté mode, add the oil, heat it up, add the onion, carrot and the garlic and sauté for 5 minutes. Add the rest of the ingredients except the cilantro, toss, put the lid on and cook on High or 15 minutes. Release the pressure naturally for 10 minutes, ladle the soup into bowls and serve with the cilantro sprinkled on top.

Nutrition: calories 199, fat 5, fiber 4, carbs 6, protein 11

Ginger Chicken Soup

Preparation time: 10 minutes *Cooking time:* 25 minutes *Servings:* 4

Ingredients:
- 1 yellow onion, chopped
- 2 tablespoons olive oil
- 1 celery stalk, chopped
- 1 carrot, peeled and sliced
- 1 tablespoon ginger, grated
- 2 garlic cloves, minced
- 2 tomatoes, cubed
- 1 pound chicken breast, boneless, skinless and cubed
- 6 cups chicken stock
- A pinch of salt and black pepper
- 2 tablespoons chives, chopped

Directions:
Set your instant pot on sauté mode, add oil, heat it up, add the onion, celery stalk, the carrot, ginger and the garlic and sauté for 5 minutes. Add the meat and brown for 5 minutes more. Add the rest of the ingredients except the chives, stir, put the lid on and cook on High for 15 minutes. Release the pressure naturally for 10 minutes, ladle the soup into bowls and serve with the chives on top.

Nutrition: calories 201, fat 8, fiber 2, carbs 5, protein 9

Cheesy Sweet Potato Cream

Preparation time: *10 minutes* ***Cooking time:*** *20 minutes* ***Servings:*** *4*

Ingredients:
- 4 sweet potatoes, peeled and cubed
- 1 yellow onion, chopped
- 4 garlic cloves, minced
- 2 tablespoons olive oil
- 6 cups chicken stock
- A pinch of salt and black pepper
- 2 cups heavy cream
- 1 cup cheddar cheese, grated

Directions:
Set your instant pot on Sauté mode, add the oil, heat it up, add the onion and the garlic and sauté for 5 minutes. Add the sweet potatoes and the other ingredients except the cream and the cheese, put the lid on and cook on High for 15 minutes. Release the pressure naturally for 10 minutes, transfer the soup to a blender, add the cream and cheese, pulse well, divide into bowls and serve.

Nutrition: calories 210, fat 7, fiber 4, carbs 6, protein 11

Corn Soup

Preparation time: *10 minutes* ***Cooking time:*** *15 minutes* ***Servings:*** *4*

Ingredients:
- 1 tablespoon avocado oil
- 4 scallions, chopped
- 2 carrots, peeled and sliced
- 4 cups corn
- 2 tomatoes, cubed
- 5 cups veggie stock
- 1 cup heavy cream
- A pinch of salt and black pepper
- 2 tablespoons chives, chopped

Directions:
Set your instant pot on Sauté mode, add the oil, heat it up, add the scallions and the carrots and sauté for 5 minutes Add the corn and the rest of the ingredients except the cream and chives, stir, put the lid on and cook on High for 10 minutes. Release the pressure naturally for 10 minutes, add the cream and the chives, stir, divide the soup into bowls.

Nutrition: calories 185, fat 6, fiber 4, carbs 8, protein 10

Hot Bell Pepper Soup

Preparation time: 10 minutes **Cooking time:** *20 minutes* **Servings:** *4*

Ingredients:

- 1 yellow onion, chopped
- 2 tablespoons olive oil
- 2 red bell peppers, roughly cubed
- 1 green bell pepper, roughly cubed
- 1 orange bell pepper, roughly cubed
- 3 tablespoons tomato paste
- 6 cups chicken stock
- 1 teaspoon garlic powder
- 1 teaspoon onion powder
- 1 teaspoon rosemary, dried
- ½ tablespoon cilantro, chopped
- ½ teaspoon red pepper flakes

Directions:

Set the instant pot on Sauté mode, add the oil, heat it up, add the onion, bell peppers, onion and garlic powder and sauté for 5 minutes Add the rest of the ingredients, put the lid on and cook on High for 15 minutes. Release the pressure naturally for 10 minutes, divide the soup into bowls and serve.

Nutrition: calories 180, fat 5, fiber 3, carbs 6, protein 10

Cabbage Soup

Preparation time: 10 minutes **Cooking time:** *15 minutes* **Servings:** *4*

Ingredients:

- 1 green cabbage head, shredded
- 1 red cabbage head, shredded
- 1 yellow onion, chopped
- 2 tablespoons olive oil
- A pinch of salt and black pepper
- 1 teaspoon sweet paprika
- 12 ounces canned tomatoes, chopped
- ¼ cup cilantro, chopped
- 4 cups chicken stock

Directions:

Set the instant pot on Sauté mode, add the oil, heat it up, add the onion and the paprika and sauté for 5 minutes. Add the cabbage and the other ingredients, stir, put the lid on and cook on High for 10 minutes. Release the pressure naturally for 10 minutes, ladle the soup into bowls and serve.

Nutrition: calories 172, fat 4, fiber 4, carbs 6, protein 9

Salsa Soup

Preparation time: 10 minutes Cooking time: 25 minutes Servings: 4

Ingredients:
- 1 pound chicken breast, skinless, boneless and cubed
- 2 tablespoons olive oil
- 1 red onion, chopped
- 3 garlic cloves, minced
- 1 cup chunky salsa
- 1 teaspoon cumin, ground
- 1 teaspoon coriander, ground
- 5 cups chicken stock
- A pinch of salt and black pepper
- 1 tablespoon cilantro, chopped

Directions:
Set your instant pot on Sauté mode, add the oil, heat it up, add the onion, garlic, cumin and coriander and sauté for 5 minutes. Add the meat and sauté for 5 minutes more. Add the rest of the ingredients, put the lid on and cook on High for 15 minutes. Release the pressure naturally for 10 minutes, divide the soup into bowls and serve.

Nutrition: calories 200, fat 4, fiber 4, carbs 7, protein 17

Dill Zucchini Soup

Preparation time: 10 minutes Cooking time: 15 minutes Servings: 4

Ingredients:
- 2 tablespoons olive oil
- 1 yellow onion, chopped
- 2 garlic cloves, minced
- 1 pound zucchinis, sliced
- 1 tablespoon dill, chopped
- 1 cup tomatoes, cubed
- 5 cups chicken stock
- A pinch of salt and black pepper

Directions:
Set your instant pot on Sauté mode, add the oil, heat it up, add the onion and the garlic, stir and sauté for 5 minutes. Add the zucchinis and the other ingredients, stir, put the lid on and cook on High for 10 minutes. Release the pressure naturally for 10 minutes, ladle the soup into bowls and serve.

Nutrition: calories 200, fat 5, fiber 4, carbs 8, protein 11

Pork and Tomato Soup

Preparation time: 10 minutes **Cooking time:** *25 minutes* **Servings:** *4*

Ingredients:

- 1 yellow onion, chopped
- 2 tablespoons olive oil
- 2 garlic cloves, minced
- 2 pounds pork stew meat, cubed
- ½ cup celery, chopped
- 5 cups beef stock
- 1 teaspoon cumin, ground
- ½ teaspoon chili powder
- 2 cups tomatoes, cubed
- A pinch of salt and black pepper
- 1 tablespoon parsley, chopped

Directions:

Set your instant pot on Sauté mode, add the onion, garlic and celery and sauté for 5 minutes. Add the meat and brown for 5 minutes more. Add the rest of the ingredients except the parsley, put the lid on and cook on High for 15 minutes. Release the pressure naturally for 10 minutes, ladle the soup into bowls, sprinkle the parsley on top and serve.

Nutrition: calories 192, fat 8, fiber 4, carbs 9, protein 12

Chicken and Green Beans Soup

Preparation time: 10 minutes **Cooking time:** *25 minutes* **Servings:** *4*

Ingredients:

- 6 cups chicken stock
- 1 yellow onion, chopped
- 2 pounds chicken breasts, skinless, boneless and cubed
- 2 cups green beans, trimmed and halved
- 2 tablespoons avocado oil
- A pinch of salt and black pepper
- ½ teaspoon cumin, ground
- ½ teaspoon thyme, dried
- 1 tablespoon tomato passata
- 1 tablespoon cilantro, chopped

Directions:

Set your instant pot on Sauté mode, add the oil, heat it up, add the onion, cumin and thyme and sauté for 5 minutes Add the meat and brown for 5 minutes more Add the rest of the ingredients, stir, put the lid on and cook on High for 15 minutes Release the pressure naturally for 10 minutes, divide the soup into bowls and serve.

Nutrition: calories 182, fat 3, fiber 4, carbs 6, protein 12

Creamy Turkey Soup

Preparation time: 10 minutes *Cooking time:* 25 minutes *Servings:* 4

Ingredients:

- 2 tablespoons olive oil
- 1 pound turkey breast, skinless, boneless and cubed
- 1 yellow onion, chopped
- 1 celery stalk, chopped
- 10 ounces canned tomatoes, chopped
- 2 garlic cloves, minced
- 5 cups chicken stock
- A pinch of salt and black pepper
- ½ cup heavy cream
- 1 tablespoon cilantro, chopped

Directions:

Set the instant pot on Sauté mode, add the oil, heat it up, add the onion, celery and the garlic and sauté for 5 minutes. Add the turkey and brown for 5 minutes more. Add the rest of the ingredients except the cream, put the lid on and cook on High for 10 minutes. Release the pressure naturally for 10 minutes, set the pot on Sauté mode again, add the cream, cook the soup for 5 minutes more, ladle into bowls and serve.

Nutrition: calories 192, fat 5, fiber 3, carbs 7, protein 16

Pork and Kale Soup

Preparation time: 10 minutes *Cooking time:* 25 minutes *Servings:* 4

Ingredients:

- 1 pound beef stew meat, cubed
- 1 cup kale, torn
- 1 yellow onion, chopped
- 3 garlic cloves, minced
- 2 tablespoons olive oil
- 3 tablespoons tomato passata
- 1 teaspoon coriander, ground
- 1 teaspoon cumin, ground
- 5 cups beef stock
- A pinch of salt and black pepper
- 1 tablespoon parsley, chopped

Directions:

Set your instant pot on Sauté mode, add the oil, heat it up, add the onion, garlic, coriander and cumin and sauté for 5 minutes. Add the meat and brown for 5 minutes more. Add the kale and the rest of the ingredients except the parsley, put the lid on and cook on High for 15 minutes. Release the pressure naturally for 10 minutes, add the parsley, ladle the soup into bowls and serve.

Nutrition: calories 261, fat 6, fiber 4, carbs 6, protein 15

Eggplant Soup

Preparation time: *10 minutes* ***Cooking time:*** *15 minutes* ***Servings:*** *4*

Ingredients:
1. 1 yellow onion, chopped
2. 1 tablespoon olive oil
3. 1 celery rib, chopped
4. 1 carrot, peeled and sliced
5. 1 pound eggplant, cubed
6. 10 ounces canned tomatoes, chopped
7. A pinch of salt and black pepper
8. 6 cups chicken stock
9. ½ teaspoon turmeric powder
10. 1 tablespoon cilantro, chopped

Directions:
Set your instant pot on Sauté mode, add the oil, heat it up, add the onion, celery and carrot and sauté for 5 minute Add the eggplants and the rest of the ingredients, put the lid on and cook on High for 10 minutes Release the pressure naturally for 10 minutes, ladle the soup into bowls and serve.

Nutrition: calories 200, fat 4, fiber 3, carbs 6, protein 12

Chicken and Broccoli Soup

Preparation time: *10 minutes* ***Cooking time:*** *25 minutes* ***Servings:*** *4*

Ingredients:
- 1 yellow onion, chopped
- 2 garlic cloves, minced
- 1 cup broccoli florets
- 1 pound chicken breast, skinless, boneless and cubed
- ½ teaspoon chili powder
- ½ teaspoon sweet paprika
- 1 celery stalk, chopped
- 2 tablespoons olive oil
- 6 cups chicken stock
- A pinch of salt and black pepper
- 1 tablespoon parsley, chopped

Directions:
Set your instant pot on Sauté mode, add the oil, heat it up, add the onion, garlic, chili powder, paprika and the celery and sauté for 5 minutes. Add the meat and brown for 5 minutes more. Add the stock rest of the ingredients, put the lid on and cook on High for 15 minutes. Release the pressure naturally for 10 minutes, ladle the soup into bowls and serve.

Nutrition: calories 200, fat 8, fiber 4, carbs 6, protein 12

Mint Zucchini and Green Beans Soup

Preparation time: 5 minutes *Cooking time:* 20 minutes *Servings:* 4

Ingredients:
- 1 yellow onion, chopped
- 2 garlic cloves, minced
- 2 zucchinis, sliced
- 1 pound green beans, trimmed and halved
- 2 tablespoons olive oil
- 2 celery stalks, chopped
- 1 carrot, peeled and sliced
- 6 cups chicken stock
- A pinch of salt and black pepper
- ¼ cup mint, chopped

Directions:
Set your instant pot on Sauté mode, add the oil, heat it up, add the onion, garlic, celery and carrots and sauté for 5 minutes Add the zucchinis and the rest of the ingredients except the mint, stir, put the lid on and cook on High for 15 minutes. Release the pressure fast for 5 minutes, divide into soup bowls and serve with the mint sprinkled on top.

Nutrition: calories 200, fat 5, fiber 3, carbs 7, protein 12

Tomato and Spinach Soup

Preparation time: 5 minutes *Cooking time:* 15 minutes *Servings:* 4

Ingredients:
- 1 pound tomatoes, cut into wedges
- 2 cups baby spinach
- 1 yellow onion, chopped
- 2 tablespoons avocado oil
- 1 cup tomato passata
- 3 garlic cloves, minced
- 5 cups chicken stock
- A pinch of salt and black pepper
- 1 tablespoon parsley, chopped

Directions:
Set your instant pot on Sauté mode, add the oil, heat it up, add the onion and the garlic and sauté for 5 minutes. Add the tomatoes and the rest of the ingredients, put the lid on and cook on High for 10 minutes. Release the pressure naturally for 10 minutes, ladle the soup into bowls and serve.

Nutrition: calories 200, fat 8, fiber 4, carbs 7, protein 14

Green Beans and Kale Soup

Preparation time: 10 minutes **Cooking time:** *15 minutes* **Servings:** *6*

Ingredients:
- 1 tablespoon olive oil
- 1 yellow onion, chopped
- 1 pound green beans, trimmed and halved
- 1 cup baby kale
- 1 cup tomatoes, cubed
- 2 garlic cloves, minced
- 5 cups chicken stock
- ½ teaspoon turmeric powder
- A pinch of salt and black pepper
- 2 tablespoons parsley, chopped

Directions:
Set your instant pot on Sauté mode, add the oil, heat it up, add the onion, turmeric and garlic stir and cook for 5 minutes. Add the green beans and the rest of the ingredients, put the lid on and cook on High for 10 minutes. Release the pressure naturally for 10 minutes, ladle the soup into bowls and serve.

Nutrition: calories 162, fat 4, fiber 4, carbs 6, protein 9

Kale Soup

Preparation time: 10 minutes **Cooking time:** *15 minutes* **Servings:** *4*

Ingredients:
- 1 yellow onion, chopped
- 2 tablespoons olive oil
- 1 carrot, sliced
- 1 pound kale, torn
- 2 celery ribs, chopped
- 5 cups chicken stock
- A pinch of salt and black pepper
- 1 cup heavy cream
- 1 tablespoon chives, chopped

Directions:
Set the instant pot on sauté mode, add the oil, heat it up, add the onion, carrot and the celery and sauté for 5 minutes Add the rest of the ingredients except the cream, put the lid on and cook on High for 10 minutes. Release the pressure naturally for 10 minutes, add the cream, blend using an immersion blender, divide into bowls and serve.

Nutrition: calories 162, fat 3, fiber 4, carbs 7, protein 5

Ginger Carrot Cream

Preparation time: 10 minutes **Cooking time:** 20 minutes **Servings:** 4

Ingredients:
1. 1 tablespoon olive oil
2. 1 yellow onion, chopped
3. 2 garlic cloves, minced
4. 1 pound carrots, chopped
5. 1 tablespoon ginger, grated
6. A pinch of salt and black pepper
7. 4 cups veggie stock
8. ½ teaspoon chili powder
9. ½ teaspoon turmeric powder
10. 1 cup heavy cream

Directions:

Set your instant pot on Sauté mode, add the oil, heat it up, add the onion, ginger, garlic, chili powder and turmeric and sauté for 5 minutes. Add the carrots, salt, pepper and the stock, stir, put the lid on and cook on High for 15 minutes. Release the pressure naturally for 10 minutes, add the cream, blend the soup using an immersion blender, divide into bowls and serve.

Nutrition: calories 152, fat 4, fiber 3, carbs 8, protein 5

Greens Soup

Preparation time: 5 minutes Cooking time: 12 minutes Servings: 6

Ingredients:
- 1 pound baby spinach
- 1 cup baby kale
- 1 cup red chard, torn
- 1 red onion, chopped
- 1 tablespoon olive oil
- 3 garlic cloves, minced
- 1 tomato, peeled and chopped
- 1 zucchini, cubed
- Salt and black pepper to the taste
- 6 cups veggie stock
- 1 tablespoon chives, chopped

Directions:

Set your instant pot on Sauté mode, add the oil, heat it up, add the onion and garlic, stir and cook for 2 minutes. Add the spinach, kale and the rest of the ingredients, put the lid on and cook on High for 10 minutes. Release the pressure fast for 5 minutes, ladle the soup into bowls and serve.

Nutrition: calories 172, fat 5, fiber 3, carbs 9, protein 12

Chickpeas Soup

*Preparation time: 10 minutes **Cooking time:** 25 minutes **Servings:** 4*

Ingredients:
- 2 celery stalks, chopped
- 1 carrot, sliced
- 1 zucchini, cubed
- 1 sweet potato, peeled and cubed
- 1 tablespoon olive oil
- 1 yellow onion, chopped
- 5 cups chicken stock
- 2 garlic cloves, minced
- 2 cups canned chickpeas, drained and rinsed
- ¼ cup tomato passata
- A pinch of salt and black pepper
- 1 tablespoon parsley, chopped

Directions:
Set your instant pot on Sauté mode, add the oil, heat it up, add the celery, carrot, zucchini, onion and garlic and sauté for 5 minutes. Add the chickpeas and the rest of the ingredients except the parsley, stir, put the lid on and cook on High for 20 minutes. Release the pressure naturally for 10 minutes ladle the soup into bowls and serve with the parsley sprinkled on top.

Nutrition: calories 162, fat 3, fiber 4, carbs 5, protein 4

Cilantro Zucchini Cream

*Preparation time: 10 minutes **Cooking time:** 15 minutes **Servings:** 4*

Ingredients:
- 1 pound zucchinis, roughly cubed
- 1 yellow onion, chopped
- 2 tablespoons olive oil
- 3 teaspoons garlic, minced
- ¼ cup cilantro, chopped
- 3 cups chicken stock
- ½ teaspoon turmeric powder
- 1 cup heavy cream
- ½ teaspoon nutmeg, ground
- A pinch of salt and black pepper

Directions:
Set the instant pot on Sauté mode, add the oil, heat it up, add the onion, garlic, turmeric and nutmeg, stir and sauté for 5 minutes. Add the zucchinis and the other ingredients except the cream, stir, put the lid on and cook on High for 10 minutes. Release the pressure naturally for 10 minutes, add the cream, blend the soup using an immersion blender, ladle into bowls and serve.

Nutrition: calories 172, fat 4, fiber 2, carbs 7, protein 10

Lemon Beans Soup

Preparation time: *10 minutes* ***Cooking time:*** *20 minutes* ***Servings:*** *4*

Ingredients:

- 1 cup canned black beans, drained and rinsed
- 1 cup canned kidney beans, drained and rinsed
- 1 cup canned chickpeas, drained and rinsed
- 2 tablespoons olive oil
- 1 yellow onion, chopped
- 5 cups chicken stock
- ¼ teaspoon lemon juice
- 1 tablespoon cilantro, chopped
- A pinch of salt and black pepper

Directions:

Set your instant pot on Sauté mode, add the oil, heat it up, add the onion and sauté for 5 minutes. Add the beans and the rest of the ingredients except the cilantro, stir, put the lid on and cook on High for 15 minutes. Release the pressure naturally for 10 minutes, ladle the soup into bowls, sprinkle the cilantro on top and serve.

Nutrition: calories 130, fat 3, fiber 4, carbs 7, protein 6

Artichoke Soup

Preparation time: *5 minutes* ***Cooking time:*** *15 minutes* ***Servings:*** *4*

Ingredients:

- 10 ounces canned artichoke hearts, drained and quartered
- 1 yellow onion, chopped
- 2 tablespoons avocado oil
- 2 garlic cloves, minced
- 5 cups chicken stock
- ¼ teaspoon black peppercorns, crushed
- 1 tablespoon parsley, chopped
- A pinch of salt and black pepper

Directions:

Set your instant pot on Sauté mode, add the oil, heat it up, add the onion, garlic and peppercorns, stir and sauté for 2 minutes. Add the artichokes and the rest of the ingredients, put the lid on and cook o High for 13 minutes. Release the pressure fast for 5 minutes, ladle the soup into bowls and serve.

Nutrition: calories 162, fat 5, fiber 4, carbs 7, protein 5

Beet Soup

Preparation time: 10 minutes *Cooking time:* 20 minutes *Servings:* 4

Ingredients:
- 1 tablespoon olive oil
- 1 yellow onion, chopped
- 4 beets, peeled and cubed
- 2 garlic cloves, minced
- ½ teaspoon chili powder
- ½ teaspoon smoked paprika
- 6 cups chicken stock
- 2 tablespoons parsley, chopped
- A pinch of salt and black pepper

Directions:
Set your instant pot on Sauté mode, add the oil, heat it up, add the onion and the garlic and sauté for 5 minutes. Add the beets and the rest of the ingredients, put the lid on and cook on High for 15 minutes. Release the pressure naturally for 10 minutes, ladle the soup into bowls and serve.

Nutrition: calories 142, fat 4, fiber 3, carbs 6, protein 6

Chives Chicken Soup

Preparation time: 10 minutes *Cooking time:* 20 minutes *Servings:* 4

Ingredients:
- 1 yellow onion, chopped
- 1 pound chicken breast, skinless, boneless and cubed
- 1 tablespoons olive oil
- 2 garlic cloves, minced
- ½ teaspoon coriander, ground
- ½ teaspoon chili powder
- 5 cups chicken stock
- ¼ cup tomato passata
- A pinch of salt and black pepper
- 1 tablespoon chives, chopped

Directions:
Set your instant pot on Sauté mode, add the oil, heat it up, add onion, garlic, coriander and chili powder and sauté for 5 minutes. Add the meat and brown for 5 minutes more. Add the rest of the ingredients except the chives, put the lid on and cook on High for 10 minutes. Release the pressure naturally for 10 minutes, ladle the soup into bowls, sprinkle the chives on top and serve.

Nutrition: calories 172, fat 3, fiber 4, carbs 6, protein 5

Mushroom and Green Beans Soup

Preparation time: 10 minutes *Cooking time:* 20 minutes *Servings:* 4
Ingredients:
- 1 yellow onion, chopped
- ½ pound white mushrooms, sliced
- 2 tablespoons olive oil
- 4 garlic cloves, minced
- 1 pound green beans, trimmed and halved
- A pinch of salt and black pepper
- 6 cups veggie stock
- 1 tablespoon sweet paprika
- ½ teaspoon turmeric powder
- 1 tablespoon parsley, chopped

Directions:
Set your instant pot on Sauté mode, add the oil, heat it up, add the onion, mushrooms and the garlic and sauté for 5 minutes. Add green beans and the rest of the ingredients except the parsley, put the lid on and cook on High for 15 minutes. Release the pressure naturally for 10 minutes, divide the soup into bowls, sprinkle the parsley on top and serve.
Nutrition: calories 120, fat 3, fiber 3, carbs 6, protein 8

Leeks and Beef Soup

Preparation time: 10 minutes *Cooking time:* 25 minutes *Servings:* 4
Ingredients:
1. 4 leeks, sliced
2. 1 pound beef stew meat, cubed
3. 1 red onion, chopped
4. ½ teaspoon rosemary, dried
5. ½ teaspoon cumin, ground
6. 2 tablespoons avocado oil
7. 1 tablespoon cilantro, chopped
8. 6 cups beef stock
9. 2 tomatoes, cubed
10. ¼ teaspoon chili powder
11. A pinch of salt and black pepper

Directions:
Set your instant pot on Sauté mode, add the oil, heat it up, add the leeks, onion, rosemary and cumin and sauté for 5 minutes. Add the meat and brown for 5 minutes more. Add the stock and the rest of the ingredients, put the lid on and cook on High for 15 minutes. Release the pressure naturally for 10 minutes, ladle the soup into bowls and serve.
Nutrition: calories 162, fat 4, fiber 4, carbs 7, protein 3

Tomato and Fennel Soup

Preparation time: 10 minutes **Cooking time:** *20 minutes* **Servings:** *4*

Ingredients:
- 2 fennel bulbs, shredded
- 1 pound tomatoes, cut into wedges
- 1 yellow onion, chopped
- 2 tablespoons olive oil
- 5 cups chicken stock
- 1 teaspoon thyme, dried
- A pinch of salt and black pepper
- 2 tablespoons tomato passata
- 1 tablespoon parsley, chopped

Directions:
Set the instant pot on Sauté mode, add the oil, heat it up, add the onion, thyme and fennel and sauté for 5 minutes. Add the tomatoes and the rest of the ingredients, put the lid on and cook on High for 15 minutes. Release the pressure naturally for 10 minutes, ladle the soup into bowls and serve.

Nutrition: calories 162, fat 10, fiber 3, carbs 8, protein 14

Beets and Cauliflower Soup

Preparation time: 10 minutes **Cooking time:** *20 minutes* **Servings:** *4*

Ingredients:
1. 1 yellow onion, chopped
2. 2 garlic cloves, minced
3. 2 beets, peeled and cubed
4. 1 pound cauliflower florets
5. 2 tablespoons avocado oil
6. ½ teaspoon chili powder
7. ½ teaspoon thyme, dried
8. ½ teaspoon turmeric powder
9. 6 cups chicken stock
10. A pinch of salt and black pepper
11. 1 tablespoon cilantro, chopped

Directions:
Set your instant pot on Sauté mode, add the oil, heat it up, add the onion, garlic, chili powder, thyme and turmeric and sauté for 5 minutes. Add the beets, cauliflower and the rest of the ingredients, put the lid on and cook on High for 15 minutes. Release the pressure naturally for 10 minutes, divide the soup into bowls and serve.

Nutrition: calories 143, fat 3, fiber 4, carbs 7, protein 6

Oregano Beef Soup

Preparation time: 10 minutes *Cooking time:* 30 minutes *Servings:* 4

Ingredients:

- 1 pound beef stew meat, cubed
- 1 red onion, chopped
- 2 carrots, chopped
- 2 tablespoons olive oil
- 6 cups beef stock
- 2 garlic cloves, minced
- ½ teaspoon sweet paprika
- 1 teaspoon coriander, ground
- 1 tablespoon oregano, chopped
- A pinch of salt and black pepper

Directions:

Set your instant pot on Sauté mode, add the oil, heat it up, add the onion, garlic, paprika and coriander, stir and cook for 5 minutes. Add the meat and brown for 5 minutes more. Add the rest of the ingredients, put the lid on and cook on High for 20 minutes. Release the pressure naturally for 10 minutes, ladle the soup into bowls and serve.

Nutrition: calories 174, fat 12, fiber 3, carbs 6, protein 15

Thyme Turkey and Carrots Soup

Preparation time: 10 minutes *Cooking time:* 25 minutes *Servings:* 6

Ingredients:

- 2 pounds turkey breast, skinless, boneless and cubed
- 2 tablespoons olive oil
- 1 yellow onion, chopped
- 2 carrots, sliced
- A pinch of salt and black pepper
- 1 teaspoon garlic powder
- 6 cups chicken stock
- 2 teaspoons thyme, dried
- 1 tablespoon parsley, chopped

Directions:

Set the instant pot on Sauté mode, add the oil, heat it up, add the onion, garlic powder, thyme and the meat and brown for 5 minutes Add the rest of the ingredients, put the lid on and cook on High for 20 minutes. Release the pressure naturally for 10 minutes, ladle the soup into bowls and serve.

Nutrition: calories 173, fat 4, fiber 5, carbs 9, protein 12

Kale and Asparagus Soup

Preparation time: 10 minutes *Cooking time:* 15 minutes *Servings:* 4

Ingredients:
- 1 yellow onion, chopped
- 1 tablespoon olive oil
- 2 garlic cloves, minced
- 1 pound kale, torn
- 4 asparagus spears, trimmed and halved
- A pinch of salt and black pepper
- 1 cup tomatoes, chopped
- 5 cups veggie stock
- 1 tablespoon parsley, chopped

Directions:
Set your instant pot on Sauté mode, add the oil, heat it up, add the onion and the garlic and sauté for 3 minutes. Add the kale and the rest of the ingredients except the parsley, put the lid on and cook on High for 12 minutes. Release the pressure naturally for 10 minutes, add the parsley, divide the soup into bowls and serve.

Nutrition: calories 130, fat 3, fiber 4, carbs 7, protein 6

Pork and Chard Soup

Preparation time: 10 minutes *Cooking time:* 25 minutes *Servings:* 4

Ingredients:
- 1 yellow onion, chopped
- 2 tablespoons olive oil
- 2 garlic cloves, minced
- 2 green chilies, minced
- 2 pounds pork stew meat, cubed
- 1 cup red chard, torn
- 1 teaspoon chili powder
- ½ teaspoon sweet paprika
- ½ teaspoon red pepper flakes, crushed
- 5 cups beef stock
- A pinch of salt and black pepper
- 1 tablespoon chives, chopped

Directions:
Set your instant pot on Sauté mode, add the oil, heat it up, add the onion, garlic, chilies, chili powder and pepper flakes and sauté for 5 minutes. Add the meat, stir and brown for 5 minutes more. Add the rest of the ingredients except the chives, stir, put the lid on and cook on High for 15 minutes. Release the pressure naturally for 10 minutes, ladle the soup into bowls, sprinkle the chives on top and serve.

Nutrition: calories 172, fat 4, fiber 3, carbs 9, protein 13

Cauliflower and Chicken Soup

Preparation time: *10 minutes* ***Cooking time:*** *25 minutes* ***Servings:*** *4*

Ingredients:

- 1 cauliflower head, florets separated
- 1 pound chicken breast, skinless, boneless and cubed
- 1 red onion, chopped
- 2 tablespoons olive oil
- 3 garlic cloves, minced
- 5 cups chicken stock
- 1 cup heavy cream
- A pinch of salt and black pepper
- 1 tablespoon cilantro, chopped

Directions:

Set your instant pot on Sauté mode, add the oil, heat it up, add the onion, garlic and the meat and brown for 5 minutes. Add the stock and the rest of the ingredients except the cream, stir, put the lid on and cook on High for 20 minutes. Release the pressure naturally for 10 minutes, add the cream, stir the soup, ladle into bowls and serve.

Nutrition: calories 172, fat 4, fiber 3, carbs 6, protein 7

Beef Meatballs Soup

Preparation time: *10 minutes* ***Cooking time:*** *20 minutes* ***Servings:*** *4*

Ingredients:

- 1 pound beef meat, ground
- 1 egg, whisked
- 1 tablespoon shallots, chopped
- 1 tablespoon chives, chopped
- 1 carrot, sliced
- 1 celery stalk, chopped
- 1 cup tomato passata
- 4 cups beef stock
- 2 tablespoons olive oil
- A pinch of salt and black pepper
- 4 garlic cloves, minced
- 1 yellow onion, chopped

Directions:

In a bowl, combine the meat with the egg, shallots, chives, salt and pepper, stir and shape medium meatballs out of this mix. Set the instant pot on Sauté mode, add the oil, heat it up, add the garlic and the yellow onion and sauté for 5 minutes. Add the meatballs and brown them for 5 minutes more. Add the rest of the ingredients, toss, put the lid on and cook on High for 10 minutes more. Release the pressure naturally for 10 minutes, ladle the soup into bowls and serve.

Nutrition: calories 182, fat 8, fiber 4, carbs 7, protein 12

Chicken and Mustard Greens Soup

Preparation time: 10 minutes **Cooking time:** *25 minutes* **Servings:** *4*

Ingredients:
- 1 tablespoon olive oil
- 1 yellow onion, chopped
- 1 cup mustard greens, torn
- 1 pound chicken breast, skinless, boneless and cubed
- ¼ cup tomato puree
- 6 cups chicken stock
- A pinch of salt and black pepper
- 1 tablespoon cilantro, chopped

Directions:
Set your instant pot on Sauté mode, add the oil, heat it up, add the onion and sauté for 5 minutes. Add the chicken and brown for 5 minutes more. Add the rest of the ingredients, stir, put the lid on and cook on High for 15 minutes. Release the pressure naturally for 10 minutes, stir, ladle the soup into bowls and serve.

Nutrition: calories 175, fat 6, fiber 3, carbs 8, protein 14

Broccoli, Tomato and Chilies Soup

Preparation time: 10 minutes **Cooking time:** *20 minutes* **Servings:** *4*

Ingredients:
- 1 cup broccoli florets
- 1 cup tomatoes, cubed
- 1 yellow onion, chopped
- 2 green chilies, chopped
- 1 tablespoon olive oil
- 4 cups chicken stock
- A pinch of salt and black pepper
- 1 cup roasted peppers, chopped
- 1 teaspoon oregano, dried
- 1 tablespoon cilantro, chopped

Directions:
Set the instant pot on Sauté mode, add the oil, heat it up, add the onion and chilies and sauté for 5 minutes. Add the broccoli and the rest of the ingredients except the cilantro, put the lid on and cook on High for 15 minutes. Release the pressure naturally for 10 minutes, ladle the soup into bowls, sprinkle the cilantro on top and serve.

Nutrition: calories 200, fat 8, fiber 4, carbs 7, protein 15

Coconut Beef Soup

Preparation time: 10 minutes *Cooking time:* 25 minutes *Servings:* 4

Ingredients:
- 2 pounds beef stew meat, cubed
- 1 yellow onion, chopped
- 2 garlic cloves, minced
- 2 tablespoons olive oil
- A pinch of salt and black pepper
- 6 cups beef stock
- 1 cup coconut cream
- 1 tablespoon cilantro, chopped
- ½ teaspoon rosemary, dried

Directions:
Set your instant pot on Sauté mode, add the oil, heat it up, add the onion, garlic and the meat and brown for 5 minutes. Add the rest of the ingredients, put the lid on and cook on High for 20 minutes. Release the pressure naturally for 10 minutes, divide the soup into bowls and serve.

Nutrition: calories 152, fat 4, fiber 5, carbs 9, protein 15

Cod and Tomato Soup

Preparation time: 10 minutes *Cooking time:* 15 minutes *Servings:* 4

Ingredients:
- 1 yellow onion, chopped
- 1 carrot, grated
- 1 pound cod fillets, boneless, skinless and cubed
- 2 garlic cloves, chopped
- 5 cups chicken stock
- 2 tablespoons avocado oil
- 1 cup tomatoes, cubed
- A pinch of salt and black pepper
- 1 cup heavy cream

Directions:
Set your instant pot on Sauté mode, add the oil, heat it up, add the onion, carrot and the garlic and sauté for 5 minutes. Add the fish and the rest of the ingredients, put the lid on and cook on High for 10 minutes. Release the pressure naturally for 10 minutes, ladle the soup into bowls and serve.

Nutrition: calories 178, fat 7, fiber 4, carbs 8, protein 11

Salmon Soup

*Preparation time: 5 minutes **Cooking time:** 20 minutes **Servings:** 6*

Ingredients:
- 2 pounds salmon fillets, boneless, skinless and cubed
- 3 garlic cloves, minced
- 1 yellow onion, chopped
- 4 cups chicken stock
- 1 tablespoon olive oil
- 1 cup tomato passata
- 1 tablespoon oregano, chopped

Directions:
Set the instant pot on Sauté mode, add the oil, heat it up, add onion, garlic, and the salmon and cook for 5 minutes. Add the rest of the ingredients, put the lid on and cook on High for 15 minutes. Release the pressure fast for 5 minutes, ladle the soup into bowls and serve.

Nutrition: calories 221, fat 11, fiber 4, carbs 7, protein 10

Cod and Beets Soup

*Preparation time: 10 minutes **Cooking time:** 20 minutes **Servings:** 4*

Ingredients:
- 1 pound cod fillets, boneless, skinless and cubed
- 2 beets, peeled and cubed
- 1 red onion, chopped
- 2 tablespoons olive oil
- 3 garlic cloves, minced
- 4 cups chicken stock
- 1 cup tomatoes, peeled and crushed
- A pinch of salt and black pepper
- 2 tablespoons parsley, chopped

Directions:
Set your instant pot on Sauté mode, add the oil, heat it up, add the onion and the garlic and cook for 5 minutes. Add the cod and the remaining ingredients except the parsley, put the lid on and cook on High for 15 minutes. Release the pressure naturally for 10 minutes, add the parsley, stir, ladle the soup into bowls and serve.

Nutrition: calories 210, fat 14, fiber 4, carbs 9, protein 17

Mustard Greens Soup

Preparation time: 10 minutes *Cooking time:* 20 minutes *Servings:* 4

Ingredients:
- 3 cups mustard greens
- 4 cups veggie stock
- 4 scallions, chopped
- ½ teaspoon sweet paprika
- ½ teaspoon chili powder
- A pinch of salt and black pepper
- ½ tablespoon basil, dried
- ½ tablespoon oregano, dried
- 2 teaspoons thyme, dried
- 2 garlic cloves, minced

Directions:
In your instant pot, combine the mustard greens with the stock, the scallions and the other ingredients, stir, put the lid on and cook on High for 20 minutes. Release the pressure naturally for 10 minutes, ladle the soup into bowls and serve.

Nutrition: calories 182, fat 7, fiber 4, carbs 9, protein 13

Salmon and Green Beans Cream

Preparation time: 10 minutes *Cooking time:* 20 minutes *Servings:* 4

Ingredients:
- 3 cups chicken stock
- 1 cup heavy cream
- 1 pound salmon fillets, skinless, boneless and cubed
- 1 cup green beans, trimmed and halved
- 1 yellow onion, chopped
- 3 garlic cloves, minced
- 1 tablespoon avocado oil
- A pinch of salt and black pepper
- 1 tablespoon oregano, chopped

Directions:
Set your instant pot on sauté mode, add the oil, heat it up, add the onion and garlic, stir and sauté for 5 minutes. Add the salmon, green beans and the rest of the ingredients, put the lid on and cook on High for 15 minutes. Release the pressure naturally for 10 minutes, ladle the soup into bowls and serve.

Nutrition: calories 186, fat 12, fiber 4, carbs 9, protein 11

Cod and Green Onions Soup

Preparation time: 5 minutes Cooking time: 15 minutes Servings: 4

Ingredients:
- 1 pound cod fillets, boneless, skinless and cubed
- 1 cup green onions, chopped
- 2 tablespoons olive oil
- 1 teaspoon garam masala
- 1 teaspoon turmeric powder
- 5 cups chicken stock
- 2 garlic cloves, minced
- 2 tablespoons cilantro, chopped

Directions:
Set your instant pot on sauté mode, add the oil, heat it up, add the onions, garlic, turmeric and garam masala and sauté for 2 minutes. Add the cod and the rest of the ingredients, put the lid on and cook on High for 13 minutes. Release the pressure fast for 5 minutes, ladle the soup into bowls and serve.

Nutrition: calories 201, fat 8, fiber 4, carbs 6, protein 8

Leeks Cream

Preparation time: 10 minutes Cooking time: 15 minutes Servings: 6

Ingredients:
- 4 leeks, sliced
- 1 yellow onion, chopped
- 2 garlic cloves, minced
- 2 tablespoons olive oil
- 5 cups veggie stock
- 1 cup heavy cream
- 1 tablespoon mint, chopped
- A pinch of salt and black pepper
- 1 teaspoon chili powder

Directions:
Set your instant pot on sauté mode, add the oil, heat it up, add the leeks, onion and garlic and sauté for 3 minutes. Add the rest of the ingredients except the cream, stir, put the lid on and cook on High for 12 minutes. Release the pressure naturally for 10 minutes, transfer the soup to a blender, add the cream, pulse well, ladle into bowls and serve.

Nutrition: calories 150, fat 8, fiber 4, carbs 7, protein 5

Instant Pot Stew Recipes

Parsley Salmon Stew

Preparation time: *5 minutes* ***Cooking time:*** *15 minutes* ***Servings:*** *4*

Ingredients:
- 1 pound salmon fillets, boneless, skinless and cubed
- 1 cup chicken stock
- 1 tablespoon avocado oil
- 1 yellow onion, chopped
- 1 tablespoon hot paprika
- 1 tablespoon tomato passata
- Salt and black pepper to the taste
- ½ bunch parsley, chopped

Directions:
Set the instant pot on Sauté mode, add the oil, heat it up, add the onion and the paprika and sauté for 5 minutes. Add the fish and the rest of the ingredients, put the lid on and cook on High for 10 minutes. Release the pressure fast for 5 minutes, divide the stew into bowls and serve.

Nutrition: calories 176, fat 8, fiber 3, carbs 8, protein 11

Corn Stew

Preparation time: *10 minutes* ***Cooking time:*** *20 minutes* ***Servings:*** *4*

Ingredients:
1. 1 tablespoon olive oil
2. 3 cups fresh corn
3. 1 yellow onion, chopped
4. 3 garlic cloves, minced
5. Salt and black pepper to the taste
6. 1 cup beef stock
7. 1 cup tomato sauce
8. 1 tablespoon chives, chopped

Directions:
Set your instant pot on Sauté mode, add the oil, heat it up, add the onion and the garlic and sauté for 5 minutes. Add the corn and the rest of the ingredients, put the lid on and cook on High for 15 minutes. Release the pressure naturally for 10 minutes, divide the stew into bowls and serve.

Nutrition: calories 271, fat 13, fiber 4, carbs 8, protein 14

Beef Stew

Preparation time: 10 minutes *Cooking time:* 30 minutes *Servings:* 4

Ingredients:
- 2 pounds beef stew meat, cubed
- 1 yellow onion, chopped
- 1 celery stalk, chopped
- 1 carrot, sliced
- 2 tablespoons olive oil
- 2 garlic cloves, chopped
- Salt and black pepper to the taste
- ½ cup beef stock
- 1 teaspoon sweet paprika
- 2 tablespoons tomato passata
- 1 tablespoon cilantro, chopped

Directions:

Set your instant pot on Sauté mode, add the oil, heat it up, add the onion, celery and garlic and sauté for 5 minutes. Add the meat and brown for 5 minutes more. Add the rest of the ingredients, put the lid on and cook on High for 20 minutes. Release the pressure naturally for 10 minutes, divide the stew into bowls and serve.

Nutrition: calories 264, fat 12, fiber 4, carbs 9, protein 18

Potato Stew

Preparation time: 10 minutes *Cooking time:* 20 minutes *Servings:* 4

Ingredients:
1. 1 pound gold potatoes, peeled and cut into wedges
2. 2 red onions, sliced
3. 4 garlic cloves, minced
4. 2 tablespoons olive oil
5. Salt and black pepper to the taste
6. 1 celery stalk, chopped
7. 2 tablespoons tomato paste
8. 1 cup chicken stock
9. 1 tablespoon cilantro, chopped

Directions:

Set your instant pot on Sauté mode, add the oil, heat it up, add the onion and the garlic and sauté for 5 minutes Add the potatoes and the rest of the ingredients, put the lid on and cook on High for 15 minutes Release the pressure naturally for 10 minutes, divide the stew into bowls and serve.

Nutrition: calories 200, fat 12, fiber 5, carbs 9, protein 16

Lentils Stew

Preparation time: 10 minutes *Cooking time:* 25 minutes *Servings:* 4

Ingredients:
- 1 yellow onion, chopped
- 2 garlic cloves, minced
- 3 cups canned lentils, drained and rinsed
- 2 tablespoons olive oil
- 2 cups chicken stock
- 4 ounces canned tomatoes, chopped
- 1 teaspoon oregano, dried
- A pinch of salt and black pepper
- ½ teaspoon red pepper flakes

Directions:

Set the instant pot on Sauté mode, add the oil, heat it up, add onion, garlic and the oregano and sauté for 5 minutes. Add the lentils and the other ingredients, put the lid on and cook on High for 20 minutes. Release the pressure naturally for 10 minutes, divide the stew into bowls and serve.

Nutrition: calories 200, fat 12, fiber 5, carbs 9, protein 10

Cinnamon Pork Stew

Preparation time: 10 minutes *Cooking time:* 25 minutes *Servings:* 4

Ingredients:
- 1 yellow onion, chopped
- 2 pounds pork stew meat, cubed
- 2 tablespoons olive oil
- 3 garlic cloves, chopped
- 1 celery stalk, chopped
- 1 cup beef stock
- 2 tablespoons tomato passata
- ½ cup tomatoes, chopped
- A pinch of salt and black pepper
- ½ teaspoon cinnamon powder
- 1 tablespoon cilantro, chopped

Directions:

Set your instant pot on Sauté mode, add the oil, heat it up, add the onion, garlic and the meat and brown for 5 minutes. Add the rest of the ingredients except the cilantro, put the lid on and cook on High for 20 minutes. Release the pressure naturally for 10 minutes, add the cilantro, stir the stew, divide it into bowls and serve.

Nutrition: calories 182, fat 8, fiber 3, carbs 10, protein 11

Spinach Stew

Preparation time: 5 minutes **Cooking time:** 15 minutes **Servings:** 4

Ingredients:
- 1 yellow onion, chopped
- 1 tablespoon olive oil
- 1 pound baby spinach
- 2 celery stalks, chopped
- 2 carrots, chopped
- 2 garlic cloves, minced
- 1 teaspoon chili powder
- ½ teaspoon coriander, ground
- A pinch of salt and black pepper
- 1 cup veggie stock
- 1 cup tomato puree

Directions:
Set your instant pot on Sauté mode, add the oil, heat it up, add the onion, celery, carrots and the garlic and sauté for 5 minutes. Add the spinach and the rest of the ingredients, put the lid on and cook on High for 10 minutes. Release the pressure fast for 5 minutes, divide the stew into bowls and serve.

Nutrition: calories 172, fat 4, fiber 4, carbs 7, protein 8

Zucchini Stew

Preparation time: 10 minutes **Cooking time:** 15 minutes **Servings:** 4

Ingredients:
- 2 tablespoons olive oil
- 1 pound zucchinis, roughly cubed
- 1 yellow onion, chopped
- A pinch of salt and black pepper
- 2 garlic cloves, minced
- 2 tablespoons tomato sauce
- ¼ cup chicken stock
- ½ teaspoon chili powder
- 1 tablespoon cilantro, chopped
- 1 teaspoon sweet paprika

Directions:
Set your instant pot on Sauté mode, add the oil, heat it up, add the onion, garlic, chili powder and the paprika and sauté for 3 minutes. Add the zucchinis and the rest of the ingredients, put the lid on and cook on High for 10 minutes. Release the pressure naturally for 10 minutes, divide the stew into bowls and serve.

Nutrition: calories 165, fat 5, fiber 3, carbs 9, protein 5

Chicken and Spinach Stew

Preparation time: 10 minutes *Cooking time:* 25 minutes *Servings:* 4

Ingredients:
- 1 tablespoon avocado oil
- 1 yellow onion, chopped
- 1 carrot, sliced
- 1 sweet potato, peeled and cubed
- 1 pound chicken breast, skinless, boneless and cubed
- 1 cup baby spinach
- A pinch of salt and black pepper
- 2 ounces canned tomatoes, chopped
- 1 cup chicken stock
- 1 tablespoon cilantro, chopped

Directions:
Set your instant pot on Sauté mode, add the oil, heat it up, add the onion, carrot and sweet potato and sauté for 5 minutes. Add the meat and sauté for 5 minutes more. Add the rest of the ingredients except the spinach, put the lid on and cook on Low for 15 minutes.. Release the pressure naturally for 10 minutes, divide the stew into bowls and serve.

Nutrition: calories 200, fat 12, fiber 4, carbs 8, protein 12

Mushroom Stew

Preparation time: 10 minutes *Cooking time:* 25 minutes *Servings:* 6

Ingredients:
- 1 tablespoon olive oil
- 1 red onion, chopped
- 3 garlic cloves, minced
- 1 pound mushrooms, halved
- 1 teaspoon rosemary, chopped
- ½ teaspoon coriander, ground
- 1 cup chicken stock
- A pinch of salt and black pepper
- 2 carrots, sliced
- 1 cup tomatoes, cubed

Directions:
Set your instant pot on Sauté mode, add the oil, heat it up, add the onion and the garlic and sauté for 5 minutes. Add the mushrooms and sauté for 5 minutes more. Add the remaining ingredients, put the lid on and cook on Low for 15 minutes. Release the pressure naturally for 10 minutes, divide the stew into bowls and serve.

Nutrition: calories 182, fat 4, fiber 4, carbs 8, protein 12

Artichokes Stew

Preparation time: 10 minutes **Cooking time:** *20 minutes* **Servings:** *4*

Ingredients:
- 10 ounces canned artichoke hearts, drained and halved
- 1 tablespoon olive oil
- 4 garlic cloves, minced
- 1 yellow onion, chopped
- A pinch of salt and black pepper
- 3 carrots, chopped
- 1 cup tomatoes, chopped
- ½ teaspoon chili powder
- 1 teaspoon cumin, ground
- 1 cup beef stock
- 1 tablespoon parsley, chopped

Directions:
Set the instant pot on Sauté mode, add the oil, heat it up, add the onion and the garlic and sauté for 5 minutes. Add the artichokes and the rest of the ingredients except the parsley, put the lid on and cook on High for 15 minutes. Release the pressure naturally for 10 minutes, add the parsley, divide the stew into bowls and serve.

Nutrition: calories 231, fat 13, fiber 3, carbs 8, protein 12

Lamb and Olives Stew

Preparation time: 10 minutes **Cooking time:** *30 minutes* **Servings:** *4*

Ingredients:
- 2 pounds lamb shoulder, cubed
- 4 garlic cloves, minced
- 1 red onion, chopped
- 1 cup kalamata olives, pitted and sliced
- 1 cup tomatoes, chopped
- 1 tablespoon olive oil
- 1 teaspoon oregano, dried
- A pinch of salt and black pepper
- ½ cup cilantro, chopped

Directions:
Set the pot on Sauté mode, add the oil, heat it up, add the onion, garlic and the oregano and sauté for 5 minutes. Add the meat and brown for 5 minutes more. Add the olives and the rest of the ingredients except the cilantro, put the lid on and cook on High for 20 minutes. Release the pressure naturally for 10 minutes, add the cilantro, divide the stew into bowls and serve.

Nutrition: calories 242, fat 12, fiber 4, carbs 9, protein 15

Green Beans Stew

Preparation time: 10 minutes *Cooking time:* 20 minutes *Servings:* 4
Ingredients:
- 1 yellow onion, chopped
- 2 pounds green beans, trimmed and halved
- 3 garlic cloves, minced
- 2 tablespoons olive oil
- A pinch of salt and black pepper
- 2 cups chicken stock
- 2 tablespoons tomato passata
- 2 carrots, chopped
- ¼ cup parsley, minced

Directions:
Set the instant pot on Sauté mode, add the oil, heat it up, add the onion and the garlic and sauté for 5 minutes. Add the green beans and the other ingredients, stir, put the lid on and cook on High for 15 minutes. Release the pressure naturally for 10 minutes, divide the stew into bowls and serve.

Nutrition: calories 251, fat 13, fiber 5, carbs 9, protein 15

Sausage Stew

Preparation time: 10 minutes *Cooking time:* 25 minutes *Servings:* 4
Ingredients:
- 1 pound pork sausage, sliced
- 2 red onions, sliced
- 2 garlic cloves, minced
- 2 tablespoons olive oil
- 14 ounces canned tomatoes, chopped
- 1 teaspoon turmeric powder
- 1 teaspoon coriander, ground
- A pinch of salt and black pepper
- ½ cup beef stock
- 1 tablespoon cilantro, chopped

Directions:
Set the instant pot on Sauté mode, add the oil, heat it up, add the onions and the garlic and sauté for 5 minutes. Add the sausage and brown for 5 minutes more. Add the rest of the ingredients, put the lid on and cook on High for 15 minutes. Release the pressure naturally for 10 minutes, divide the stew into bowls and serve.

Nutrition: calories 200, fat 7, fiber 3, carbs 9, protein 12

Parsnips and Chicken Stew

Preparation time: 10 minutes Cooking time: 25 minutes Servings: 4

Ingredients:
- 1 pound chicken breast, skinless, boneless and cubed
- 1 red onion, chopped
- 2 tablespoons olive oil
- A pinch of salt and black pepper
- ¼ pound parsnips, sliced
- 1 cup chicken stock
- 1 tablespoon tomato paste
- 1 tablespoon cilantro, chopped

Directions:
Set the instant pot on Sauté mode, add the oil, heat it up, add the onion and the meat and sauté for 5 minutes. Add the parsnips and the rest of the ingredients, put the lid on and cook on High for 20 minutes. Release the pressure naturally for 10 minutes, divide the stew into bowls and serve.

Nutrition: calories 242, fat 12, fiber 4, carbs 9, protein 13

Turkey and Spinach Stew

Preparation time: 10 minutes Cooking time: 25 minutes Servings: 4

Ingredients:
- 1 pound turkey breast, skinless, boneless and cubed
- 1 yellow onion, chopped
- 2 garlic cloves, minced
- 1 cup tomatoes, chopped
- 1 tablespoon olive oil
- 2 cups spinach, torn
- 1 cup chicken stock
- 1 teaspoon sweet paprika
- Salt and black pepper to the taste

Directions:
Set your instant pot on Sauté mode, add the oil, heat it up, add the onion, garlic and the paprika and sauté for 5 minutes. Add the meat and brown for 5 minutes more. Add the rest of the ingredients, put the lid on and cook on High for 15 minutes. Release the pressure naturally for 10 minutes, divide the stew into bowls and serve.

Nutrition: calories 263, fat 11, fiber 3, carbs 6, protein 17

Lime Chicken Stew

Preparation time: 10 minutes *Cooking time:* 25 minutes *Servings:* 4

Ingredients:

- 1 yellow onion, chopped
- 1 pound chicken breast, skinless, boneless and cubed
- 2 tablespoons olive oil
- 2 cups chicken stock
- 10 ounces canned tomatoes, chopped
- 1 teaspoon cumin, ground
- ½ teaspoon coriander, ground
- A pinch of salt and black pepper
- ½ cup cilantro, chopped
- Juice of 1 lime

Directions:

Set the instant pot on Sauté mode, add the oil, heat it up, add the onion, cumin and coriander and sauté for 5 minutes. Add the meat and brown for 5 minutes more. Add the rest of the ingredients, put the lid on and cook on High for 15 minutes. Release the pressure naturally for 10 minutes, divide the stew into bowls and serve.

Nutrition: calories 253, fat 12, fiber 5, carbs 8, protein 16

Peas Stew

Preparation time: 10 minutes *Cooking time:* 20 minutes *Servings:* 4

Ingredients:

- 1 yellow onion, chopped
- 4 garlic cloves, minced
- 1 tablespoon olive oil
- 2 cups peas
- ½ teaspoon chili powder
- ½ teaspoon sweet paprika
- ¼ teaspoon thyme, dried
- A pinch of salt and black pepper
- 1 cup chicken stock
- 3 tablespoons tomato paste
- 1 tablespoon chives, chopped

Directions:

Set your instant pot on sauté mode, add the oil, heat it up, add the onion and the garlic and sauté for 5 minutes. Add the peas, chili powder and the rest of the ingredients except the chives, put the lid on and cook on High for 15 minutes. Release the pressure naturally for 10 minutes, divide the stew into bowls and serve.

Nutrition: calories 272, fat 12, fiber 4, carbs 7, protein 11

Brussels Sprouts Stew

Preparation time: 10 minutes **Cooking time:** 20 minutes **Servings:** 4

Ingredients:
- 1 pound Brussels sprouts, halved
- 1 red onion, chopped
- 2 garlic cloves, minced
- 1 tablespoon avocado oil
- A pinch of salt and black pepper
- ½ tablespoon tarragon, chopped
- 1 cup chicken stock
- ½ cup tomato passata

Directions:
Set your instant pot on sauté mode, add the oil, heat it up, add the onion and the garlic and sauté for 5 minutes. Add the sprouts and the rest of the ingredients, put the lid on and cook on Low for 15 minutes. Release the pressure naturally for 10 minutes, divide the stew into bowls and serve.

Nutrition: calories 239, fat 14, fiber 4, carbs 9, protein 6

Beef and Peppers Stew

Preparation time: 5 minutes **Cooking time:** 25 minutes **Servings:** 4

Ingredients:
- 1 pound beef stew meat, cubed
- 2 tablespoons olive oil
- 1 red onion, chopped
- 2 garlic cloves, minced
- 1 red bell pepper, cut into strips
- 1 green bell pepper, cut into strips
- 1 cup beef stock
- 2 tablespoons tomato paste
- A pinch of salt and black pepper
- 2 tablespoons thyme, chopped

Directions:
Set your instant pot on sauté mode, add the oil, heat it up, add the onion and the garlic and sauté for 5 minutes. Add the meat and brown for 5 minutes more. Add the rest of the ingredients, put the lid on and cook on High for 15 minutes. Release the pressure fast for 5 minutes, divide the stew into bowls and serve.

Nutrition: calories 221, fat 11, fiber 4, carbs 6, protein 14

Tomato Stew

Preparation time: 10 minutes *Cooking time:* 20 minutes *Servings:* 4

Ingredients:
- 2 pounds tomatoes, cut into wedges
- 2 garlic cloves, minced
- 1 cup chicken stock
- ½ teaspoon sweet paprika
- 1 red chili pepper, chopped
- 1 yellow onion, chopped
- 2 tablespoons olive oil
- A pinch of salt and black pepper
- 1 tablespoon basil, chopped

Directions:
Set your instant pot on Sauté mode, add the oil, heat it up, add the garlic, chili pepper and the onion and sauté for 5 minutes. Add the tomatoes and the rest of the ingredients except the basil, put the lid on and cook on Low for 15 minutes. Release the pressure naturally for 10 minutes, divide the stew into bowls, sprinkle the basil and serve.

Nutrition: calories 231, fat 12, fiber 3, carbs 7, protein 9

Turkey Stew

Preparation time: 10 minutes *Cooking time:* 30 minutes *Servings:* 4

Ingredients:
- 1 yellow onion, chopped
- 1 pound turkey breast, skinless, boneless and cubed
- 2 garlic cloves, minced
- 1 cup chicken stock
- 1 teaspoon coriander, ground
- 1 teaspoon cumin, ground
- 12 ounces tomato sauce
- 1 tablespoon avocado oil
- 1 tablespoon parsley, chopped

Directions:
Set the instant pot on Sauté mode, add the oil, heat it up, add the onion and the garlic and sauté for 5 minutes. Add the meat and brown it for 5 minutes more. Add the rest of the ingredients, put the lid on and cook on Low for 20 minutes. Release the pressure naturally for 10 minutes, divide the stew into bowls and serve.

Nutrition: calories 233, fat 12, fiber 4, carbs 7, protein 15

Okra Stew

*Preparation time: 10 minutes **Cooking time:** 20 minutes **Servings:** 4*

Ingredients:
- 1 pound okra, sliced
- 1 red onion, chopped
- 2 garlic cloves, minced
- 1 cup chicken stock
- 1 cup tomato sauce
- Salt and black pepper to the taste
- 1 teaspoon chili powder
- 1 teaspoon cumin, ground
- 1 tablespoon cilantro, chopped

Directions:
In your instant pot, combine the okra with the onion, the garlic and the other ingredients, put the lid on and cook on High for 20 minutes. Release the pressure naturally for 10 minutes, divide the stew into bowls and serve.

Nutrition: calories 221, fat 12, fiber 4, carbs 7, protein 11

Beans and Tomatoes Stew

*Preparation time: 10 minutes **Cooking time:** 25 minutes **Servings:** 4*

Ingredients:
- 1 cup canned black beans, drained and rinsed
- 1 cup canned red kidney beans, drained and rinsed
- 1 pound cherry tomatoes, halved
- 1 red onion, chopped
- 2 tablespoons olive oil
- 2 garlic cloves, minced
- 1 teaspoon rosemary, dried
- 1 tablespoon oregano, chopped
- A pinch of salt and black pepper
- 2 cups chicken stock

Directions:
Set your instant pot on Sauté mode, add the oil, heat it up, add the onion, garlic and rosemary and sauté for 5 minutes. Add the beans, tomatoes and the rest of the ingredients, put the lid on and cook on High for 20 minutes. Release the pressure naturally for 10 minutes, divide the stew into bowls and serve.

Nutrition: calories 230, fat 14, fiber 4, carbs 7, protein 11

Salsa Pork Stew

Preparation time: *5 minutes* **Cooking time:** *25 minutes* **Servings:** *4*

Ingredients:
- 1 pound pork stew meat, cubed
- 1 red onion, chopped
- 2 garlic cloves, minced
- 2 tablespoons olive oil
- ½ cup canned black beans, drained and rinsed
- ½ cup cherry tomatoes, halved
- 2 cups beef stock
- 10 ounces Salsa Verde
- 1 teaspoon chili powder
- A pinch of salt and black pepper
- 1 tablespoon chives, chopped

Directions:
Set the instant pot on Sauté mode, add the oil, heat it up, add the onion and the garlic and sauté for 5 minutes. Add the meat and brown for 5 minutes more. Add the rest of the ingredients, toss, put the lid on and cook on High for 15 minutes. Release the pressure fast for 5 minutes, divide the stew into bowls, and serve.

Nutrition: calories 201, fat 7, fiber 4, carbs 7, protein 9

Kale Stew

Preparation time: *10 minutes* **Cooking time:** *20 minutes* **Servings:** *4*

Ingredients:
- 1 pound baby kale
- 1 red onion, chopped
- 2 garlic cloves, minced
- ½ cup chicken stock
- ½ cup tomato sauce
- A pinch of salt and black pepper
- 1 tablespoon cilantro, chopped

Directions:
In your instant pot, combine the kale with the onion and the other ingredients, put the lid on and cook on High for 20 minutes. Release the pressure naturally for 10 minutes, divide the stew into bowls and serve.

Nutrition: calories 192, fat 8, fiber 4, carbs 8, protein 12

Sage Turkey Stew

Preparation time: 10 minutes **Cooking time:** 20 minutes **Servings:** 4
Ingredients:
- 2 pounds turkey breast, skinless, boneless and cubed
- 1 yellow onion, chopped
- 3 garlic cloves, minced
- 2 tablespoons olive oil
- 1 cup tomato sauce
- 1 cup chicken stock
- 1 tablespoon sage, chopped
- A pinch of salt and black pepper

Directions:
Set your instant pot on Sauté mode, add the oil, heat it up, add the onion and the garlic and sauté for 5 minutes. Add the meat and brown for 5 minutes more. Add the rest of the ingredients, put the lid on and cook on High for 10 minutes. Release the pressure naturally for 10 minutes, divide the stew into bowls and serve.

Nutrition: calories 200, fat 12, fiber 4, carbs 6, protein 9

Cabbage and Bacon Stew

Preparation time: 10 minutes **Cooking time:** 20 minutes **Servings:** 4
Ingredients:
- 2 cups bacon, chopped
- 1 red onion, chopped
- 4 garlic cloves, minced
- 1 carrot, peeled and grated
- 1 teaspoon olive oil
- 1 green cabbage head, shredded
- A pinch of salt and black pepper
- ½ cup chicken stock
- ½ teaspoon sweet paprika
- 2 tablespoons dill, chopped

Directions:
Set your instant pot on sauté mode, add the oil, heat it up, add the bacon and cook for 5 minutes. Add the onion and the garlic and sauté for 3 minutes more. Add the cabbage and the rest of the ingredients, put the lid on and cook on High for 12 minutes. Release the pressure naturally for 10 minutes, divide the stew into bowls and serve.

Nutrition: calories 195, fat 4, fiber 5, carbs 9, protein 6

Shrimp and Olives Stew

Preparation time: 5 minutes **Cooking time:** *12 minutes* **Servings:** *4*

Ingredients:
- 1 pound shrimp, peeled and deveined
- 1 cup black olives, pitted and halved
- 1 tomato, cubed
- 1 red onion, sliced
- 5 ounces canned tomatoes, chopped
- 1 tablespoon cilantro, chopped
- ¼ cup chicken stock

Directions:
In your instant pot, combine the shrimp with the olives and the other ingredients, put the lid on and cook on Low for 12 minutes. Release the pressure fast for 5 minutes, divide the mix into bowls and serve.

Nutrition: calories 160, fat 4, fiber 3, carbs 7, protein 9

Green Beans and Tuna Stew

Preparation time: 10 minutes **Cooking time:** *20 minutes* **Servings:** *4*

Ingredients:
- 1 tablespoon olive oil
- 1 yellow onion, chopped
- 1 pound tuna, skinless, boneless and cubed
- 2 garlic cloves, minced
- 2 cups green beans, trimmed and halved
- 4 ounces canned tomatoes, chopped
- 1 tablespoon parsley, chopped

Directions:
Set the instant pot on Sauté mode, add the oil, heat it up, add the onion and the garlic and sauté for 5 minutes. Add the tuna and the rest of the ingredients, put the lid on and cook on High for 15 minutes. Release the pressure fast for 5 minutes, divide the stew into bowls and serve.

Nutrition: calories 200, fat 8, fiber 5, carbs 8, protein 10

Veggie Quinoa Stew

Preparation time: *10 minutes* ***Cooking time:*** *20 minutes* ***Servings:*** *4*

Ingredients:

- 1 tablespoon olive oil
- 1 red onion, chopped
- 2 garlic cloves, minced
- 1 cup quinoa, rinsed
- 3 cups chicken stock
- 1 eggplant, cubed
- 1 zucchini, cubed
- 1 tomato, cubed
- ½ teaspoon cumin, ground
- ½ teaspoon turmeric powder
- A pinch of salt and black pepper
- 1 teaspoon lemon juice

Directions:

Set the instant pot on sauté mode, add the oil, heat it up, add the onion and the garlic and sauté for 5 minutes. Add the quinoa, veggies and the remaining ingredients, put the lid on and cook on High for 15 minutes. Release the pressure naturally for 10 minutes, stir the stew, divide it into bowls and serve.

Nutrition: calories 200, fat 12, fiber 4, carbs 7, protein 14

Pork and Rice Stew

Preparation time: *10 minutes* ***Cooking time:*** *30 minutes* ***Servings:*** *4*

Ingredients:

- 1 yellow onion, chopped
- 1 tablespoon olive oil
- 2 garlic cloves, minced
- 1 pound pork stew meat, cubed
- 1 cup black rice
- 2 cups beef stock
- 10 ounces canned tomatoes, chopped
- ½ teaspoon chili powder
- A pinch of salt and black pepper
- Juice of ½ lemon
- 1 tablespoon cilantro, chopped

Directions:

Set your instant pot on sauté mode, add the oil, heat it up, add the onion and the garlic and sauté for 5 minutes. Add the meat and brown for 5 minutes more. Add the remaining ingredients, put the lid on and cook on High for 20 minutes. Release the pressure naturally for 10 minutes, divide the stew into bowls and serve.

Nutrition: calories 200, fat 12, fiber 4, carbs 7, protein 14

Turkey and Broccoli Stew

Preparation time: 5 minutes *Cooking time:* 25 minutes *Servings:* 4

Ingredients:
- 1 yellow onion, chopped
- 2 tablespoons olive oil
- 4 garlic cloves, minced
- 1 pound turkey breast, skinless, boneless and cubed
- 1 cup broccoli florets
- 1 teaspoon sweet paprika
- ¼ teaspoon chili powder
- A pinch of salt and black pepper
- ½ cup chicken stock
- 1 tablespoon parsley, chopped

Directions:
Set your instant pot on sauté mode, add the oil, heat it up, add the onion, garlic, paprika and chili powder and sauté for 5 minutes. Add the meat and brown for 5 minutes more. Add the rest of the ingredients, put the lid on and cook on High for 15 minutes. Release the pressure fast for 5 minutes, divide the stew into bowls and serve.

Nutrition: calories 212, fat 6, fiber 3, carbs 5, protein 7

Corn and Shrimp Stew

Preparation time: 5 minutes *Cooking time:* 10 minutes *Servings:* 4

Ingredients:
- 2 tablespoons olive oil
- 1 cup corn
- 1 cup chicken stock
- 1 pound shrimp, peeled, deveined
- 1 yellow onion, chopped
- 1 cup tomatoes, chopped
- A pinch of salt and black pepper
- 1 tablespoon cilantro, chopped

Directions:
Set your instant pot on sauté mode, add the oil, heat it up, add the onion and the corn and sauté for 2 minutes. Add the shrimp and the rest of the ingredients, toss, put the lid on and cook on High for 8 minutes. Release the pressure fast for 5 minutes, divide the stew into bowls and serve.

Nutrition: calories 181, fat 5, fiber 2, carbs 5, protein 10

Cod, Tomato and Mango Stew

Preparation time: 5 minutes **Cooking time:** *15 minutes* **Servings:** *4*

Ingredients:
- 1 tablespoon olive oil
- 1 pound cod fillets, boneless, skinless and cubed
- 1 yellow onion, chopped
- 1 cup cherry tomatoes, halved
- 1 mango, peeled and cubed
- A pinch of salt and black pepper
- ½ teaspoon turmeric powder
- 1 cup veggie stock
- 1 teaspoon sweet paprika
- 1 tablespoon chives, chopped

Directions:
Set your instant pot on sauté mode, add the oil, heat it up, add the onion, turmeric and paprika and sauté for 2 minutes. Add the fish and the rest of the ingredients, toss, put the lid on and cook on High for 13 minutes. Release the pressure fast for 5 minutes, divide the stew into bowls and serve.

Nutrition: calories 181, fat 9, fiber 4, carbs 6, protein 7

Fennel Stew

Preparation time: 5 minutes **Cooking time:** *20 minutes* **Servings:** *4*

Ingredients:
- 4 garlic cloves, minced
- 1 yellow onion, chopped
- 2 fennel bulbs, sliced
- 2 tablespoons olive oil
- 2 tomatoes, cubed
- 1 teaspoon coriander, ground
- 1 teaspoon chili powder
- 1 cup tomato passata
- 1 cup veggie stock
- A pinch of salt and black pepper

Directions:
Set your instant pot on sauté mode, add the oil, heat it up, add the onion, coriander, chili powder and the garlic, stir and sauté for 5 minutes. Add the fennel and the rest of the ingredients, put the lid on and cook on Low for 15 minutes. Release the pressure fast for 5 minutes, divide the stew into bowls and serve.

Nutrition: calories 198, fat 8, fiber 4, carbs 9, protein 5

Curry Shrimp Stew

Preparation time: 5 minutes *Cooking time:* 15 minutes *Servings:* 4

Ingredients:
- 1 tablespoon olive oil
- 1 yellow onion, chopped
- 1 celery stalk, chopped
- 1 teaspoon curry powder
- 1 cup tomato passata
- 1 pound shrimp, peeled and deveined
- 1 cup coconut cream
- Salt and black pepper to the taste

Directions:
Set your instant pot on Sauté mode, add oil, heat it up, add the onion, celery and curry powder and sauté for 5 minutes. Add the shrimp and the rest of the ingredients, put the lid on and cook on Low for 10 minutes. Release the pressure fast for 5 minutes, divide the stew into bowls and serve.

Nutrition: calories 174, fat 7, fiber 3, carbs 5, protein 6

Lamb and Okra Stew

Preparation time: 10 minutes *Cooking time:* 30 minutes *Servings:* 4

Ingredients:
- 1 tablespoon olive oil
- 1 yellow onion, chopped
- 2 garlic cloves, minced
- 1 pound pork shoulder, cubed
- 1 cup okra, sliced
- 1 teaspoon smoked paprika
- 1 teaspoon cumin, ground
- 1 cup beef stock
- ½ cup tomato passata
- A pinch of salt and black pepper

Directions:
Set your instant pot on Sauté mode, add the oil, heat it up, add the onion, garlic, cumin and paprika, stir and sauté for 5 minutes. Add the meat and brown for 5 minutes more. Add the rest of the ingredients, put the lid on and cook on High for 20 minutes. Release the pressure naturally for 10 minutes, divide the stew into bowls and serve.

Nutrition: calories 200, fat 14, fiber 4, carbs 6, protein 11

Garlic Chicken and Endives Stew

Preparation time: 10 minutes **Cooking time:** *20 minutes* **Servings:** *4*

Ingredients:
- 1 yellow onion, chopped
- 1 tablespoon olive oil
- 2 pounds chicken breasts, skinless, boneless and cubed
- 1 cup tomato passata
- 3 garlic cloves, minced
- 2 endives, shredded
- A pinch of salt and black pepper
- 1 tablespoon rosemary, chopped

Directions:
Set your instant pot on sauté mode, add the oil, heat it up, add the onion, garlic and the meat and cook for 5 minutes. Add the rest of the ingredients, put the lid on and cook on High for 15 minutes. Release the pressure naturally for 10 minutes, divide the stew into bowls and serve.

Nutrition: calories 177, fat 7, fiber 2, carbs 6, protein 14

Thyme Lamb Stew

Preparation time: 10 minutes **Cooking time:** *30 minutes* **Servings:** *4*

Ingredients:
- 1 yellow onion, chopped
- 2 pounds lamb stew meat, cubed
- 1 celery stalk, chopped
- 2 tablespoons olive oil
- 3 carrots, chopped
- 1 cup beef stock
- 2 garlic clove, minced
- Salt and black pepper to the taste
- 1 tablespoon tomato passata

Directions:
Set your instant pot on sauté mode, add the oil, heat it up, add the onion, celery, carrots and the garlic and sauté for 5 minutes. Add the meat and brown for 5 minutes more. Add the rest of the ingredients, put the lid on and cook on High for 15 minutes. Release the pressure naturally for 10 minutes, divide the stew into bowls and serve/

Nutrition: calories 220, fat 12, fiber 4, carbs 7, protein 16

Salmon, Cod and Mushrooms Stew

*Preparation time: 10 minutes **Cooking time:** 12 minutes **Servings:** 4*

Ingredients:
- 1 pound salmon fillets, boneless, skinless and cubed
- 1 pound cod fillets, boneless, skinless and cubed
- 1 cup white mushrooms, sliced
- 1 cup chicken stock
- 10 ounces canned tomatoes, chopped
- A pinch of salt and black pepper
- 1 tablespoon cilantro, chopped

Directions:
In your instant pot, combine the salmon with the cod, mushrooms and the remaining ingredients, put the lid on and cook on High for 12 minutes. Release the pressure naturally for 10 minutes, divide the stew into bowls and serve.

Nutrition: calories 205, fat 7, fiber 4, carbs 6, protein 10

Shrimp and Avocado Stew

*Preparation time: 5 minutes **Cooking time:** 10 minutes **Servings:** 4*

Ingredients:
- 1 cup chicken stock
- 1 pound shrimp, peeled, deveined
- 2 avocados, peeled, pitted and cubed
- 2 shallots, chopped
- 2 garlic cloves, minced
- 2 tablespoons olive oil
- ¼ teaspoon turmeric powder
- 1 tablespoon basil, chopped

Directions:
Set the instant pot on Sauté mode, add the oil, heat it up, add the shallots, garlic and turmeric, stir and sauté for 2 minutes. Add the shrimp and the rest of the ingredients, toss, put the lid on and cook on High for 8 minutes. Release the pressure fast for 5 minutes, divide the mix into bowls and serve.

Nutrition: calories 190, fat 8, fiber 4, carbs 5, protein 9

Shrimp and Fennel Stew

Preparation time: 10 minutes **Cooking time:** 15 minutes **Servings:** 4

Ingredients:
- 1 pound shrimp, peeled, deveined
- 2 fennel bulbs, sliced
- 1 yellow onion, chopped
- 1 tablespoon olive oil
- 1 cup chicken stock
- ¼ cup tomato passata
- A pinch of sea salt and pepper

Directions:
Set the instant pot on Sauté mode, add the oil, heat it up, add the onion and the fennel and sauté for 5 minutes. Add the shrimp and the rest of the ingredients, put the lid on and cook on High for 10 minutes. Release the pressure naturally for 10 minutes, divide the stew into bowls and serve.

Nutrition: calories 190, fat 4, fiber 1, carbs 5, protein 6

Cod and Okra Stew

Preparation time: 5 minutes **Cooking time:** 15 minutes **Servings:** 4

Ingredients:
- 1 pound cod fillets, boneless and cubed
- 1 cup okra, sliced
- 1 cup tomatoes, chopped
- 1 yellow onion, chopped
- 2 tablespoons olive oil
- 3 garlic cloves, minced
- 1 cup chicken stock
- ½ cup tomato passata
- ½ cup cilantro, chopped
- A pinch of salt and black pepper

Directions:
Set your instant pot on Sauté mode, add the oil, heat it up, add the onion, garlic and the okra and cook for 5 minutes. Add the cod and the rest of the ingredients, put the lid on and cook on High for 10 minutes. Release the pressure fast for 5 minutes, divide the stew into bowls and serve.

Nutrition: calories 179, fat 4, fiber 2, carbs 6, protein 9

Orange Salmon Stew

Preparation time: 10 minutes *Cooking time:* 20 minutes *Servings:* 4

Ingredients:

- 1 pound salmon fillets, boneless, skinless and cubed
- Juice of 1 orange
- Zest of 1 orange, grated
- 4 scallions, chopped
- 3 garlic cloves, minced
- 1 cup chicken stock
- A pinch of salt and black pepper
- 1 teaspoon rosemary, dried
- 1 tablespoon chives, chopped

Directions:

Set your instant pot on Sauté mode, add the oil, heat it up, add the scallions, garlic, rosemary and the orange zest and sauté for 5 minutes. Add the salmon and the rest of the ingredients, put the lid on and cook on Low for 15 minutes. Release the pressure naturally for 10 minutes, divide the stew into bowls and serve.

Nutrition: calories 200, fat 12, fiber 4, carbs 7, protein 16

Curry Lamb Stew

Preparation time: 5 minutes *Cooking time:* 25 minutes *Servings:* 4

Ingredients:

- 1 tablespoon olive oil
- 1 pound lamb shoulder, cubed
- 1 yellow onion, chopped
- 1 tablespoon curry paste
- 1 teaspoon chili powder
- 1 tablespoon basil, chopped
- 2 cups beef stock
- A pinch of salt and black pepper
- ¼ cup heavy cream

Directions:

Set your instant pot on Sauté mode, add the oil, heat it up, add the onion, curry paste and chili powder and sauté for 5 minutes. Add the meat and brown for 5 minutes more. Add the rest of the ingredients except the cream, put the lid on and cook on High for 10 minutes. Release the pressure fast for 5 minutes, add the cream, toss, set the pot on Sauté mode and cook the stew for 5 minutes more. Divide the stew into bowls and serve.

Nutrition: calories 241, fat 12, fiber 3, carbs 6, protein 14

Ginger Mussels Stew

Preparation time: 5 minutes *Cooking time:* 12 minutes *Servings:* 4

Ingredients:
- 1 pound mussels, scrubbed
- 1 tablespoon olive oil
- 3 scallions, chopped
- ½ cup tomato passata
- 1 tablespoon ginger, grated
- 1 cup veggie stock
- 2 garlic cloves, minced
- A pinch of salt and black pepper
- ¼ cup cilantro, chopped

Directions:
Set the instant pot on Sauté mode, add the oil, heat it up, add the scallions, ginger and garlic and sauté for 2 minutes. Add the mussels and the other ingredients, toss, put the lid on and cook on High for 10 minutes. Release the pressure fast for 5 minutes, divide the stew into bowls and serve.

Nutrition: calories 140, fat 9, fiber 4, carbs 5, protein 6

Ground Pork Stew

Preparation time: 10 minutes *Cooking time:* 20 minutes *Servings:* 4

Ingredients:
- 1 pound pork stew meat, ground
- 1 cup tomatoes, cubed
- 1 yellow onion, chopped
- 2 tablespoons olive oil
- 1 cup beef stock
- ½ cup tomato passata
- A pinch of salt and black pepper
- 4 garlic cloves, minced
- 1 bunch parsley, chopped

Directions:
Set your instant pot on Sauté mode, add the oil, heat it up, add the onion, garlic and the meat and brown for 5 minutes Add the tomatoes and the rest of the ingredients, put the lid on and cook on High for 15 minutes Release the pressure naturally for 10 minutes, divide the stew into bowls and serve.

Nutrition: calories 198, fat 9, fiber 4, carbs 7, protein 14

Dill Avocado and Tomato Stew

Preparation time: 5 minutes **Cooking time:** *10 minutes* **Servings:** *4*

Ingredients:
- 1 tablespoon olive oil
- 2 shallots, chopped
- 1 pound tomatoes, cut into wedges
- 2 avocados, peeled, pitted and cubed
- 1 tablespoon balsamic vinegar
- ½ cup veggie stock
- A pinch of salt and black pepper
- 1 tablespoon dill, chopped

Directions:
Set your instant pot on Sauté mode, add the oil, heat it up, add the shallots and sauté for 2 minutes. Add the tomatoes, avocados and the rest of the ingredients, put the lid on and cook on High for 8 minutes. Release the pressure fast for 5 minutes, divide the stew into bowls and serve.

Nutrition: calories 203, fat 8, fiber 2, carbs 6, protein 11

Chicken and Sprouts Stew

Preparation time: 10 minutes **Cooking time:** *20 minutes* **Servings:** *4*

Ingredients:
- 1 pound chicken breast, skinless, boneless and cubed
- ¼ pound Brussels sprouts, trimmed and halved
- 1 tablespoon olive oil
- 1 yellow onion, chopped
- A pinch of salt and black pepper
- ½ teaspoon thyme, dried
- 1 cup chicken stock
- 1 cup tomatoes, chopped
- 1 tablespoon oregano, chopped

Directions:
Set your instant pot on Sauté mode, add the oil, heat it up, add the onion, thyme and the meat and brown for 5 minutes. Add the rest of the ingredients, toss, put the lid on and cook on Low for 15 minutes. Release the pressure naturally for 10 minutes, divide the stew into bowls and serve.

Nutrition: calories 191, fat 9, fiber 3, carbs 6, protein 16

Millet Stew

Preparation time: 10 minutes **Cooking time:** *20 minutes* **Servings:** *4*

Ingredients:
- 1 cup millet
- 3 cups chicken stock
- 1 yellow onion, chopped
- 2 tablespoons olive oil
- A pinch of salt and black pepper
- 1 cup canned tomatoes, chopped
- 2 tablespoons sweet paprika
- 1 bunch cilantro, chopped

Directions:
Set the instant pot on Sauté mode, add the oil, heat it up, add the onion and the paprika and sauté for 5 minutes. Add the millet and the other ingredients, toss, put the lid on and cook on High for 15 minutes. Release the pressure naturally for 10 minutes, divide the stew into bowls and serve.

Nutrition: calories 671, fat 15.6, fiber 27.5, carbs 87.5, protein 27.1

Balsamic Oyster Stew

Preparation time: 10 minutes **Cooking time:** *20 minutes* **Servings:** *6*

Ingredients:
- 2 garlic cloves, minced
- 1 red onion, chopped
- 1 cup roasted red peppers
- 2 tablespoons balsamic vinegar
- 1 pound oysters, shucked
- Salt and black pepper to the taste
- 1 teaspoon red pepper flakes
- 2 tablespoons olive oil
- 1 tablespoon basil, chopped

Directions:
Set the instant pot on Sauté mode, add the oil, heat it up, add the onion and the garlic and sauté for 5 minutes Add the oysters and the other ingredients, toss, put the lid on and cook on High for 15 minutes Release the pressure naturally for 10 minutes, divide the stew into bowls and serve.

Nutrition: calories 264, fat 9.3, fiber 1.2, carbs 2.3, protein 1.2

Turkey and Lentils Stew

Preparation time: 10 minutes *Cooking time:* 30 minutes *Servings:* 4

Ingredients:
- 1 pound turkey breast, skinless, boneless and cubed
- 1 yellow onion, chopped
- 1 tablespoon olive oil
- 1 cup celery, chopped
- 2 garlic cloves, minced
- 1 cup lentils, dried
- ½ teaspoon smoked paprika
- Salt and black pepper to the taste
- ½ cup cilantro, chopped

Directions:
Set the instant pot on Sauté mode, add the oil, heat it up, add the onion and the garlic and sauté for 5 minutes. Add the meat and brown for 5 minutes more. Add the rest of the ingredients, toss, put the lid on and cook on High for 20 minutes. Release the pressure naturally for 10 minutes, divide the stew into bowls and serve.

Nutrition: calories 325, fat 17.3, fiber 6.8, carbs 26.4, protein 16.4

Basil Pork, Tomato and Eggplant Stew

Preparation time: 10 minutes *Cooking time:* 30 minutes *Servings:* 4

Ingredients:
- 2 pounds pork stew meat, cubed
- 2 cups tomatoes, chopped
- 1 eggplant, chopped
- 1 yellow onion, chopped
- 2 garlic cloves, minced
- Salt and black pepper to the taste
- 2 tablespoons olive oil
- 1 carrot, chopped
- 1 tablespoon ginger, grated
- ½ cup cilantro, chopped
- 6 tablespoons Greek yogurt

Directions:
Set the instant pot on Sauté mode, add the oil, heat it up, add the onion, ginger and the garlic and sauté for 5 minutes. Add the meat and brown for 5 minutes more. Add the tomatoes, eggplant and the other ingredients, toss, put the lid on and cook on High for 20 minutes. Release the pressure naturally for 10 minutes, divide the stew into bowls and serve.

Nutrition: calories 355, fat 14.3, fiber 6.7, carbs 22.6, protein 15.4

Chicken and Walnuts Stew

Preparation time: 10 minutes **Cooking time:** *25 minutes* **Servings:** *4*

Ingredients:

- 2 pounds chicken breast, skinless, boneless and cubed
- 2 tablespoons olive oil
- 1 red onion, chopped
- 3 garlic cloves, minced
- Salt and black pepper to the taste
- 1 teaspoon ginger, grated
- 2 cups chicken stock
- 2/3 cup walnuts, chopped
- ¼ cup tomatoes, cubed
- ½ teaspoon sweet paprika
- 2 tablespoons cilantro, chopped

Directions:

Set the instant pot on Sauté mode, add the oil, heat it up, add the onion, garlic and ginger and sauté for 5 minutes. Add the meat and brown for 5 minutes more. Add the rest of the ingredients, toss, put the lid on and cook on High for 15 minutes. Release the pressure naturally for 10 minutes, divide the stew into bowls and serve.

Nutrition: calories 309, fat 25.4, fiber 4, carbs 15.3, protein 6.7

Sea Bass Stew

Preparation time: 10 minutes **Cooking time:** *20 minutes* **Servings:** *4*

Ingredients:

- 1 red onion, chopped
- 2 tablespoons olive oil
- 1 pound sea bass fillets, boneless, skinless and cubed
- 2 garlic cloves, minced
- ½ teaspoon sweet paprika
- 1 cup chicken stock
- ½ cup tomato passata
- ½ teaspoon coriander, ground
- ½ teaspoon cumin, ground
- Salt and black pepper to the taste
- 1 red bell pepper, chopped
- ½ cup black olives, pitted and halved
- 1 tablespoon chives, chopped

Directions:

Set the instant pot on Sauté mode, add the oil, heat it up, add the onion and the garlic and sauté for 2 minutes. Add the paprika, coriander, cumin and bell pepper and sauté for 5 minutes more. Add the fish and the remaining ingredients, toss, put the lid on and cook on High for 13 minutes. Release the pressure naturally for 10 minutes, divide the stew into bowls and serve.

Nutrition: calories 272, fat 15, fiber 3.6, carbs 14, protein 2.3

Trout Stew

*Preparation time: 10 minutes **Cooking time:** 20 minutes **Servings:** 4*

Ingredients:
- 2 garlic cloves, minced
- 2 tablespoons olive oil
- 1 yellow onion, chopped
- 1 pound trout fillets, boneless, skinless and cubed
- 1 cup tomatoes, chopped
- 1 tablespoon lemon juice
- 1 cup chicken stock
- 1 zucchini, cubed
- ½ cup tomato passata
- 1 bunch parsley, chopped
- Salt and white pepper to the taste

Directions:
Set the instant pot on Sauté mode, add the oil, heat it up, add the garlic and the onion and sauté for 5 minutes. Add the fish, tomatoes and the other ingredients, toss, put the lid on and cook on High for 15 minutes. Release the pressure naturally for 10 minutes, divide the stew into bowls and serve.

Nutrition: calories 300, fat 14.3, fiber 4.5, carbs 16.1, protein 11

Veggies Stew

*Preparation time: 10 minutes **Cooking time:** 30 minutes **Servings:** 4*

Ingredients:
- 1 yellow onion, chopped
- 1 cup zucchinis, cubed
- 1 cup eggplant, cubed
- 2 tablespoons olive oil
- 1 fennel bulb, chopped
- 1 endive, trimmed and shredded
- 1 carrot, peeled and sliced
- ½ cup tomato passata
- 1 red bell pepper, chopped
- 2 garlic cloves, minced
- 1 cup green beans, trimmed and halved
- ½ green cabbage head, shredded
- 1 teaspoon thyme, dried
- Salt and black pepper to the taste
- 2 cups veggie stock
- 1 tablespoon cilantro, chopped

Directions:
Set the instant pot on Sauté mode, add the oil, heat it up, add the onion and the garlic and sauté for 5 minutes. Add the zucchinis, eggplant, fennel and the other ingredients, toss, put the lid on and cook on High for 20 minutes. Release the pressure naturally for 10 minutes, divide the stew into bowls and serve.

Nutrition: calories 450, fat 12, fiber 13, carbs 47, protein 34

Green Beans and Olives Stew

Preparation time: 10 minutes *Cooking time:* 20 minutes *Servings:* 4

Ingredients:

- 1 yellow onion, chopped
- 2 garlic cloves, minced
- 1 pound green beans, trimmed and halved
- 1 cup black olives, pitted and halved
- ½ cup kalamata olives, pitted and halved
- 2 tablespoons olive oil
- 1 teaspoon cumin, ground
- 1 cup tomatoes, chopped
- Juice of 1 lime
- ½ cup tomato passata
- 1 cup chicken stock
- Salt and black pepper to the taste
- 1 tablespoon cilantro, chopped

Directions:

Set the instant pot on Sauté mode, add the oil, heat it up, add the onion and the garlic and sauté for 5 minutes. Add the green beans, the olives and the other ingredients, toss, put the lid on and cook on High for 15 minutes. Release the pressure naturally for 10 minutes, divide the stew into bowls and serve.

Nutrition: calories 235, fat 12.3, fiber 3.5, carbs 16.3, protein 10.2

Onions and Shrimp Stew

Preparation time: 5 minutes *Cooking time:* 15 minutes *Servings:* 4

Ingredients:

- 2 tablespoons olive oil
- 2 red onions, chopped
- 2 scallions, chopped
- 2 pounds shrimp, peeled, deveined
- 3 garlic cloves, chopped
- 2 cups chicken stock
- 2 tablespoons tomato passata
- 1 teaspoon rosemary, ground
- 1 teaspoon chili powder
- ½ teaspoon fennel seeds, crushed
- Salt and black pepper to the taste

Directions:

Set the instant pot on Sauté mode, add the oil, heat it up, add the onions, garlic and scallions and sauté for 5 minutes. Add the shrimp, stock and the other ingredients, toss, put the lid on and cook on High for 10 minutes. Release the pressure fast for 5 minutes, divide the stew into bowls and serve.

Nutrition: calories 221, fat 8, fiber 8, carbs 33.1, protein 8.9

Instant Pot Snack and Appetizer Recipes

Chicken Sliders
Preparation time: 10 minutes **Cooking time:** *20 minutes* **Servings:** *12*

Ingredients:

- 4 chicken breasts, skinless, boneless and halved
- 2 tablespoons honey
- 7 tablespoons butter
- 1 cup buffalo wing sauce
- 24 potato rolls, tops cut off
- 1 cup celery, chopped
- 2 cup Monterey Jack cheese, shredded
- 1 tablespoon parsley, chopped

Directions:

In your instant pot, combine the chicken with the honey, 4 tablespoons butter and the buffalo sauce, toss, put the lid on and cook on High for 10 minutes. Release the pressure naturally for 10 minutes, shred the meat and transfer the whole mix to a bowl. Spread the remaining butter on the roll bottoms, divide the meat, cheese and parsley, put the tops, arrange all the rolls in a baking dish and cook at 375 degrees F for 10 minutes. Arrange the sliders on a platter and serve as an appetizer.

Nutrition: calories

Spicy Meatballs
Preparation time: 10 minutes **Cooking time:** *10 minutes* **Servings:** *10*

Ingredients:

- 2 pounds beef stew meat, ground
- 2 eggs, whisked
- 1 tablespoon cilantro, chopped
- 2 tablespoons almond flour
- 12 ounces chili sauce
- ½ cup water
- ½ tablespoon red pepper, crushed
- A pinch of cayenne pepper
- A pinch of salt and black pepper
- 1 tablespoon green onions, chopped

Directions:

In a bowl, combine the meat with the eggs, cilantro and the flour, stir well and shape medium meatballs out of this mix. In your instant pot, combine the meatballs with the remaining ingredients except the green onions, toss, put the lid on and cook on High for 10 minutes. Release the pressure naturally for 10 minutes, arrange the meatballs on a platter, sprinkle the green onions on top and serve.

Nutrition: calories

Onion Dip

Preparation time: 10 minutes **Cooking time:** *12 minutes* **Servings:** *8*

Ingredients:
- 8 ounces cream cheese, soft
- 1 cup Swiss cheese, grated
- 1 cup yellow onion, chopped
- 1 cup mayonnaise
- 1 cup water

Directions:
In a baking pan combine the cream cheese with the Swiss cheese, onion and mayo and whisk well. Put the water in the instant pot, add the trivet inside, put the baking pan in the machine, put the lid on and cook on High for 12 minutes. Release the pressure naturally for 10 minutes, divide the dip into bowls and serve.

Nutrition: calories

Hummus

Preparation time: 10 minutes **Cooking time:** *30 minutes* **Servings:** *8*

Ingredients:
- 1 cup chickpeas
- 3 cups veggie stock
- A pinch of salt and black pepper
- 2 tablespoons olive oil
- 4 tablespoons tahini paste
- ¼ cup lemon juice
- 1 teaspoon cumin, ground
- 2 garlic cloves, minced

Directions:
Put the chickpeas in the instant pot, add the stock, salt and pepper, put the lid on and cook on High for 30 minutes. Release the pressure naturally for 10 minutes, transfer the chickpeas to a blender, add 1 cup of the cooking liquid, also add the rest of the ingredients, pulse well, divide into bowls and serve as a party dip.

Nutrition: calories 300, fat 12, fiber 4, carbs 12, protein 5

Honey Wings

*Preparation time: 10 minutes **Cooking time:** 12 minutes **Servings:** 8*

Ingredients:
- 2 pounds chicken wings
- 1 tablespoon garlic, minced
- 1 cup bbq sauce
- ½ cup brown sugar
- 2 tablespoons Worcestershire sauce
- ½ cup water
- ½ cup honey
- A pinch of cayenne pepper

Directions:
In your instant pot, combine the chicken wings with the garlic, bbq sauce and the other ingredients, toss, put the lid on and cook on High for 12 minutes. Release the pressure naturally for 10 minutes, arrange the chicken wings on a platter and serve as an appetizer.

Nutrition: calories 234, fat 11, fiber 3, carbs 20, protein 12

Almond and Spring Onions Dip

*Preparation time: 5 minutes **Cooking time:** 8 minutes **Servings:** 4*

Ingredients:
- 8 ounces cream cheese, soft
- 1 cup almonds, chopped
- 1 cup spring onions, chopped
- A pinch of salt and black pepper
- 1 and ½ teaspoons turmeric powder
- 1 tablespoon lemon juice
- 1 cup water

Directions:
In a bowl, combine the cream cheese with the almonds, spring onions and the other ingredients except the water, whisk them well and transfer to a big ramekin. Put the water in the instant pot, add the trivet inside, put the ramekin in the trivet, put the lid on and cook on High for 8 minutes. Release the pressure fast for 5 minutes and serve the mix as a party dip.

Nutrition: calories 132, fat 1, fiber 2, carbs 6, protein 5

Basil Tomato Dip

Preparation time: 10 minutes *Cooking time:* 15 minutes *Servings:* 4

Ingredients:
- 1 pound tomatoes, roughly chopped
- 2 garlic cloves, minced
- 4 scallions, chopped
- ½ cup veggie stock
- 1 tablespoon lime juice
- 1 tablespoon olive oil
- A pinch of salt and black pepper
- 1 tablespoon basil, chopped

Directions:
Set the instant pot on Sauté mode, add the oil, heat it up, add the garlic and the scallions and sauté for 2 minutes. Add the tomatoes and the other ingredients, toss, put the lid on and cook on High for 13 minutes. Release the pressure naturally for 10 minutes, transfer the mix to your blender, pulse well, divide into bowls and serve as a dip.

Nutrition: calories 140, fat 4, fiber 3, carbs 6, protein 6

Balsamic Shrimp Platter

Preparation time: 5 minutes *Cooking time:* 8 minutes *Servings:* 4

Ingredients:
- 2 pounds shrimp, peeled and deveined
- 1 tablespoon olive oil
- 1 tablespoon balsamic vinegar
- ¼ cup chicken stock
- 1 teaspoon sweet paprika
- 2 spring onions, chopped
- ½ teaspoon chili powder

Directions:
Set the instant pot on Sauté mode, add the oil, heat it up, add the shrimp, vinegar and the other ingredients except the spring onions, toss, put the lid on and cook on High for 8 minutes. Release the pressure fast for 5 minutes, arrange the shrimp on a platter and serve as an appetizer.

Nutrition: calories 170, fat 9, fiber 4, carbs 7, protein 6

Shrimp Bites

Preparation time: 5 minutes **Cooking time:** 10 minutes **Servings:** 4

Ingredients:
- 1 tablespoon lemon juice
- 1 tablespoon olive oil
- 1 pound shrimp, peeled and deveined
- 2 garlic cloves, minced
- 1 tablespoon chives, chopped

Directions:
In your instant pot, combine the shrimp with the lemon juice and the other ingredients, toss, put the lid on and cook on High for 10 minutes. Release the pressure fast for 5 minutes, arrange the shrimp bites on a platter and serve.

Nutrition: calories 180, fat 3, fiber 3, carbs 7, protein 9

Zucchini Salsa

Preparation time: 5 minutes **Cooking time:** 10 minutes **Servings:** 4

Ingredients:
- 1 pound zucchinis, roughly cubed
- 1 tablespoon avocado oil
- 1 red onion, thinly sliced
- 1 tablespoon balsamic vinegar
- ¼ cup veggie stock
- 1 cup cherry tomatoes, halved
- 1 cup black olives, pitted and halved
- Zest and juice of 1 lime
- ½ cup spring onions, chopped
- ¼ cup cilantro, chopped

Directions:
In the instant pot, combine the zucchinis with the oil, the onion and the other ingredients, toss, put the lid on and cook on High for 10 minutes. Release the pressure fast for 5 minutes, divide the salsa into cups and serve as an appetizer.

Nutrition: calories 150, fat 9, fiber 2, carbs 6, protein 6

Basil Olives Salsa

Preparation time: *5 minutes* ***Cooking time:*** *6 minutes* ***Servings:*** *4*

Ingredients:
- 1 cup kalamata olives, pitted and halved
- 1 cup black olives, pitted and halved
- 1 cup green olives, pitted and halved
- 1 cup tomatoes, cubed
- 1 cup cucumber, cubed
- ½ cup veggie stock
- 1 red onion, sliced
- ½ cup balsamic vinegar
- 1 tablespoon olive oil
- 2 tablespoons basil, chopped

Directions:
In the instant pot, combine the olives with the tomatoes, the cucumber and the other ingredients, toss, put the lid on and cook on High for 6 minutes. Release the pressure fast for 5 minutes, divide the salsa into small bowls and serve.

Nutrition: calories 173, fat 9, fiber 3, carbs 5, protein 8

Kale Dip

Preparation time: *5 minutes* ***Cooking time:*** *15 minutes* ***Servings:*** *4*

Ingredients:
- 1 pound kale, torn
- 1 cup heavy cream
- 2 red onions, chopped
- A pinch of salt and black pepper
- 2 tablespoons olive oil
- 4 garlic cloves, roasted and minced
- 2 tablespoons lime juice
- 1 tablespoon chives, chopped

Directions:
Set the instant pot on Sauté mode, add the oil, heat it up, add the onions and the garlic and sauté for 5 minutes. Add the kale and the other ingredients, toss, put the lid on and cook on High for 10 minutes. Release the pressure fast for 5 minutes, blend the mix using an immersion blender, divide into bowls and serve.

Nutrition: calories 183, fat 9, fiber 4, carbs 7, protein 5

Mint Spinach Salad

*Preparation time: 5 minutes **Cooking time:** 6 minutes **Servings:** 4*

Ingredients:
- 1 pound spinach leaves, torn
- 4 scallions, chopped
- 2 tomatoes, cubed
- 1 cucumber, cubed
- 1 avocado, peeled, pitted and cubed
- ½ cup black olives, pitted and cubed
- 1 tablespoon olive oil
- ½ cup heavy cream
- 2 tablespoons mint leaves, chopped
- A pinch of salt and black pepper

Directions:
In the instant pot, combine the spinach with the scallions, the tomatoes and the other ingredients, toss, put the lid on and cook on Low for 6 minutes. Release the pressure fast for 5 minutes, divide the salad into bowls and serve as an appetizer.

Nutrition: calories 180, fat 9, fiber 2, carbs 6, protein 9

Green Beans Salsa

*Preparation time: 10 minutes **Cooking time:** 15 minutes **Servings:** 6*

Ingredients:
- 1 pound green beans, trimmed and halved
- 1 cup black olives, pitted and halved
- 1 cup red onion, chopped
- 1 cup tomatoes, cubed
- 1 cup veggie stock
- 1 tablespoon sweet paprika
- 1 tablespoon balsamic vinegar
- 2 tablespoons olive oil
- 2 garlic cloves, minced

Directions:
In your instant pot, combine the green beans with the olives and the other ingredients, toss, put the lid on and cook on High for 15 minutes. Release the pressure naturally for 10 minutes, divide the salsa into bowls and serve as an appetizer.

Nutrition: calories 210, fat 7, fiber 4, carbs 6, protein 10

Rosemary Salmon Bites

Preparation time: 10 minutes **Cooking time:** *10 minutes* **Servings:** *4*

Ingredients:
- 1 tablespoon avocado oil
- 1 pound salmon fillets, boneless, skinless and roughly cubed
- A pinch of salt and black pepper
- ½ cup bbq sauce
- 1 teaspoon rosemary, dried
- 1 tablespoon lime juice

Directions:
In your instant pot, combine the salmon cubes with the oil and the other ingredients, toss, put the lid on and cook on High for 10 minutes. Release the pressure naturally for 10 minutes, arrange the salmon bites on a platter and serve.

Nutrition: calories 180, fat 9, fiber 4, carbs 6, protein 8

Pesto Shrimp

Preparation time: 5 minutes **Cooking time:** *6 minutes* **Servings:** *4*

Ingredients:
- 2 pounds shrimp, peeled and deveined
- 2 tablespoons basil pesto
- Juice of 1 lime
- 1 tablespoon olive oil
- A pinch of salt and black pepper
- 1 tablespoon balsamic vinegar
- ½ cup chicken stock

Directions:
In your instant pot, combine the shrimp with the basil pesto and the other ingredients, toss, put the lid on and cook on High for 6 minutes. Release the pressure fast for 5 minutes, arrange the shrimp on a platter and serve as an appetizer.

Nutrition: calories 177, fat 8, fiber 2, carbs 6, protein 7

Peppers Dip

Preparation time: 10 minutes *Cooking time:* 15 minutes *Servings:* 4

Ingredients:
- 1 pound roasted bell peppers, peeled and chopped
- 6 ounces cream cheese
- 1 red onion, chopped
- 2 tablespoons garlic, chopped
- 1 cup heavy cream
- 1 cup tomatoes, crushed
- 1 tablespoon basil, chopped
- 1 cup water

Directions:
In a bowl, combine the bell peppers with the cream cheese and the other ingredients except the water, whisk well and pour into a ramekin. Put the water in the instant pot, add the trivet inside, put the ramekin in the machine, put the lid on and cook on High for 15 minutes. Release the pressure naturally for 10 minutes, divide the mix into smaller bowls and serve as an appetizer.

Nutrition: calories 221, fat 12, fiber 4, carbs 7, protein 11

Shrimp and Spinach Bowls

Preparation time: 5 minutes *Cooking time:* 6 minutes *Servings:* 4

Ingredients:
- 2 pounds shrimp, peeled and deveined
- 2 cups baby spinach
- 4 scallions, chopped
- 2 tablespoons olive oil
- ½ cup chicken stock
- 2 garlic cloves, minced
- 1 teaspoon chili powder
- 1 tablespoon chives, chopped

Directions:
In your instant pot, combine the shrimp with the spinach, scallions and the other ingredients, toss, put the lid on and cook on High for 6 minutes. Release the pressure fast for 5 minutes, divide the mix into small bowls and serve as an appetizer.

Nutrition: calories 180, fat 9, fiber 3, carbs 5, protein 7

Herbed Tomato Salsa

Preparation time: *5 minutes* ***Cooking time:*** *8 minutes* ***Servings:*** *4*

Ingredients:
- 2 pounds cherry tomatoes, halved
- ¼ cup heavy cream
- 1 cup black olives, pitted and halved
- 1 avocado, peeled, pitted and cubed
- 2 tablespoons olive oil
- 2 tablespoons balsamic vinegar
- 2 scallions, chopped
- 1 tablespoon oregano, chopped
- 1 tablespoon cilantro, chopped
- 1 tablespoon chives, chopped

Directions:

In your instant pot, combine the tomatoes with the olives, the cream and the other ingredients, toss, put the lid on and cook on High for 8 minutes Release the pressure fast for 5 minutes, divide the mix into small cups and serve as an appetizer.

Nutrition: calories 140, fat 4, fiber 3, carbs 5, protein 4

Salmon Salad

Preparation time: *5 minutes* ***Cooking time:*** *10 minutes* ***Servings:*** *4*

Ingredients:
- 2 pounds salmon fillets, boneless, skinless and cubed
- 1 cup baby arugula
- 1 carrot, peeled and grated
- 1 cup tomatoes, cubed
- 1 tablespoon balsamic vinegar
- ½ cup heavy cream
- 1 cup avocado, peeled, pitted and cubed
- 2 tablespoons olive oil
- 1 red onion, chopped
- 2 teaspoons garlic, minced
- 2 teaspoons oregano, dried
- 1 tablespoon parsley, chopped

Directions:

Set your instant pot on Sauté mode, add the oil, heat it up, add the carrot, onion and the garlic and sauté for 2 minutes. Add the salmon, arugula and the rest of the ingredients, toss, put the lid on and cook on High for 8 minutes. Release the pressure fast for 5 minutes, divide the mix into small bowls and serve.

Nutrition: calories 176, fat 4, fiber 3, carbs 6, protein 7\

Tuna and Shrimp Salad

*Preparation time: 10 minutes **Cooking time:** 12 minutes **Servings:** 4*
Ingredients:
- 1 pound tuna fillets, boneless, skinless and roughly cubed
- 1 pound shrimp, peeled and deveined
- 2 tablespoons olive oil
- 2 tomatoes, cubed
- 2 red onions, chopped
- ½ cup chives, chopped
- 1 cup baby spinach
- ½ cup chicken stock
- 1 tablespoon basil, chopped
- A pinch of salt and black pepper

Directions:
Set your instant pot on Sauté mode, add the oil, heat it up, add the onions and sauté for 2 minutes. Add the tuna, shrimp and the other ingredients, toss, put the lid on and cook on High for 10 minutes. Release the pressure naturally for 10 minutes, transfer the mix bowls and serve as an appetizer.
Nutrition: calories 181, fat 4, fiber 3, carbs 7, protein 15

Shrimp Dip

*Preparation time: 5 minutes **Cooking time:** 8 minutes **Servings:** 4*
Ingredients:
- 1 pound shrimp, peeled, deveined, cooked and chopped
- 1 red onion, chopped
- 1 tablespoon olive oil
- 3 garlic cloves, minced
- 4 ounces cream cheese, soft
- 1 teaspoon hot paprika
- 1 tablespoon basil, chopped
- 1 tablespoon chives, chopped
- 1 cup heavy cream
- A pinch of salt and black pepper
- 1 teaspoon lemon juice
- 1 cup water

Directions:
In a bowl, combine the shrimp with the onion, the oil, garlic and the other ingredients except the water, whisk well and transfer to 4 ramekins. Put the water in the instant pot, add the trivet, put the ramekins inside, put the lid on and cook on High for 8 minutes. Release the pressure fast for 5 minutes, and serve the mix as a party dip.
Nutrition: calories 201, fat 9, fiber 4, carbs 7, protein 10

Fennel Dip

Preparation time: 10 minutes **Cooking time:** *12 minutes* **Servings:** *8*
Ingredients:
- 2 fennel bulbs, shredded
- 8 ounces cream cheese, soft
- 1 cup mozzarella cheese, grated
- ½ cup chicken stock
- ½ cup heavy cream
- A pinch of salt and black pepper
- 3 garlic cloves, minced
- 1 teaspoon sweet paprika
- 1 tablespoon chives, chopped

Directions:
In your instant pot, combine the fennel bulbs with the cream cheese, the mozzarella and the other ingredients, whisk, put the lid on and cook on High for 12 minutes. Release the pressure naturally for 10 minutes, divide the mix into bowls and serve as a party dip.
Nutrition: calories 200, fat 8, fiber 2, carbs 6, protein 8

Artichoke Salsa

Preparation time: 5 minutes **Cooking time:** *12 minutes* **Servings:** *4*
Ingredients:
- 2 cups canned artichoke hearts, drained and halved
- 1 cup heavy cream
- 1 cup baby spinach
- 2 spring onions, chopped
- 2 tomatoes, cubed
- 1 teaspoon chili powder
- ½ cup kalamata olives, pitted and halved
- A pinch of salt and black pepper
- 2 garlic cloves, chopped
- 2 tablespoons olive oil
- 2 tablespoons lemon juice
- 2 tablespoons chives, chopped

Directions:
Set the instant pot on Sauté mode, add the oil, heat it up, add the spring onions, garlic and chili powder, stir and sauté for 2 minutes. Add the artichokes, baby spinach and the other ingredients, toss gently, put the lid on and cook on High for 10 minutes. Release the pressure fast for 5 minutes, divide the mix into bowls and serve as an appetizer.
Nutrition: calories 171, fat 3, fiber 4, carbs 7, protein 5

Carrot Dip

*Preparation time: 5 minutes **Cooking time:** 8 minutes **Servings:** 4*

Ingredients:
- 1 pound carrots, peeled and grated
- 1 cup heavy cream
- 2 cups cream cheese, soft
- 1 tablespoon lime juice
- A pinch of salt and black pepper
- 1 teaspoon turmeric powder
- 1 tablespoon chives, chopped
- 1 cup water

Directions:
In a bowl, combine the carrots with the cream , cream cheese and the other ingredients except the water, whisk well and divide into 4 ramekins Put the water in your instant pot, add the trivet, put the ramekins inside, put the lid on and cook on High for 8 minutes. Release the pressure fast for 5 minutes, and serve the mix as a party dip.

Nutrition: calories 162, fat 3, fiber 4, carbs 7, protein 6

Pistachio Dip

*Preparation time: 5 minutes **Cooking time:** 6 minutes **Servings:** 6*

Ingredients:
- 2 cups heavy cream
- 1 cup pistachios, toasted and chopped
- A pinch of salt and black pepper
- 1 teaspoon turmeric powder
- 1 teaspoon rosemary, dried
- ¼ cup chives, chopped
- 2 tablespoons olive oil
- 1 cup water

Directions:
In a blender, combine the cream with the pistachios, salt, pepper and the other ingredients except the water, pulse well and divide into 6 ramekins. Put the water in the instant pot, add the trivet inside, put the ramekins into the pot, put the lid on and cook on High for 6 minutes. Release the pressure fast for 5 minutes and serve the dip right away.

Nutrition: calories 294, fat 18, fiber 1, carbs 21, protein 10

Balsamic Tomato Platter

Preparation time: 5 minutes *Cooking time:* 15 minutes *Servings:* 6

Ingredients:

- 1 pound mixed tomatoes, halved
- 1/3 cup basil, chopped
- 2 garlic cloves, minced
- A pinch of salt and black pepper
- 2 tablespoons olive oil
- 1 tablespoon balsamic vinegar
- ½ teaspoon rosemary, dried
- ½ teaspoon chili powder
- 1 cup water

Directions:

In a bowl, combine the tomatoes with the basil, the garlic and the other ingredients except the water and toss. Put the water in the instant pot, add the steamer basket inside, put the tomatoes in the pot, put the lid on and cook on High for 15 minutes. Release the pressure fast for 5 minutes, arrange the tomatoes on a platter and serve.

Nutrition: calories 162, fat 4 fiber 7, carbs 29, protein 4

Spinach Dip

Preparation time: 10 minutes *Cooking time:* 12 minutes *Servings:* 4

Ingredients:

- 3 tablespoons avocado oil
- 2 garlic cloves, minced
- 2 tablespoons chives, chopped
- 1 pound baby spinach
- 1 cup heavy cream
- 4 tablespoons parmesan, grated
- ½ cup mozzarella cheese, grated
- ½ teaspoon basil, dried
- Salt and black pepper to the taste
- 1 cup water

Directions:

In a bowl, combine the spinach with the cream, the chives and the other ingredients except the water, whisk well and divide into 4 ramekins. Put the water in the instant pot, add the trivet inside, put the ramekins in the pot, put the lid on and cook on High for 12 minutes. Release the pressure naturally for 10 minutes and serve the dip right away.

Nutrition: calories 223, fat 11.2, fiber 5.34, carbs 15.5, protein 7.4

Olives and Artichokes Tapenade

Preparation time: 5 minutes **Cooking time:** *8 minutes* **Servings:** *4*

Ingredients:

- 2 cups black olives, pitted and chopped
- ½ cup kalamata olives, pitted and chopped
- 2 tablespoons cheddar cheese, shredded
- 1/3 cup oregano, chopped
- 12 ounces canned artichokes, drained and chopped
- 2 tablespoons olive oil
- 2 tablespoons lemon juice
- 1 cup heavy cream
- 2 garlic cloves, minced
- ½ teaspoon chili powder
- 1 cup water

Directions:

In your blender, combine the olives with the artichokes, the cheese and the other ingredients except the water, pulse well and divide into 4 ramekins. Put the water in the instant pot, add the trivet inside, put the ramekins in the pot, put the lid on and cook on High for 8 minutes. Release the pressure fast for 5 minutes and serve the tapenade as a snack.

Nutrition: calories 200, fat 5.6, fiber 4.5, carbs 12.4, protein 4.6

Lentils Balls

Preparation time: 10 minutes **Cooking time:** *15 minutes* **Servings:** *8*

Ingredients:

- 2 cups canned lentils, drained and rinsed
- 1 cup chives, chopped
- 2 tablespoons cilantro, chopped
- 1 yellow onion, chopped
- 5 garlic cloves, minced
- 1 teaspoon turmeric powder
- A pinch of salt and black pepper
- ¼ teaspoon cumin powder
- 1 teaspoon lemon juice
- 2 tablespoons almond flour
- 1 cup water
- Cooking spray

Directions:

In your food processor, combine the lentils with the chives, cilantro and the other ingredients except the water and the cooking spray, pulse well and shape medium balls out of this mix. Put the water in the instant pot, add the steamer basket inside, arrange the balls in the pot, grease them with cooking spray, put the lid on and cook on High for 15 minutes. Release the pressure naturally for 10 minutes, arrange the balls on a platter and serve as an appetizer.

Nutrition: calories 112, fat 6.2, fiber 2, carbs 12.3, protein 3.1

Lemon Dip

*Preparation time: 5 minutes **Cooking time:** 6 minutes **Servings:** 6*

Ingredients:
- ¼ cup Greek yogurt
- 1 cup heavy cream
- 2 tablespoons tahini paste
- Juice of 1 lemon
- Zest of 1 lemon, grated
- 1 tablespoon olive oil
- A pinch of salt and black pepper
- 1 tablespoon chives, chopped
- 1 cup water

Directions:
In a bowl, combine the yogurt with the cream, the tahini paste and the other ingredients except the water, whisk well, and divide into 6 ramekins. Put the water in the instant pot, add the trivet inside, put the ramekins in the pot, put the lid on and cook on High for 6 minutes. Release the pressure fast for 5 minutes, and serve the dip right away.

Nutrition: calories 255, fat 11.4, fiber 4.5, carbs 17.4, protein 6.5

Red Beans Spread

*Preparation time: 10 minutes **Cooking time:** 10 minutes **Servings:** 4*

Ingredients:
- 2 cups canned red beans, drained and rinsed
- 1 red onion , chopped
- 1 cup heavy cream
- 2 tablespoons avocado oil
- 4 garlic cloves, minced
- 1 tablespoon cilantro, chopped
- Juice of ½ lemon
- Zest of ½ lemon, grated
- Salt and black pepper to the taste

Directions:
Set the instant pot on Sauté mode, add the oil, heat it up, add the onion and the garlic and sauté for 2 minutes. Add the beans, the cream and the other ingredients, toss, put the lid on and cook on High for 8 minutes. Release the pressure naturally for 10 minutes, transfer the mix to a blender, pulse well, divide into bowls and serve as a party spread.

Nutrition: calories 274, fat 11.7, fiber 6.5, carbs 18.5, protein 16.5

Ground Pork Dip

Preparation time: 10 minutes *Cooking time:* 20 minutes *Servings:* 8

Ingredients:

- 1 pound pork meat, ground
- 2 tablespoons olive oil
- 1 cup beef stock
- 1 cup heavy cream
- ¼ cup mozzarella, shredded
- 1 red onion, chopped
- 1 teaspoon chili powder
- ½ teaspoon sweet paprika
- ¼ cup parsley, chopped

Directions:

Set the instant pot on Sauté mode, add the oil, heat it up, add the onion and the meat and brown for 5 minutes. Add the rest of the ingredients except the cheese, stir, put the lid on and cook on High for 10 minutes. Release the pressure naturally for 10 minutes, set the pot on Sauté mode again, add the cheese, cook the mix for 5 minutes more, divide into bowls and serve as a party dip.

Nutrition: calories 133, fat 9.7, fiber 1.7, carbs 6.4, protein 5.4

Parsley Eggplant Salsa

Preparation time: 5 minutes *Cooking time:* 20 minutes *Servings:* 4

Ingredients:

- 1 pound eggplant, roughly cubed
- 2 tablespoons olive oil
- 2 tablespoons lime juice
- 4 scallions, chopped
- 1 cup tomatoes, cubed
- 1 cup kalamata olives, pitted and halved
- ½ cup tomato passata
- ½ teaspoon sweet paprika
- 2 garlic cloves, minced
- Salt and black pepper to the taste
- 1 tablespoon parsley, chopped

Directions:

Set the instant pot on Sauté mode, add the oil, heat it up, add the scallions and sauté for 5 minutes. Add the eggplant, lime juice and the other ingredients, toss, put the lid on and cook on High for 15 minutes. Release the pressure fast for 5 minutes, divide the salsa into bowls and serve cold.

Nutrition: calories 121, fat 4.3, fiber 1, carbs 1.4, protein 4.3

Carrot Fritters

Preparation time: 5 minutes **Cooking time:** *14 minutes* **Servings:** *8*

Ingredients:
- 2 garlic cloves, minced
- ½ cup spring onions, chopped
- 1 pound carrots, peeled and grated
- 1 egg, whisked
- 2 tablespoons almond flour
- ½ teaspoon turmeric powder
- Salt and black pepper to the taste
- 2 tablespoons parsley, chopped
- Juice of ½ lime
- 2 tablespoons olive oil
- 1 cup tomato passata

Directions:

In a bowl, combine the garlic with the spring onions, the carrots and the other ingredients except the oil and the tomato passata, stir well, shape medium balls out of this mix and flatten them a bit. Set the instant pot on Sauté mode, add the oil, heat it up, add the fritters and cook them for 2 minutes on each side. Add the passata, put the lid on and cook on High for 10 minutes. Release the pressure fast for 5 minutes, arrange the fritters on a platter and serve as an appetizer.

Nutrition: calories 209, fat 11.2, fiber 3, carbs 4.4, protein 4.8

Bulgur Balls

Preparation time: 10 minutes **Cooking time:** *15 minutes* **Servings:** *6*

Ingredients:
- 1 cup Greek yogurt
- 2 cups bulgur, cooked
- ½ teaspoon cumin, ground
- 1 cup carrot, peeled and grated
- 2 garlic cloves, minced
- A pinch of salt and black pepper
- ¼ cup parsley, chopped
- ¼ cup shallots, chopped
- ½ teaspoon cinnamon powder
- 1 cup water
- Cooking spray

Directions:

In a bowl, combine the bulgur with the carrot, the yogurt and the other ingredients except the water and the cooking spray, stir well and shape medium balls out of this mix. Put the water in the instant pot, add the steamer basket inside, arrange the bulgur balls into the pot, grease them with the cooking spray, put the lid on and cook on High for 12 minutes. Release the pressure naturally for 10 minutes, arrange the balls on a platter and serve.

Nutrition: calories 300, fat 9.6, fiber 4.6, carbs 22.6, protein 6.6

Cucumber Dip

Preparation time: 5 minutes *Cooking time:* 5 minutes *Servings:* 6

Ingredients:
- 1 pound cucumber, cubed
- 1 cup heavy cream
- 1 tablespoon chives, chopped
- 1 tablespoon parsley, chopped
- 1 ounce feta cheese, crumbled

Directions:
In a bowl, combine the cucumber with the cream and the other ingredients except the water, whisk and divide into 6 small ramekins. Put the water in the instant pot, add the basket inside, put the ramekins in the pot, put the lid on and cook on High for 5 minutes. Release the pressure fast for 5 minutes and serve the mix as a party dip.

Nutrition: calories 162, fat 3.4, fiber 2, carbs 6.4, protein 2.4

Tuna Avocado Bowls

Preparation time: 5 minutes *Cooking time:* 5 minutes *Servings:* 4

Ingredients:
- 2 avocados, halved, pitted and roughly cubed
- 1 tablespoon olive oil
- 10 ounces canned tuna, drained and flaked
- ¼ cup black olives, pitted and halved
- 2 tablespoons basil pesto
- Salt and black pepper to the taste
- 1 tablespoon walnuts, chopped
- 1 tablespoon basil, chopped

Directions:
In your instant pot, combine the avocados with the oil, tuna and the other ingredients, toss, put the lid on and cook on High for 5 minutes. Release the pressure fast for 5 minutes, divide the mix into cups and serve.

Nutrition: calories 233, fat 9, fiber 3.5, carbs 11.4, protein 5.6

Plums and Shrimp Bowls

*Preparation time: 5 minutes **Cooking time:** 6 minutes **Servings:** 4*

Ingredients:
- 1 pound shrimp, peeled and deveined
- 1 tablespoon olive oil
- 4 scallions, chopped
- 1 cup cherry tomatoes, cubed
- 4 plums, pitted and cubed
- ½ cup chicken stock
- ½ teaspoon chili powder
- 1 tablespoon chives, chopped

Directions:
In your instant pot, combine the shrimp with the oil, scallions and the other ingredients, toss, put the lid on and cook on High for 6 minutes. Release the pressure fast for 5 minutes, divide the mix into small bowls and serve as an appetizer.

Nutrition: calories 30, fat 1, fiber 0, carbs 4, protein 2

Mustard Cucumber Spread

*Preparation time: 5 minutes **Cooking time:** 5 minutes **Servings:** 12*

Ingredients:
- 1 pound cucumber, cubed
- 5 ounces cream cheese, soft
- ½ cup heavy cream
- 1 tablespoon chives, chopped
- 1 teaspoon mustard
- Salt and black pepper to the taste
- 1 cup water

Directions:
In a bowl, combine the cucumber with the cream cheese and the other ingredients except the water, whisk well and divide into 4 ramekins. Put the water in the instant pot, add the trivet inside, put the ramekins in the pot, put the lid on and cook on High for 5 minutes. Release the pressure fast for 5 minutes and serve the mix as a party spread.

Nutrition: calories 187, fat 12.4, fiber 2.1, carbs 4.5, protein 8.2

Cucumber Avocado Rolls

Preparation time: 5 minutes **Cooking time:** *5 minutes* **Servings:** *4*

Ingredients:
- 1 big cucumber, sliced lengthwise
- 2 tablespoons cream cheese
- 1 avocado, peeled, pitted, halved and sliced
- Salt and black pepper to the taste
- 1 teaspoon lime juice
- 1 tablespoon chives
- 1 cup water

Directions:
Arrange cucumber slices on a working surface, spread the cream cheese on each side, divide the avocado slices, season with salt and pepper, sprinkle the chives, drizzle the lime juice and roll them. Put the water in the instant pot, add the trivet inside, put the rolls in the pot, put the lid on and cook on High for 5 minutes. Release the pressure fast for 5 minutes, arrange all the rolls on a platter and serve as an appetizer.

Nutrition: calories 200, fat 6, fiber 3.4, carbs 7.6, protein 3.5

Stuffed Tomatoes

Preparation time: 5 minutes **Cooking time:** *10 minutes* **Servings:** *4*

Ingredients:
- 4 tomatoes, tops cut off and insides scooped
- 2 tablespoons olive oil
- ¼ teaspoon chili powder
- ½ cup feta cheese, crumbled
- ½ cup kalamata olives, chopped
- ¼ cup basil, chopped
- Salt and black pepper to the taste
- 1 cup water

Directions:
In a bowl, combine the cheese with the oil, olives and the other ingredients except the water and the tomatoes, stir well and stuff the tomatoes with this mix. Put the water in the instant pot, add the trivet inside, arrange the tomatoes in the pot, put the lid on and cook on High for 10 minutes. Release the pressure fast for 5 minutes, arrange the tomatoes on a platter and serve as an appetizer.

Nutrition: calories 136, fat 8.6, fiber 4.8, carbs 5.6, protein 5.1

Basil Spread

*Preparation time: 5 minutes **Cooking time:** 6 minutes **Servings:** 6*

Ingredients:
- 2 garlic cloves, minced
- 1 tablespoon olive oil
- 1 cup basil, chopped
- 1 cup Greek yogurt
- 1 tablespoon balsamic vinegar
- 1 tablespoon chives, chopped
- Salt and black pepper to the taste
- 1 cup water

Directions:
In a blender, combine the garlic with the basil, the yogurt and the other ingredients except the water, pulse well and divide into 6 small ramekins. Put the water in the instant pot, add the trivet inside, put the ramekins in the pot, put the lid on and cook on High for 6 minutes. Release the pressure fast for 5 minutes and serve the spread right away.

Nutrition: calories 160, fat 13.7, fiber 5.5, carbs 10.1, protein 2.2

Mango Salsa

*Preparation time: 5 minutes **Cooking time:** 5 minutes **Servings:** 4*

Ingredients:
- Salt and black pepper to the taste
- 1 cup black olives, pitted and halved
- 1 cup tomatoes, cubed
- 1 red onion, chopped
- 2 mangos, peeled and chopped
- ½ cup Greek yogurt
- ¼ cup cilantro, chopped
- 3 tablespoons lime juice

Directions:
In your instant pot, combine the mangos with the olives, the tomatoes and the other ingredients, toss, put the lid on and cook on High for 5 minutes. Release the pressure fast for 5 minutes, divide the salsa into bowls and serve.

Nutrition: calories 62, fat 4.7, fiber 1.3, carbs 3.9, protein 2.3

Creamy Spinach Bowls

Preparation time: *5 minutes* **Cooking time:** *6 minutes* **Servings:** *4*

Ingredients:
- 1 pound baby spinach
- 2 shallots, chopped
- 2 tablespoons mint, chopped
- ¾ cup tomatoes, cubed
- ½ Greek yogurt
- Salt and black pepper to the taste

Directions:
In your instant pot, combine the spinach with the mint, shallots and the other ingredients, toss, put the lid on and cook on High for 6 minutes. Release the pressure fast for 5 minutes, divide the mix into bowls and serve as an appetizer.

Nutrition: calories 204, fat 11.5, fiber 3.1, carbs 4.2, protein 5.9

Feta Dip

Preparation time: *10 minutes* **Cooking time:** *10 minutes* **Servings:** *8*

Ingredients:
- 8 ounces baby spinach
- 1 and ½ cups feta cheese, crumbled
- 1 cup heavy cream
- ¾ cup basil, chopped
- A pinch of salt and black pepper
- 1 cup water

Directions:
In a blender, combine the spinach with the cream, and the other ingredients except the water, pulse well and spread into a baking dish. Put the water in the instant pot, add the trivet inside, put the baking dish into the pot, put the lid on and cook on High for 10 minutes. Release the pressure naturally for 10 minutes and serve as a party dip.

Nutrition: calories 186, fat 12.4, fiber 0.9, carbs 2.6, protein 1.5

Avocado Dip

Preparation time: *5 minutes* ***Cooking time:*** *5 minutes* ***Servings:*** *6*

Ingredients:
- ½ cup Greek yogurt
- 1 green chili, minced
- ½ teaspoon rosemary, dried
- 1 tablespoon chives, chopped
- Salt and black pepper to the taste
- 3 avocados, pitted, peeled and chopped
- 1 cup cilantro, chopped
- 2 tablespoons lemon juice
- 1 tablespoon olive oil
- 1 cup water

Directions:
In a blender, combine the yogurt with the chili, rosemary and the other ingredients except the water, pulse well and divide into 6 small ramekins. Put the water in the instant pot, add the trivet inside, put the ramekins inside, put the lid on and cook on High for 5 minutes. Release the pressure fast for 5 minutes and serve cold as a party dip.

Nutrition: calories 200, fat 14.5, fiber 3.8, carbs 8.1, protein 7.6

Tomato and Goat Cheese Bowls

Preparation time: *5 minutes* ***Cooking time:*** *8 minutes* ***Servings:*** *4*

Ingredients:
- 3 ounces goat cheese, crumbled
- 1 pound cherry tomatoes, halved
- 2 tablespoons chives, chopped
- 1 tablespoon balsamic vinegar
- 1 tablespoon rosemary, chopped
- ½ cup heavy cream
- Salt and black pepper to the taste
- 2 tablespoons olive oil

Directions:
In your instant pot, combine the tomatoes with the vinegar, the chives and the other ingredients except the cheese and toss gently. Sprinkle the cheese on top, put the lid on and cook on High for 8 minutes. Release the pressure fast for 5 minutes, divide the tomato mix into small bowls and serve as an appetizer.

Nutrition: calories 220, fat 11.5, fiber 4.8, carbs 8.9, protein 5.6

Lentils and Chickpeas Salsa

*Preparation time: 5 minutes **Cooking time:** 15 minutes **Servings:** 4*

Ingredients:
- 4 scallions, chopped
- 2 tablespoons olive oil
- 1 cup cherry tomatoes, halved
- ½ cup black olives, pitted and halved
- 1 cup baby spinach
- ½ cup veggie stock
- 1 cup canned chickpeas, drained and rinsed
- 1 cup canned lentils, drained and rinsed
- Salt and black pepper to the taste
- 2 tablespoons lemon juice
- 1 tablespoon chives, chopped

Directions:
Set the instant pot on Sauté mode, add the oil, heat it up, add the scallions and sauté for 2 minutes. Add the tomatoes, black olives and the other ingredients, toss, put the lid on and cook on High for 13 minutes. Release the pressure fast for 5 minutes, divide the mix into small bowls and serve as an appetizer.

Nutrition: calories 224, fat 5.1, fiber 1, carbs 9.9, protein 15.1

Ginger Dip

*Preparation time: 5 minutes **Cooking time:** 6 minutes **Servings:** 6*

Ingredients:
- 2 tablespoons ginger, grated
- 2 cups heavy cream
- 3 tablespoons chives, chopped
- 2 tablespoons olive oil
- 1 cup cream cheese, soft
- 1 cup water

Directions:
In your blender, combine the ginger with the cream, chives and the other ingredients except the water, pulse well and divide into 6 small ramekins. Put the water in the instant pot, add the trivet inside, put the ramekins in the pot, put the lid on and cook on High for 6 minutes. Release the pressure fast for 5 minutes and serve the mix as a party dip.

Nutrition: calories 213, fat 4.9, fiber 4.1, carbs 8.8, protein 17.8

Instant Pot Poultry Recipes

Cilantro Chicken

Preparation time: 10 minutes **Cooking time:** *20 minutes* **Servings:** *4*

Ingredients:
- 1 cup cilantro, chopped
- 1 red onion, chopped
- 2 tablespoons olive oil
- 4 garlic cloves, minced
- 1 tablespoon oregano, chopped
- 1 cup heavy cream
- 1 pound chicken breast, skinless, boneless and halved
- A pinch of salt and black pepper

Directions:
Set the instant pot on Sauté mode, add the oil, heat it up, add the onion and the garlic and sauté for 5 minutes. Add the chicken breasts, cilantro and the other ingredients, toss, put the lid on and cook on High for 15 minutes. Release the pressure naturally for 10 minutes, divide everything between plates and serve.

Nutrition: calories 263, fat 12, fiber 3, carbs 6, protein 14

Tomato Chicken Breast

Preparation time: 10 minutes Cooking time: 25 minutes Servings: 4

Ingredients:
- 1 pound chicken breasts, skinless, boneless and cubed
- 2 tablespoons olive oil
- 1 cup scallions, chopped
- 1 teaspoon chili powder
- A pinch of salt and black pepper
- 1 cup tomato sauce
- 1 tablespoon oregano, chopped

Directions:
Set the instant pot on Sauté mode, add the oil, heat it up, add the scallions and chili powder and sauté for 5 minutes. Add the meat, tomato sauce and the other ingredients, toss, put the lid on and cook on High for 20 minutes. Release the pressure naturally for 10 minutes, divide everything between plates and serve.

Nutrition: calories 162, fat 8, fiber 2, carbs 5, protein 9

Turkey and Sauce

*Preparation time: 10 minutes **Cooking time:** 25 minutes **Servings:** 4*

Ingredients:
- 2 tablespoons avocado oil
- 1 red onion, chopped
- 1 pound turkey breast, skinless, boneless and cut into strips
- ¾ cup chicken stock
- 2 tablespoons walnuts, chopped
- 1 tablespoon lemon juice
- 3 tablespoons Dijon mustard
- A pinch of salt and black pepper
- 1 tablespoon cilantro, chopped

Directions:
Set your instant pot on sauté mode, add the oil, heat it up, add the onion and the meat and brown for 5 minutes. Add the stock, walnuts and the other ingredients, toss well, put the lid on and cook on High for 20 minutes. Release the pressure naturally for 10 minutes, divide the mix between plates and serve.

Nutrition: calories 200, fat 9, fiber 2, carbs 5, protein 10

Orange Turkey

*Preparation time: 10 minutes **Cooking time:** 25 minutes **Servings:** 4*

Ingredients:
- 1 pound turkey breasts, skinless, boneless and roughly cubed
- 1 cup baby spinach
- 1 tablespoon orange zest, grated
- 2 scallions, chopped
- 2 tablespoons olive oil
- 1 cup orange juice
- ½ cup chicken stock
- 1 tablespoon oregano, chopped
- A pinch of salt and black pepper
- 1 teaspoon turmeric powder

Directions:
Set the instant pot on Sauté mode, add the oil, heat it up, add the scallions and orange zest and sauté for 2 minutes. Add the meat and brown for 3 minutes more. Add the rest of the ingredients, toss, put the lid on and cook on High for 20 minutes. Release the pressure naturally for 10 minutes, divide the mix between plates and serve.

Nutrition: calories 200, fat 7, fiber 2, carbs 6, protein 11

Cinnamon Turkey and Sweet Potatoes

Preparation time: 10 minutes *Cooking time:* 25 minutes *Servings:* 4

Ingredients:
- 1 pound turkey breasts, skinless, boneless and cubed
- 2 sweet potatoes, peeled and roughly cubed
- 1 red onion, chopped
- 2 tablespoons olive oil
- ½ teaspoon cinnamon, ground
- 1 teaspoon sweet paprika
- 1 cup chicken stock
- ½ cup parsley, chopped

Directions:

Set your instant pot on Sauté mode, add the oil, heat it up, add onion, cinnamon and the paprika and sauté for 2 minutes. Add the meat and brown for 3 minutes more. Add the rest of the ingredients, toss, put the lid on and cook on High for 20 minutes. Release the pressure naturally for 10 minutes, divide the mix between plates and serve.

Nutrition: calories 210, fat 8, fiber 2, carbs 6, protein 11

Parmesan Chicken Wings

Preparation time: 10 minutes *Cooking time:* 20 minutes *Servings:* 4

Ingredients:
- 1 cup chicken stock
- 2 tablespoons olive oil
- 1 pound chicken wings, halved
- 1 cup parmesan, grated
- 1 yellow onion, chopped
- ½ teaspoon chili powder
- ½ teaspoon cumin, ground
- 1 teaspoon oregano, dried
- A pinch of salt and black pepper
- 1 tablespoon hot paprika
- 1 tablespoon chives, chopped

Directions:

Set your instant pot on Sauté mode, add the oil, heat it up, add the onion, chili powder, cumin, oregano and paprika and sauté for 5 minutes. Add the rest of the ingredients except the cheese, toss, put the lid on and cook on High for 15 minutes. Release the pressure naturally for 10 minutes, sprinkle the cheese on top, leave the mix aside for a couple of minutes, divide between plates and serve.

Nutrition: calories 220, fat 8, fiber 2, carbs 5, protein 11

Oregano Turkey and Green Beans

Preparation time: 10 minutes Cooking time: 25 minutes Servings: 4

Ingredients:
- 1 pound turkey breasts, skinless, boneless and roughly cubed
- 1 cup green beans, trimmed and halved
- 2 tablespoons olive oil
- 1 yellow onion, chopped
- 1 tablespoon tomato sauce
- Salt and black pepper to the taste
- 2 teaspoons sweet paprika
- 1 cup chicken stock
- 1 tablespoon oregano, chopped

Directions:

Set the instant pot on Sauté mode, add the oil, heat it up, add the meat, onion and the paprika and sauté for 5 minutes. Add the green beans and the other ingredients, toss, put the lid on and cook on High for 20 minutes. Release the pressure naturally for 10 minutes, divide the mix into bowls and serve.

Nutrition: calories 192, fat 12, fiber 3, carbs 5, protein 12

Lime Chicken

*Preparation time: 10 minutes **Cooking time:** 20 minutes **Servings:** 4*

Ingredients:
- 1 pound chicken breasts, skinless, boneless and halved
- 1 tablespoon lime zest, grated
- 1 cup lime juice
- ½ teaspoon coriander, ground
- 2 tablespoons olive oil
- 4 scallions, chopped
- 1 green bell pepper, roughly chopped
- 1 carrot, peeled and grated
- 2 teaspoons chives, chopped
- 1 cup chicken stock

Directions:

Set the instant pot on Sauté mode, add the oil, heat it up, add the scallions, bell pepper and the carrot and sauté for 5 minutes. Add the meat and brown for 5 minutes more. Add the rest of the ingredients, put the lid on and cook on High for 10 minutes. Release the pressure naturally for 10 minutes, divide the mix between plates and serve.

Nutrition: calories 200, fat 7, fiber 1, carbs 5, protein 12

Peppercorn Turkey

Preparation time: 10 minutes **Cooking time:** *25 minutes* **Servings:** *4*

Ingredients:

- 1 pound turkey breast, skinless, boneless and cut into strips
- 1 tablespoon black peppercorns, crushed
- 2 tablespoons avocado oil
- 1 red onion, chopped
- ½ teaspoon fennel seeds, crushed
- A pinch of salt and black pepper
- 1 cup chicken stock
- 3 garlic cloves, minced
- 2 teaspoons cumin, ground
- 1 tablespoon chives, chopped

Directions:

Set the instant pot on Sauté mode, add the oil, heat it up, add the onion, peppercorns, garlic and cumin and sauté for 5 minutes. Add the meat and brown for 5 minutes more. Add the rest of the ingredients, toss, put the lid on and cook on High for 15 minutes. Release the pressure naturally for 10 minutes, divide the mix between plates and serve.

Nutrition: calories 231, fat 7, fiber 2, carbs 6, protein 12

Turkey and Zucchinis

Preparation time: 10 minutes **Cooking time:** *25 minutes* **Servings:** *4*

Ingredients:

- 1 pound turkey breast, skinless, boneless and cubed
- 2 zucchinis, sliced
- 1 yellow onion, chopped
- 2 tablespoons olive oil
- 2 garlic cloves, minced
- 1 teaspoon coriander, ground
- ½ teaspoon cumin, ground
- A pinch of salt and black pepper
- 1 cup chicken stock
- ½ cup tomato passata
- 1 tablespoon basil, chopped

Directions:

Set your instant pot on Sauté mode, add the oil, heat it up, add the onion, garlic, coriander and cumin and sauté for 5 minutes. Add the meat and brown for 5 minutes more. Add the rest of the ingredients, toss, put the lid on and cook on High for 15 minutes. Release the pressure naturally for 10 minutes, divide everything between plates and serve.

Nutrition: calories 252, fat 12, fiber 4, carbs 7, protein 13

Chicken and Artichokes

Preparation time: 10 minutes *Cooking time:* 20 minutes *Servings:* 4

Ingredients:
- 1 pound chicken breasts, skinless, boneless and cubed
- 4 ounces canned artichoke hearts, drained and quartered
- 1 red onion, chopped
- 2 tablespoons olive oil
- A pinch of salt and black pepper
- 1 teaspoon black peppercorns, crushed
- 2 garlic cloves, minced
- 1 cup chicken stock
- 1 tablespoon chives, chopped

Directions:
Set the instant pot on Sauté mode, add the oil, heat it up, add the onion, garlic and peppercorns, stir and sauté for 5 minutes. Add the meat and brown for 5 minutes more. Add the rest of the ingredients, toss, put the lid on and cook on High for 10 minutes. Release the pressure naturally for 10 minutes, divide everything between plates and serve.

Nutrition: calories 221, fat 14, fiber 3, carbs 7, protein 14

Turkey and Pesto

Preparation time: 10 minutes *Cooking time:* 25 minutes *Servings:* 4

Ingredients:
- 1 pound turkey breast, skinless, boneless and cut into strips
- 2 tablespoons olive oil
- 4 scallions, chopped
- 2 tablespoons basil pesto
- 1 tablespoon pine nuts, toasted
- 1 cup tomatoes, cubed
- 1 cup chicken stock
- A handful cilantro, chopped
- A pinch of salt and black pepper

Directions:
Set your instant pot on Sauté mode, add the oil, heat it up, add scallions, pesto and pine nuts and sauté for 2 minutes. Add the turkey and brown for 3 minutes more. Add the rest of the ingredients, put the lid on and cook on High for 20 minutes. Release the pressure naturally for 10 minutes, divide the mix between plates and serve.

Nutrition: calories 263, fat 14, fiber 1, carbs 8, protein 12

Ginger Chicken Mix

Preparation time: *10 minutes* ***Cooking time:*** *25 minutes* ***Servings:*** *4*
Ingredients:
- 1 pound chicken breast, skinless, boneless and cubed
- 2 tablespoons olive oil
- 1 tablespoon ginger, grated
- 1 cup tomato passata
- 1 carrot, peeled and sliced
- 1 zucchini, sliced
- 1 eggplant, cubed
- A pinch of salt and black pepper
- 1 tablespoon sweet paprika
- 2 garlic cloves, minced
- 1 cup chicken stock
- 1 tablespoon cilantro, chopped

Directions:
Set your instant pot on Sauté mode, add the oil, heat it up, add the ginger, garlic and the paprika and sauté for 2 minutes. Add the meat and brown for 3 minutes more. Add the rest of the ingredients, put the lid on and cook on High for 20 minutes. Release the pressure naturally for 10 minutes, divide everything between plates and serve.
Nutrition: calories 263, fat 12, fiber 3, carbs 6, protein 14

Turkey and Apples

Preparation time: *10 minutes* ***Cooking time:*** *20 minutes* ***Servings:*** *4*
Ingredients:
- 1 pound turkey breast, skinless, boneless and sliced
- 2 green apples, cored and cut into wedges
- 1 cup chicken stock
- 1 teaspoon garam masala
- ½ teaspoon cumin, ground
- 1 tablespoon olive oil
- 1 teaspoon chili powder
- 1 teaspoon basil, chopped
- 1 tablespoon rosemary, chopped
- A pinch of salt and black pepper

Directions:
Set the instant pot on Sauté mode, add the oil, heat it up, add the meat and brown for 5 minutes. Add the apples, garam masala and the rest of the ingredients, put the lid on and cook on High for 15 minutes. Release the pressure naturally for 10 minutes, divide the mix between plates and serve.
Nutrition: calories 253, fat 13, fiber 2, carbs 7, protein 16

Creamy Chicken and Carrots

Preparation time: *10 minutes* ***Cooking time:*** *20 minutes* ***Servings:*** *4*

Ingredients:
- 1 pound chicken breast, skinless, boneless and cubed
- 1 cup baby carrots, peeled
- 1 red onion, chopped
- 2 tablespoons avocado oil
- 4 garlic cloves, minced
- ¼ cup chives, chopped
- A pinch of salt and black pepper
- 1 cup heavy cream
- ¼ cup chicken stock

Directions:

Set your instant pot on Sauté mode, add the oil, heat it up, add the onion, garlic and the meat and brown for 7 minutes. Add the rest of the ingredients, toss, put the lid on and cook on High for 13 minutes. Release the pressure naturally for 10 minutes, divide everything between plates and serve.

Nutrition: calories 234, fat 14, fiber 4, carbs 7, protein 15

Tarragon Turkey Mix

Preparation time: *10 minutes* ***Cooking time:*** *25 minutes* ***Servings:*** *4*

Ingredients:
- 1 pound turkey breast, skinless, boneless and sliced
- 1 yellow onion, chopped
- 2 tablespoons olive oil
- 1 tablespoon tarragon, chopped
- ½ teaspoon turmeric powder
- ½ teaspoon chili powder
- 3 garlic cloves, minced
- 1 cup chicken stock
- A pinch of salt and black pepper
- 1 tablespoon chives, chopped

Directions:

Set pot on Sauté mode, add the oil, heat it up, add the meat, onion and the garlic and sauté for 2 minutes. Add the turmeric and chili powder, toss and cook the mix for 3 minutes more. Add the rest of the ingredients, put the lid on and cook on High for 20 minutes. Release the pressure naturally for 10 minutes, divide the mix between plates and serve.

Nutrition: calories 263, fat 13, fiber 2, carbs 7, protein 15

Turkey and Asparagus

Preparation time: 5 minutes **Cooking time:** 20 minutes **Servings:** 4

Ingredients:
- 1 pound turkey breasts, skinless, boneless and sliced
- 2 tablespoons olive oil
- 4 scallions, chopped
- 1 asparagus bunch, trimmed and steamed
- ½ cup tomatoes, cubed
- 1 cup chicken stock
- 1 teaspoon basil, chopped
- A pinch of salt and black pepper

Directions:
Set the instant pot on Sauté mode, add the oil, heat it up, add the scallions and the meat and brown for 5 minutes. Add the asparagus and the other ingredients, toss gently, put the lid on and cook on High for 15 minutes. Release the pressure fast for 5 minutes, divide everything between plates and serve.

Nutrition: calories 200, fat 13, fiber 2, carbs 5, protein 16

Honey Chicken Wings

Preparation time: 5 minutes **Cooking time:** 20 minutes **Servings:** 4

Ingredients:
- 1 pound chicken wings, halved
- 2 tablespoons olive oil
- 1 tablespoon honey
- 1 cup chicken stock
- A pinch of salt and black pepper
- 1 tablespoon mustard
- 4 scallions, sliced
- 1 tablespoon chives, chopped

Directions:
Set the instant pot on Sauté mode, add the oil, heat it up, add the scallions and sauté for 2 minutes. Add the honey and the other ingredients except the chicken wings, toss and cook for 3 minutes more. Add the wings, toss, put the lid on and cook on High for 15 minutes. Release the pressure fast for 5 minutes, divide the mix between plates and serve.

Nutrition: calories 200, fat 12, fiber 2, carbs 6, protein 15

Turkey and Cauliflower Mix

Preparation time: *10 minutes* **Cooking time:** *25 minutes* **Servings:** *4*

Ingredients:

- 1 pound turkey breast, skinless, boneless and sliced
- 1 cup cauliflower florets
- 2 tablespoons avocado oil
- 1 yellow onion, sliced
- 3 garlic cloves, minced
- A pinch of salt and black pepper
- 1 cup chicken stock
- 1 cup tomato passata
- 1 teaspoon turmeric powder
- 1 tablespoon cilantro, chopped

Directions:

Set the instant pot on Sauté mode, add the oil, heat it up, add the onion, garlic and turmeric and sauté for 5 minutes. Add the meat and brown for 5 minutes more. Add the rest of the ingredients, toss, put the lid on and cook on High for 15 minutes. Release the pressure naturally for 10 minutes, divide the mix between plates and serve.

Nutrition: calories 253, fat 14, fiber 2, carbs 7, protein 16

Chicken and Masala Broccoli

Preparation time: 10 minutes **Cooking time:** 25 minutes **Servings:** 4

Ingredients:

1. 4 garlic cloves, chopped
2. 1 yellow onion, chopped
3. 1 cup broccoli florets
4. 1 tablespoon avocado oil
5. 1 teaspoon garam masala
6. 1 pound chicken breasts, skinless and halved
7. ½ teaspoon fennel seeds, crushed
8. 1 teaspoon rosemary, dried
9. 1 cup chicken stock
10. A pinch of salt and black pepper
11. 1 tablespoon cilantro, chopped

Directions:

Set the instant pot on Sauté mode, add the oil, heat it up, add the onion, garlic and the garam masala and sauté for 2 minutes. Add the chicken and brown for 3 minutes more. Add the remaining ingredients, toss, put the lid on and cook on High for 20 minutes. Release the pressure naturally for 10 minutes, divide the mix between plates and serve.

Nutrition: calories 273, fat 13, fiber 3, carbs 7, protein 17

Chicken and Fennel Mix

Preparation time: 10 minutes Cooking time: 25 minutes Servings: 4

Ingredients:

- 1 pound chicken breast, skinless, boneless and sliced
- 1 fennel bulb, sliced
- 1 yellow onion, chopped
- 2 tablespoons olive oil
- 1 teaspoon rosemary, dried
- 1 teaspoon black peppercorns, crushed
- ¼ cup tomato passata
- 1 cup chicken stock
- Juice of 1 lemon
- 1 tablespoon chives, chopped

Directions:

Set the instant pot on Sauté mode, add the oil, heat it up, add the onion, rosemary and black peppercorns and sauté for 2 minutes. Add the meat and brown for 3 minutes more. Add the rest of the ingredients except the chives, put the lid on and cook on High for 20 minutes. Release the pressure naturally for 10 minutes, divide the mix between plates and serve with the chives sprinkled on top.

Nutrition: calories 276, fat 15, fiber 3, carbs 7, protein 16

Turkey with Berries Mix

Preparation time: 10 minutes Cooking time: 25 minutes Servings: 4

Ingredients:

1. 1 pound turkey breast, skinless, boneless and sliced
2. 1 cup blackberries
3. 4 scallions, chopped
4. 1 tablespoon balsamic vinegar
5. 2 tablespoons avocado oil
6. A pinch of salt and black pepper
7. 1 tablespoon cilantro, chopped
8. 1 cup orange juice

Directions:

Set your instant pot on Sauté mode, add the oil, heat it up, add the scallions and the meat and brown for 5 minutes. Add the rest of the ingredients, put the lid on and cook on High for 20 minutes. Release the pressure naturally for 10 minutes, divide the mix between plates and serve.

Nutrition: calories 252, fat 15, fiber 2, carbs 6, protein 15

Turkey and Avocado Mix

*Preparation time: 10 minutes **Cooking time:** 25 minutes **Servings:** 4*

Ingredients:

- 1 pound turkey breasts, skinless, boneless and cubed
- 1 avocado, peeled, pitted and roughly cubed
- 4 scallions, chopped
- 2 tablespoons olive oil
- 1 tablespoons lemon zest, grated
- 1 tablespoon lemon juice
- 1 cup chicken stock
- 1 tablespoon sweet paprika
- A pinch of salt and black pepper
- 1 tablespoon chives, chopped

Directions:

Set the instant pot on Sauté mode, add the oil, heat it up, add the scallions, paprika, lemon juice and lemon zest and sauté for 2 minutes. Add the meat and brown for 3 minutes more. Add the rest of the ingredients, put the lid on and cook on High for 20 minutes. Release the pressure naturally for 10 minutes, divide everything between plates and serve.

Nutrition: calories 234, fat 12, fiber 3, carbs 5, protein 7

Chicken with Tomatoes and Olives

*Preparation time: 10 minutes **Cooking time:** 25 minutes **Servings:** 4*

Ingredients:

- 1 pound chicken breast, skinless, boneless and sliced
- 1 cup cherry tomatoes, halved
- 1 cup black olives, pitted and halved
- 2 tablespoons olive oil
- 1 teaspoon hot paprika
- 1 yellow onion, chopped
- 1 cup chicken stock
- A pinch of salt and black pepper
- 1 tablespoon parsley, chopped

Directions:

Set the instant pot on Sauté mode, add the oil, heat it up, add the onion and the paprika and sauté for 2 minutes. Add the chicken and brown for 3 minutes more. Add the rest of the ingredients, toss, put the lid on and cook on High for 20 minutes. Release the pressure naturally for 10 minutes, divide everything between plates and serve.

Nutrition: calories 263, fat 14, fiber 3, carbs 7, protein 16

Parsley Chicken and Endives Mix

Preparation time: 10 minutes Cooking time: 20 minutes Servings: 4
Ingredients:
- 1 pound chicken thighs, boneless and skinless
- 2 endives, shredded
- 1 red onion, chopped
- 2 tablespoons avocado oil
- ½ cup tomato passata
- ½ cup chicken stock
- A pinch of salt and black pepper
- 1 tablespoon parsley, chopped

Directions:
Set your instant pot on Sauté mode, add the oil, heat it up, add the onion and the chicken and brown for 5 minutes. Add the rest of the ingredients, put the lid on and cook on High for 15 minutes. Release the pressure naturally for 10 minutes, divide the mix between plates and serve.

Nutrition: calories 263, fat 12, fiber 2, carbs 7, protein 18

Chicken Salsa

Preparation time: 10 minutes Cooking time: 25 minutes Servings: 4
Ingredients:
- 1 pound chicken breasts, skinless, boneless and cubed
- A pinch of salt and black pepper
- 2 scallions, chopped
- 1 tablespoon olive oil
- 1 teaspoon chili powder
- 1 cup tomatoes, cubed
- 1 cup zucchinis, cubed
- ½ cup black olives, pitted and halved
- 1 avocado, peeled, pitted and cubed
- 1 cup chicken stock
- 1 tablespoon basil, chopped
- 1 tablespoon balsamic vinegar

Directions:
Set the instant pot on Sauté mode, add the oil, heat it up, add the scallions, chili powder and the chicken and brown for 5 minutes. Add the tomatoes and the other ingredients, toss, put the lid on and cook on High for 20 minutes. Release the pressure naturally for 10 minutes, divide the mix between plates and serve.

Nutrition: calories 201, fat 7, fiber 3, carbs 6, protein 8

Chicken Chili

Preparation time: 10 minutes **Cooking time:** *25 minutes* **Servings:** *4*
Ingredients:

- 1 cup canned kidney beans, drained and rinsed
- 1 pound chicken breast, skinless, boneless and cubed
- 1 yellow onion, chopped
- 2 garlic cloves, minced
- 2 tablespoons olive oil
- ½ teaspoon sweet paprika
- 1 tablespoon chili powder
- 1 cup chicken stock
- 1 cup tomato sauce
- A pinch of salt and black pepper
- 1 tablespoon cilantro, chopped

Directions:
Set the instant pot on Sauté mode, add the oil, heat it up, add the onion and the garlic and sauté for 2 minutes. Add the meat, paprika and chili powder and brown for 3 minutes more. Add the rest of the ingredients, toss, put the lid on and cook on High for 20 minutes. Release the pressure naturally for 10 minutes, divide the mix into bowls and serve.
Nutrition: calories 263, fat 12, fiber 3, carbs 7, protein 15

Coconut Turkey Mix

Preparation time: 10 minutes **Cooking time:** *25 minutes* **Servings:** *4*
Ingredients:

- 1 yellow onion, sliced
- 1 pound turkey breasts, skinless, boneless and cubed
- 1 cup coconut cream
- 2 tablespoons olive oil
- 1 tablespoon balsamic vinegar
- ½ teaspoon chili powder
- 1 tablespoon cumin, ground
- 1 cup chicken stock
- A pinch of salt and black pepper
- 2 tablespoons chives, chopped

Directions:
Set your instant pot on Sauté mode, add the oil, heat it up, add the onion, chili powder, cumin and the turkey and brown for 5 minutes. Add the rest of the ingredients, toss, put the lid on and cook on High for 20 minutes. Release the pressure naturally for 10 minutes, divide everything between plates and serve.
Nutrition: calories 214, fat 14, fiber 2, carbs 6, protein 15

Chicken Curry

Preparation time: 10 minutes *Cooking time:* 25 minutes *Servings:* 4

Ingredients:
- 1 pound chicken breasts, skinless, boneless and cubed
- 1 tablespoon olive oil
- 1 red onion, chopped
- ½ teaspoon chili powder
- ½ teaspoon cumin, ground
- 1 cup heavy cream
- 1 tablespoon green curry paste
- 1 tablespoon coriander, chopped

Directions:
Set your instant pot on Sauté mode, add the oil, heat it up, add the onion, chili powder and curry paste and sauté for 2 minutes. Add the meat and brown for 3 minutes more. Add the rest of the ingredients, put the lid on and cook on High for 20 minutes. Release the pressure naturally for 10 minutes, divide the curry into bowls and serve.

Nutrition: calories 231, fat 12, fiber 4, carbs 7, protein 15

Duck and Tomato Sauce

Preparation time: 10 minutes *Cooking time:* 30 minutes *Servings:* 4

Ingredients:
- 2 pounds duck breast, skinless, boneless and cubed
- 2 tablespoons olive oil
- 1 yellow onion, sliced
- 2 garlic cloves, minced
- 1 cup chicken stock
- 1 cup tomato passata
- 1 teaspoon coriander, ground
- ½ teaspoon sweet paprika
- 1 tablespoon parsley, chopped

Directions:
Set your instant pot on Sauté mode, add the oil, heat it up, add the onion, garlic, coriander and paprika and sauté for 5 minutes. Add the meat and brown for 5 minutes more. Add the rest of the ingredients, put the lid on and cook on High for 20 minutes. Release the pressure naturally for 10 minutes, divide everything between plates and serve.

Nutrition: calories 263, fat 12, fiber 5, carbs 7, protein 16

Chicken and Peas Mix

Preparation time: 10 minutes *Cooking time:* 25 minutes *Servings:* 4

Ingredients:
- 2 tablespoons olive oil
- 2 pound chicken breasts, skinless, boneless and sliced
- 1 cup green peas
- ½ cup scallions, chopped
- ½ cup tomatoes, cubed
- A pinch of salt and black pepper
- 1 cup chicken stock
- 1 teaspoon sweet paprika
- 1 tablespoon dill, chopped

Directions:
Set your instant pot on Sauté mode, add the oil, heat it up, add the scallions and the paprika and sauté for 2 minutes. Add the meat and brown for 3 minutes more. Add the rest of the ingredients, toss, put the lid on and cook on High for 20 minutes. Release the pressure naturally for 10 minutes, divide the mix into bowls and serve.

Nutrition: calories 242, fat 14, fiber 3, carbs 7, protein 14

Chicken with Green Rice

Preparation time: 10 minutes *Cooking time:* 25 minutes *Servings:* 4

Ingredients:
- 2 pounds chicken breasts, skinless, boneless and cubed
- 1 tablespoon cilantro, chopped
- 1 tablespoon oregano, chopped
- 1 yellow onion, chopped
- 2 tablespoons olive oil
- 1 cup wild rice
- 2 tablespoons green onions, chopped
- 3 cups chicken stock
- ½ teaspoon turmeric powder
- A pinch of salt and black pepper

Directions:
Set the instant pot on Sauté mode, add the oil, heat it up, add the onion green onions, turmeric and the meat and brown for 5 minutes Add the rest of the ingredients, toss, put the lid on and cook on High for 20 minutes. Release the pressure naturally for 10 minutes, divide everything between plates and serve.

Nutrition: calories 232, fat 12, fiber 2, carbs 6, protein 15

Italian Chicken Mix

Preparation time: *10 minutes* **Cooking time:** *25 minutes* **Servings:** *4*
Ingredients:
- 1 pound chicken breasts, skinless, boneless and roughly cubed
- 2 tablespoons olive oil
- 1 red onion, sliced
- 1 cup chicken stock
- 1 tablespoon oregano, chopped
- 1 tablespoon Italian seasoning
- 1 tablespoon cilantro, chopped
- A pinch of salt and black pepper **Directions:**

Set the instant pot on Sauté mode, add the oil, heat it up, add the onion and Italian seasoning and sauté for 5 minutes. Add the meat and brown for 5 minutes more. Add the rest of the ingredients, toss, put the lid on and cook on High for 15 minutes. Release the pressure naturally for 10 minutes, divide the mix between plates and serve.

Nutrition: calories 263, fat 14, fiber 4, carbs 6, protein 18

Chicken with Mushrooms

Preparation time: *10 minutes* **Cooking time:** *25 minutes* **Servings:** *4*
Ingredients:
- 1 pound chicken breast, skinless, boneless and sliced
- 1 yellow onion, chopped
- 1 teaspoon chili powder
- 1 cup white mushrooms, sliced
- 2 tablespoons olive oil
- ½ cup heavy cream
- 1 tablespoon olive oil
- ½ cup chicken stock
- ¼ cup chives, chopped

Directions:
Set the instant pot on Sauté mode, add the oil, heat it up, add the onion and the chili powder and sauté for 2 minutes Add the meat and the mushrooms and brown for 3 minutes more Add the remaining ingredients, toss, put the lid on and cook on High for 20 minutes Release the pressure naturally for 10 minutes, divide everything between plates and serve.

Nutrition: calories 262, fat 16, fiber 2, carbs 8, protein 16

Turkey and Corn Mix

Preparation time: 10 minutes *Cooking time:* 25 minutes *Servings:* 4

Ingredients:
- 1 cup corn
- 1 pound turkey breast, skinless, boneless and roughly cubed
- 1 yellow onion, chopped
- 2 tablespoons olive oil
- ½ cup tomato passata
- ½ cup chicken stock
- 1 tablespoon cilantro, chopped
- A pinch of salt and black pepper

Directions:
Set the instant pot on Sauté mode, add the oil, heat it up, add the onion and the meat and brown for 5 minutes. Add the rest of the ingredients, put the lid on and cook on High for 20 minutes. Release the pressure naturally for 10 minutes, divide everything between plates and serve.

Nutrition: calories 283, fat 16, fiber 2, carbs 6, protein 17

Chicken and Chickpeas Mix

Preparation time: 10 minutes *Cooking time:* 25 minutes *Servings:* 4

Ingredients:
1. 2 tablespoons olive oil
2. 1 red onion, chopped
3. 2 pounds chicken thighs, boneless, skinless and roughly cubed
4. 1 cup canned chickpeas, drained and rinsed
5. ½ cup tomato passata
6. ½ teaspoon cumin, ground
7. ½ teaspoon garam masala
8. 1 cup chicken stock
9. A pinch of salt and black pepper
10. 1 tablespoon chives, chopped

Directions:
Set your instant pot on Sauté mode, add the oil, heat it up, add the onion, cumin and garam masala and sauté for 2 minutes. Add the meat and brown for 3 minutes more Add the rest of the ingredients, put the lid on and cook on High for 20 minutes Release the pressure naturally for 10 minutes, divide the mix between plates and serve.

Nutrition: calories 291, fat 17, fiber 3, carbs 7, protein 16

Chicken and Leeks Mix

Preparation time: 10 minutes **Cooking time:** *25 minutes* **Servings:** *4*

Ingredients:
- 3 garlic cloves, minced
- 2 leeks, sliced
- 1 red onion, chopped
- 2 pounds chicken breasts, skinless, boneless and sliced
- 2 tablespoons avocado oil
- 1 green chili, chopped
- A pinch of salt and black pepper
- 1 cup chicken stock
- ½ teaspoon sweet paprika
- 1 tablespoon cilantro, chopped

Directions:
Set your instant pot on Sauté mode, add the oil, heat it up, add the leeks, onion, and garlic and sauté for 5 minutes. Add the chicken and brown for 5 minutes more. Add the rest of the ingredients, put the lid on and cook on High for 15 minutes. Release the pressure naturally for 10 minutes, divide everything between plates and serve.

Nutrition: calories 226, fat 9, fiber 1, carbs 6, protein 12

Turmeric Turkey and Chives

Preparation time: 10 minutes **Cooking time:** *25 minutes* **Servings:** *4*

Ingredients:
- 1 yellow onion, chopped
- 2 tablespoons olive oil
- 1 pound turkey breast, skinless, boneless and cubed
- 1 teaspoon turmeric powder
- ½ cup chives, chopped
- 1 cup chicken stock
- A pinch of salt and black pepper

Directions:
Set your instant pot on Sauté mode, add the oil, heat it up, add the onion and the meat and brown for 5 minutes. Add the rest of the ingredients, put the lid on and cook on High for 20 minutes. Release the pressure naturally for 10 minutes, divide the mix between plates and serve.

Nutrition: calories 283, fat 11, fiber 2, carbs 8, protein 15

Chicken and Black Beans

*Preparation time: 10 minutes **Cooking time:** 25 minutes **Servings:** 4*

Ingredients:
- 1 pound chicken breasts, skinless, boneless and cubed
- 1 cup canned black beans, drained and rinsed
- 1 red onion, chopped
- 2 tablespoons olive oil
- A pinch of salt and black pepper
- 1 cup chicken stock
- 1 teaspoon sweet paprika
- 1 tablespoon cilantro, chopped

Directions:
Set the instant pot on Sauté mode, add the oil, heat it up, add the meat and the onion, stir and sauté for 5 minutes. Add the remaining ingredients, put the lid on and cook on High for 20 minutes. Release the pressure naturally for 10 minutes, divide the mix between plates and serve.

Nutrition: calories 221, fat 12, fiber 2, carbs 5, protein 17

Chicken and Brussels Sprouts Mix

*Preparation time: 10 minutes **Cooking time:** 25 minutes **Servings:** 4*

Ingredients:
- 1 tablespoon olive oil
- 1 red onion, chopped
- 1 pound chicken breast, skinless, boneless and cubed
- 2 garlic cloves, minced
- 1 teaspoon sweet paprika
- A pinch of salt and black pepper
- 1 cup Brussels sprouts, halved
- 1 cup chicken stock
- ½ cup tomato passata
- ½ teaspoon coriander, ground

Directions:
Set the instant pot on sauté mode, add the oil, heat it up, add the onion, chicken, garlic and paprika and brown for 5 minutes. Add the rest of the ingredients, put the lid on and cook on High for 20 minutes. Release the pressure naturally for 10 minutes, divide the mix between plates and serve.

Nutrition: calories 227, fat 12, fiber 3, carbs 7, protein 18

Chives Duck

Preparation time: 10 minutes **Cooking time:** *20 minutes* **Servings:** *4*

Ingredients:
- 1 pound duck breasts, boneless, skinless and sliced
- 1 tablespoon olive oil
- 1 red bell pepper, cut into strips
- 1 yellow onion, chopped
- 1 cup chicken stock
- ½ cup heavy cream
- A pinch of salt and black pepper
- 1 tablespoon chives, chopped

Directions:
Set the instant pot on Sauté mode, add the oil, heat it up, add the onion and the bell pepper and sauté for 5 minutes. Add the duck and the rest of the ingredients except the chives, put the lid on and cook on High for 15 minutes. Release the pressure naturally for 10 minutes, divide everything between plates, sprinkle the chives on top and serve.

Nutrition: calories 293, fat 15, fiber 4, carbs 6, protein 14

Chicken and Squash

Preparation time: 10 minutes **Cooking time:** *20 minutes* **Servings:** *4*

Ingredients:
- 1 pound chicken breasts, skinless, boneless and halved
- 3 scallions, chopped
- 1 butternut squash, peeled and cubed
- 1 cup chicken stock
- 1 tablespoon tomato sauce
- A pinch of salt and black pepper
- 1 teaspoon chili powder
- 1 tablespoon cilantro, chopped

Directions:
In your instant pot, combine the chicken with the scallions, the squash and the other ingredients, toss , put the lid on and cook on High for 20 minutes Release the pressure naturally for 10 minutes, divide the mix between plates and serve.

Nutrition: calories 223, fat 9, fiber 2, carbs 4, protein 11

Turkey and Cucumber Mix

Preparation time: *10 minutes* ***Cooking time:*** *25 minutes* ***Servings:*** *4*

Ingredients:
- 1 pound turkey breasts, skinless, boneless and roughly cubed
- 1 teaspoon cumin, ground
- ½ teaspoon garam masala
- 1 cup chicken stock
- 1 tablespoon olive oil
- 1 yellow onion, chopped
- 2 cucumbers, cubed
- 1 tablespoon cilantro, chopped

Directions:
Set instant pot on Sauté mode, add the oil, heat it up, add the onion, cumin and garam masala and sauté for 5 minutes. Add the meat and brown for 5 minutes more. Add the rest of the ingredients, toss, put the lid on and cook on High for 15 minutes. Release the pressure naturally for 10 minutes, divide the mix between plates and serve.

Nutrition: calories 210, fat 11, fiber 2, carbs 7, protein 14

Chicken and Pomegranate Bowls

Preparation time: *10 minutes* ***Cooking time:*** *30 minutes* ***Servings:*** *4*

Ingredients:
- 1 pound chicken breast, skinless, boneless and sliced
- 1 cup pomegranate seeds
- 4 scallions, chopped
- 2 tablespoons olive oil
- 1 cup chicken stock
- 1 tablespoon sweet paprika
- A pinch of salt and black pepper
- 1 tablespoon chives, chopped

Directions:
Set the instant pot on Sauté mode, add the oil, heat it up, add the scallions and the paprika and sauté for 5 minutes. Add the meat and brown for 5 minutes more. Add the rest of the ingredients, put the lid on and cook on High for 20 minutes. Release the pressure naturally for 10 minutes, divide everything between plates and serve.

Nutrition: calories 263, fat 8, fiber 2, carbs 7, protein 12

Basil Turkey and Avocado

Preparation time: 10 minutes **Cooking time:** *20 minutes* **Servings:** *4*

Ingredients:
- 1 pound turkey breasts, skinless, boneless and cubed
- 1 cup avocado, peeled, pitted and cubed
- 1 cup tomato sauce
- 1 tablespoon basil, chopped
- 4 garlic cloves, minced
- ¼ cup chicken stock

Directions:
In your instant pot, combine the turkey with the avocado and the rest of the ingredients, put the lid on and cook on High for 20 minutes. Release the pressure naturally for 10 minutes, divide everything between plates and serve.

Nutrition: calories 220, fat 8, fiber 2, carbs 7, protein 15

Chicken and Sweet Chili Mix

Preparation time: 10 minutes **Cooking time:** *25 minutes* **Servings:** *4*

Ingredients:
- 1 pound chicken breasts, skinless, boneless and cubed
- ¼ cup sweet chili sauce
- 2 tablespoons olive oil
- 1 teaspoon Italian seasoning
- A pinch of cayenne pepper
- 1 cup tomato, cubed
- 1 yellow onion, chopped
- 1 cup chicken stock

Directions:
Set the instant pot on Sauté mode, add the oil, heat it up, add the onion, chili sauce and the Italian seasoning and sauté for 5 minutes. Add the meat and brown for 5 minutes more. Add the other ingredients, put the lid on and cook on High for 15 minutes. Release the pressure naturally for 10 minutes, divide everything between plates and serve.

Nutrition: calories 282, fat 12, fiber 2, carbs 6, protein 18

Chicken and Yogurt Sauce

Preparation time: 5 minutes **Cooking time:** 25 minutes **Servings:** 4

Ingredients:
- 1 pound chicken breasts, skinless, boneless and halved
- 2 cups Greek yogurt
- 2 teaspoons cumin, ground
- A pinch of salt and black pepper
- 2 teaspoons garam masala
- ¼ cup cilantro, chopped

Directions:
In your instant pot, combine the chicken with the yogurt and the other ingredients, toss, put the lid on and cook on High for 25 minutes. Release the pressure fast for 5 minutes, divide everything between plates and serve.

Nutrition: calories 285, fat 16, fiber 4, carbs 8, protein 18

Duck and Lime Black Beans

Preparation time: 10 minutes **Cooking time:** 25 minutes **Servings:** 4

Ingredients:
- 1 pound duck breasts, skinless, boneless and cubed
- 1 tablespoon olive oil
- 1 cup chicken stock
- A pinch of salt and black pepper
- 1 cup canned black beans, drained and rinsed
- 2 tablespoons lime juice
- 1 tablespoon lime zest, grated
- 1 tablespoon tomato paste

Directions:
Set your instant pot on Sauté mode, add the oil, heat it up, add the meat and brown for 5 minutes. Add the stock and the rest of the ingredients, put the lid on and cook on High for 20 minutes. Release the pressure naturally for 10 minutes, divide everything into bowls and serve.

Nutrition: calories 292, fat 17, fiber 2, carbs 7, protein 16

Chicken Wings and BBQ Sauce

Preparation time: 10 minutes **Cooking time:** *25 minutes* **Servings:** *4*

Ingredients:
- 1 pound chicken wings, halved
- 1 cup bbq sauce
- A pinch of salt and black pepper
- 6 scallions, chopped
- ½ teaspoon garlic powder
- ¼ cup cilantro, chopped
- 1 cup chicken stock

Directions:
In your instant pot, combine the chicken wings with the sauce and the other ingredients, toss, put the lid on and cook on High for 25 minutes. Release the pressure naturally for 10 minutes, divide everything between plates and serve.

Nutrition: calories 224, fat 11, fiber 2, carbs 9, protein 11

Chicken and Rhubarb Mix

Preparation time: 10 minutes **Cooking time:** *20 minutes* **Servings:** *4*

Ingredients:
- 2 pounds chicken breast, skinless, boneless and cubed
- 1 cup rhubarb, sliced
- 1 tablespoon avocado oil
- A pinch of salt and black pepper
- 1 teaspoon cayenne pepper
- 1 cup chicken stock
- 1 cup tomatoes, cubed
- 1 tablespoon cilantro, chopped

Directions:
Set your instant pot on Sauté mode, add the oil, heat it up, add the meat and brown for 5 minutes. Add the rest of the ingredients, put the lid on and cook on High for 15 minutes. Release the pressure naturally for 10 minutes, divide everything between plates and serve.

Nutrition: calories 229, fat 9, fiber 4, carbs 7, protein 16

Instant Pot Meat Recipes

Cinnamon Roast

Preparation time: 10 minutes **Cooking time:** *40 minutes* **Servings:** *4*

Ingredients:
- 2 pound pork roast
- 2 tablespoons olive oil
- 2 cups beef stock
- 2 red onions, sliced
- 1 tablespoon cinnamon powder
- 2 garlic cloves, minced
- Salt and black pepper to the taste
- 2 tablespoons cilantro, chopped

Directions:
In your instant pot, combine pork roast with the oil, the stock and the other ingredients, rub well, put the lid on and cook on High for 20 minutes. Release the pressure naturally for 10 minutes, slice the roast, divide between plates and serve with a side salad.

Nutrition: calories 254, fat 12, fiber 2, carbs 6, protein 16

Pork with Thyme Mushrooms

Preparation time: 10 minutes **Cooking time:** *40 minutes* **Servings:** *4*

Ingredients:
- 2 pounds pork roast
- 1 cup white mushrooms, halved
- 2 tablespoons olive oil
- 1 tablespoon thyme, chopped
- ½ cup beef stock
- 2 garlic cloves, minced
- ½ teaspoon chili powder
- A pinch of salt and black pepper
- 1 teaspoon smoked paprika

Directions:
In your instant pot, combine roast with the mushrooms, the oil and the other ingredients, toss, put the lid on and cook on High for 40 minutes. Release the pressure naturally for 10 minutes, slice the roast, divide it between plates and serve.

Nutrition: calories 243, fat 15, fiber 3, carbs 6, protein 20

Creamy Beef

Preparation time: 10 minutes *Cooking time:* 40 minutes *Servings:* 4

Ingredients:
- 2 pounds beef stew meat, cubed
- 2 tablespoons olive oil
- 1 red onion, chopped
- 1 cup heavy cream
- 1 cup beef stock
- 1 teaspoon chili powder
- ½ teaspoon rosemary, dried
- 2 garlic cloves, minced
- 2 tablespoons cilantro, chopped
- A pinch of salt and black pepper

Directions:
Set your instant pot on Sauté mode, add the oil, heat it up, add onion, chili powder, garlic and rosemary and sauté for 5 minutes. Add the meat and brown for 5 minutes more. Add the rest of the ingredients, put the lid on and cook on High for 30 minutes. Release the pressure naturally for 10 minutes, divide everything between plates and serve.

Nutrition: calories 263, fat 14, fiber 3, carbs 6, protein 16

Cilantro Beef Mix

Preparation time: 10 minutes *Cooking time:* 40 minutes *Servings:* 4

Ingredients:
- 2 pounds beef, cubed
- ½ cup cilantro, chopped
- 1 yellow onion, chopped
- 2 tablespoons avocado oil
- 2 garlic cloves, minced
- 1 cup tomato puree
- A pinch of salt and black pepper

Directions:
Set your instant pot on Sauté mode, add oil, heat it up, add the onion and garlic and sauté for 5 minutes. Add the meat and brown for 5 minutes more. Add the rest of the ingredients, put the lid on and cook on High for 30 minutes. Release the pressure naturally for 10 minutes, divide the mix between plates and serve.

Nutrition: calories 264, fat 14, fiber 4, carbs 7, protein 15

Pork and Cumin Green Beans

Preparation time: 10 minutes *Cooking time:* 40 minutes *Servings:* 4

Ingredients:
- 2 pounds pork stew meat, roughly cubed
- 1 cup green beans, trimmed and halved
- 1 teaspoon cumin, ground
- 2 tablespoons olive oil
- 1 yellow onion, chopped
- A pinch of salt and black pepper
- 1 cup beef stock
- 6 garlic cloves, chopped

Directions:
Set your instant pot on Sauté mode, add the oil, heat it up, add the onion and the garlic and sauté for 5 minutes. Add the meat and brown for 5 minutes more. Add the rest of the ingredients, put the lid on and cook on High for 30 minutes. Release the pressure naturally for 10 minutes, divide the mix between plates and serve.

Nutrition: calories 263, fat 12, fiber 4, carbs 6, protein 16

Beef with Oregano Tomatoes

Preparation time: 10 minutes *Cooking time:* 40 minutes *Servings:* 4

Ingredients:
- 2 pounds beef roast, sliced
- 1 cup tomatoes, cubed
- 1 tablespoon oregano, chopped
- 1 cup beef stock
- 1 yellow onion, chopped
- 2 tablespoons olive oil
- A pinch of salt and black pepper
- ½ teaspoon chili powder
- 2 garlic cloves, minced
- 1 tablespoon chives, chopped

Directions:
Set your instant pot on Sauté mode, add the oil, heat it up, add the onion, garlic and chili powder and sauté for 5 minutes. Add the roast and brown for 5 minutes. Add the rest of the ingredients, put the lid on and cook on High for 30 minutes. Release the pressure naturally for 10 minutes, divide the mix between plates and serve.

Nutrition: calories 263, fat 14, fiber 4, carbs 6, protein 18

Garlicky Beef

Preparation time: 10 minutes *Cooking time:* 40 minutes *Servings:* 4

Ingredients:
- 2 pounds beef roast, cubed
- 1 tablespoon avocado oil
- 1 red onion, chopped
- ½ teaspoon cumin, ground
- ½ teaspoon rosemary, dried
- A pinch of salt and black pepper
- 1 cup beef stock
- 4 garlic cloves, minced
- 1 tablespoon capers, drained and chopped
- 1 tablespoon parsley, chopped

Directions:
Set the instant pot on Sauté mode, add the oil, heat it up, add the onion and the garlic and sauté for 5 minutes. Add the meat and brown for 5 minutes more. Add the rest of the ingredients, put the lid on and cook on High for 30 minutes. Release the pressure naturally for 10 minutes, divide the mix between plates and serve.

Nutrition: calories 264, fat 14, fiber 4, carbs 6, protein 17

Basil Pork Mix

Preparation time: 10 minutes *Cooking time:* 35 minutes *Servings:* 4

Ingredients:
- 2 tablespoons avocado oil
- 2 pounds pork stew meat, cubed
- 1 red onion, chopped
- 2 tablespoons basil, chopped
- 1 tablespoon almonds, chopped
- 2 garlic cloves, minced
- 2 cups beef stock
- A pinch of salt and black pepper

Directions:
Set the instant pot on Sauté mode, add the oil, heat it up, add the onion, garlic and the almonds and sauté for 5 minutes. Add the meat and brown for 5 minutes more. Add the rest of the ingredients, put the lid on and cook on High for 25 minutes. Release the pressure naturally for 10 minutes, divide the mix between plates and serve.

Nutrition: calories 263, fat 14, fiber 3, carbs 7, protein 20

Sage Beef

Preparation time: 10 minutes **Cooking time:** *40 minutes* **Servings:** *4*

Ingredients:
- 1 tablespoon sage, chopped
- 2 tablespoons olive oil
- 1 red onion, chopped
- 2 pounds beef stew meat, cubed
- 2 cups beef stock
- 2 garlic cloves, minced
- A pinch of salt and black pepper
- ¼ cup tomato passata

Directions:
Set your instant pot on Sauté mode, add the oil, heat it up, add the onion and the garlic and sauté for 5 minutes. Add the meat and brown for 5 minutes more. Add the rest of the ingredients, put the lid on and cook on High for 30 minutes. Release the pressure naturally for 10 minutes, divide the mix between plates and serve.

Nutrition: calories 263, fat 14, fiber 5, carbs 7, protein 15

Pork and Carrots Mix

Preparation time: 10 minutes **Cooking time:** *35 minutes* **Servings:** *4*

Ingredients:
- 2 pounds pork stew meat, cubed
- 2 cups baby carrots, peeled
- 1 red onion, chopped
- 1 tablespoon olive oil
- 1 and ½ cups beef stock
- 1 tablespoon parsley, chopped
- ½ teaspoon chili powder
- A pinch of salt and black pepper

Directions:
Set your instant pot on Sauté mode, add the oil, heat it up, add the onion and chili powder and sauté for 5 minutes. Add the meat and brown for 5 minutes more. Add the rest of the ingredients, toss, put the lid on and cook on High for 25 minutes. Release the pressure naturally for 10 minutes, divide everything between plates and serve.

Nutrition: calories 253, fat 14, fiber 3, carbs 7, protein 17

Beef and Eggplant Mix

*Preparation time: 10 minutes **Cooking time:** 30 minutes **Servings:** 4*

Ingredients:
- 2 tablespoons olive oil
- 1 pound beef stew meat, roughly cubed
- 1 eggplant, cubed
- 1 red onion, chopped
- 1 cup beef stock
- ½ teaspoon sweet paprika
- ½ teaspoon rosemary, dried
- ¼ teaspoon red pepper flakes
- A pinch of salt and black pepper
- 2 spring onions, chopped

Directions:
Set your instant pot on Sauté mode, add the oil, heat it up, add the onion and the meat and brown for 5 minutes. Add the rest of the ingredients, toss, put the lid on and cook on High for 25 minutes. Release the pressure naturally for 10 minutes, divide the mix between plates and serve.

Nutrition: calories 276, fat 14, fiber 3, carbs 7, protein 20

Rosemary Pork and Asparagus

*Preparation time: 10 minutes **Cooking time:** 35 minutes **Servings:** 4*

Ingredients:
- 2 pounds pork stew meat, cut into strips
- 1 red onion, chopped
- 4 asparagus spears, trimmed and halved
- 1 tablespoon avocado oil
- 1 cup beef stock
- ½ cup tomato passata
- 2 teaspoons sweet paprika
- 1 tablespoon chives, chopped

Directions:
Set your instant pot on Sauté mode, add the oil, heat it up, add the onion, paprika and the meat and brown for 5 minutes. Add the rest of the ingredients except the asparagus, toss, put the lid on and cook on High for 20 minutes. Release the pressure naturally for 10 minutes, set the pot on Sauté mode again, add the asparagus, cook for 5 minutes more, divide the mix between plates and serve.

Nutrition: calories 287, fat 16, fiber 4, carbs 6, protein 20

Beef and Sprouts

Preparation time: 10 minutes **Cooking time:** *35 minutes* **Servings:** *4*

Ingredients:

- 2 pounds beef roast, cubed
- 2 cups Brussels sprouts, trimmed and halved
- 1 red onion, chopped
- 2 tablespoon olive oil
- 3 garlic cloves, chopped
- 1 teaspoon curry powder
- ½ teaspoon coriander, ground
- A pinch of salt and black pepper
- 1 cup tomato puree
- 1 tablespoon cilantro, chopped

Directions:

Set the instant pot on Sauté mode, add the oil, heat it up, add the onion and the garlic and sauté for 5 minutes. Add the meat, curry powder and the coriander and brown for 5 minutes more. Add the rest of the ingredients, toss, put the lid on and cook on High for 25 minutes more. Release the pressure naturally for 10 minutes, divide the mix between plates and serve.

Nutrition: calories 264, fat 8, fiber 3, carbs 6, protein 17

Lamb and Basil Olives

Preparation time: 10 minutes **Cooking time:** *30 minutes* **Servings:** *4*

Ingredients:

- 2 pounds lamb shanks
- 2 tablespoons avocado oil
- 3 scallions, chopped
- 1 cup green olives, pitted and halved
- 1 tablespoon basil, chopped
- 2 garlic cloves, minced
- 1 teaspoon sweet paprika
- 2 cups beef stock
- A pinch of salt and black pepper
- 1 tablespoon chives, chopped

Directions:

Set your instant pot on Sauté mode, add the oil, heat it up, add the scallions, olives, basil, garlic and the paprika and sauté for 5 minutes. Add lamb shanks and brown them for 5 minutes more. Add the rest of the ingredients, put the lid on and cook on High for 20 minutes. Release the pressure naturally for 10 minutes, divide everything between plates and serve.

Nutrition: calories 275, fat 13, fiber 4, carbs 7, protein 20

Lamb and Spicy Tomato Mix

Preparation time: 10 minutes *Cooking time:* 30 minutes *Servings:* 4

Ingredients:

- 1 pound lamb shoulder, roughly cubed
- 1 yellow onion, chopped
- 2 tablespoons avocado oil
- ¼ pound cherry tomatoes, halved
- ½ teaspoon chili powder
- ½ teaspoon hot paprika
- 4 garlic cloves, minced
- 1 tablespoon thyme, chopped
- 1 cup beef stock
- A pinch of salt and black pepper

Directions:

Set your instant pot on Sauté mode, add the oil, heat it up, add the onion, garlic, chili powder and the paprika and sauté for 5 minutes. Add the meat and brown for 5 minutes more. Add the tomatoes and the remaining ingredients, toss, put the lid on and cook on High for 20 minutes. Release the pressure naturally for 10 minutes, divide the mix between plates and serve.

Nutrition: calories 263, fat 12, fiber 4, carbs 7, protein 12

Marjoram Beef

Preparation time: 10 minutes *Cooking time:* 40 minutes *Servings:* 4

Ingredients:

- 2 pounds beef roast, sliced
- 2 tablespoons avocado oil
- 2 tablespoons marjoram, chopped
- 1 red onion, chopped
- ½ teaspoon coriander, ground
- ½ teaspoon fennel seeds, crushed
- 4 garlic cloves, minced
- 1 cup beef stock
- 1 cup tomato passata
- A pinch of salt and black pepper
- 1 tablespoon parsley, chopped

Directions:

Set your instant pot on Sauté mode, add the oil, heat it up, add the onion, garlic, coriander and the fennel seeds and sauté for 5 minutes. Add the meat and brown for 5 minutes more. Add the rest of the ingredients, put the lid on and cook on High for 30 minutes. Release the pressure naturally for 10 minutes, divide the mix between plates and serve.

Nutrition: calories 263, fat 12, fiber 3, carbs 7, protein 10

Lamb and Curry Artichokes

Preparation time: 10 minutes *Cooking time:* 35 minutes *Servings:* 4
Ingredients:

- 2 pounds lamb shoulder, cubed
- 1 cup canned artichoke hearts, drained and rinsed
- 1 tablespoon curry powder
- 2 tablespoons avocado oil
- 1 yellow onion, chopped
- 1 cup coconut milk
- ½ cup heavy cream
- A pinch of salt and black pepper
- 1 tablespoon dill, chopped

Directions:

Set your instant pot on Sauté mode, add the oil, heat it up, add the onion, artichokes and the curry powder and sauté for 5 minutes. Add the meat and brown for 5 minutes more. Add the rest of the ingredients, put the lid on and cook on High for 25 minutes. Release the pressure naturally for 10 minutes, divide the mix between plates and serve.

Nutrition: calories 233, fat 7, fiber 2, carbs 6, protein 12

Pork Chops and Capers

Preparation time: 10 minutes *Cooking time:* 30 minutes *Servings:* 4
Ingredients:

- 4 pork chops
- 2 tablespoons avocado oil
- 2 scallions, chopped
- 1 teaspoon cumin, ground
- 1 tablespoon capers, drained
- ½ teaspoon coriander, ground
- ½ teaspoon chili powder
- 1 teaspoon sweet paprika
- A pinch of salt and black pepper
- ½ cup tomatoes, chopped
- 2 tablespoons parsley, chopped

Directions:

Set your instant pot on Sauté mode, add the oil, heat it up, add the scallions, capers, cumin, chili powder and the paprika and sauté for 5 minutes. Add the pork chops and brown for 5 minutes more. Add the rest of the ingredients, put the lid on and cook on High for 20 minutes. Release the pressure naturally for 10 minutes, divide the mix between plates and serve.

Nutrition: calories 235, fat 12, fiber 5, carbs 7, protein 10

Ginger Lamb

Preparation time: 10 minutes **Cooking time:** 30 minutes **Servings:** 4

Ingredients:
- 2 pounds lamb shoulder, cubed
- 1 tablespoon ginger, grated
- 2 tablespoons olive oil
- 1 red onion, sliced
- 1 carrot, peeled and sliced
- 1 teaspoon cumin, ground
- 1 teaspoon sweet paprika
- 3 tablespoons almonds, toasted and chopped
- 1 cup beef stock
- A pinch of salt and black pepper

Directions:
Set the instant pot on Sauté mode, add the oil, heat it up, add the onion, cumin, paprika and the ginger and sauté for 5 minutes. Add the meat and brown for 5 minutes more. Add the rest of the ingredients, toss, put the lid on and cook on High for 20 minutes. Release the pressure naturally for 10 minutes, divide the mix between plates and serve.

Nutrition: calories 211, fat 9, fiber 2, carbs 6, protein 12

Lamb and Spinach

Preparation time: 10 minutes **Cooking time:** 30 minutes **Servings:** 4

Ingredients:
- 2 pounds lamb shoulder, cubed
- 2 cups baby spinach
- 1 red onion, chopped
- 2 tablespoons olive oil
- ½ teaspoon curry powder
- ½ teaspoon rosemary, dried
- 1 teaspoon sweet paprika
- 2 garlic cloves, minced
- 2 tablespoons tomato paste
- A pinch of salt and black pepper
- A handful cilantro, chopped

Directions:
Set your instant pot on Sauté mode, add the oil, heat it up, add the onion, curry powder, rosemary, paprika and the garlic and sauté for 5 minutes. Add the meat and brown for 5 minutes more. Add the rest of the ingredients, put the lid on and cook on High for 20 minutes. Release the pressure naturally for 10 minutes, divide everything between plates and serve.

Nutrition: calories 254, fat 12, fiber 3, carbs 6, protein 16

Lamb and Lentils

Preparation time: 10 minutes *Cooking time:* 30 minutes *Servings:* 4

Ingredients:
- 2 pounds lamb shoulder, roughly cubed
- 2 tablespoons olive oil
- 1 yellow onion, chopped
- 1 cup canned lentils, drained and rinsed
- 2 cups beef stock
- ¼ cup tomato sauce
- 1 tablespoon chives, chopped
- A pinch of salt and black pepper
- 1 tablespoon cilantro, chopped

Directions:
Set the instant pot on Sauté mode, add the oil, heat it up, add the onion and the meat and brown for 5 minutes. Add the rest of the ingredients, toss, put the lid on and cook on High for 25 minutes. Release the pressure naturally for 10 minutes, divide the mix between plates and serve.

Nutrition: calories 232, fat 10, fiber 5, carbs 7, protein 11

Lamb and Cumin Chickpeas

Preparation time: 10 minutes *Cooking time:* 25 minutes *Servings:* 4

Ingredients:
- 2 pounds lamb meat, ground
- 1 cup cherry tomatoes, cubed
- 1 cup canned chickpeas, drained and rinsed
- 1 yellow onion, chopped
- 2 tablespoons olive oil
- ½ teaspoon cumin, ground
- ½ teaspoon chili powder
- 2 spring onions, chopped
- A pinch of salt and black pepper
- 1 cup beef stock
- 1 tablespoon chives, chopped

Directions:
Set the instant pot on Sauté mode, add the oil, heat it up, add the onion, cumin, chili powder and spring onions, stir and sauté for 5 minutes. Add the meat and brown for 5 minutes more. Add the rest of the ingredients, toss, put the lid on and cook on High for 15 minutes. Release the pressure naturally for 10 minutes, divide the mix into bowls and serve.

Nutrition: calories 243, fat 11, fiber 4, carbs 6, protein 10

Lamb and Beans

Preparation time: 10 minutes **Cooking time:** 35 minutes **Servings:** 4
Ingredients:
- 2 pounds lamb shoulder, cubed
- 2 tablespoons olive oil
- 1 yellow onion, chopped
- 1 cup canned black beans, drained and rinsed
- 1 cup canned red kidney beans, drained and rinsed
- 1 cup beef stock
- ¼ cup tomato passata
- 3 garlic cloves, minced
- A pinch of salt and black pepper
- ½ bunch cilantro, chopped

Directions:
Set your instant pot on Sauté mode, add the oil, heat it up, add the onion, garlic and the meat and brown for 5 minutes. Add the rest of the ingredients, put the lid on and cook on High for 30 minutes. Release the pressure naturally for 10 minutes, divide the mix between plates and serve.

Nutrition: calories 232, fat 12, fiber 4, carbs 6, protein 9

Pork and Potatoes

Preparation time: *10 minutes* ***Cooking time:*** *35 minutes* ***Servings:*** *4*
Ingredients:
- 2 pounds shoulder, cubed
- 1 red onion, chopped
- 1 yellow onion, chopped
- 3 garlic cloves, minced
- 2 tablespoons olive oil
- 2 red potatoes, peeled and cut into wedges
- 1 cup tomato passata
- 1 tablespoon rosemary, chopped
- A pinch of salt and black pepper
- 2 tablespoons cilantro, chopped

Directions:
Set your instant pot on Sauté mode, add the oil, heat it up, add the red, yellow onions and the garlic and sauté for 5 minutes. Add the meat and brown for 5 minutes more. Add the rest of the ingredients, put the lid on and cook on High for 25 minutes. Release the pressure naturally for 10 minutes, divide the mix between plates and serve.

Nutrition: calories 274, fat 9, fiber 5, carbs 6, protein 12

Garlic Lamb Chops Mix

*Preparation time: 10 minutes **Cooking time:** 30 minutes **Servings:** 4*

Ingredients:
- 4 lamb chops
- 2 tablespoons avocado oil
- 4 garlic cloves, minced
- A pinch of salt and black pepper
- 1 teaspoon turmeric powder
- 1 teaspoon chili powder
- ½ teaspoon coriander, ground
- 1 cup beef stock
- 1 tablespoon cilantro, chopped

Directions:
Set your instant pot on Sauté mode, add the oil, heat it up, add the meat, garlic, turmeric and chili powder and brown for 5 minutes. Add the rest of the ingredients, put the lid on and cook on High for 25 minutes. Release the pressure naturally for 10 minutes, divide everything between plates and serve.

Nutrition: calories 232, fat 9, fiber 3, carbs 6, protein 10

Balsamic Pork and Bok Choy

*Preparation time: 10 minutes **Cooking time:** 30 minutes **Servings:** 4*

Ingredients:
- 2 pounds pork stew meat, roughly cubed
- 2 tablespoons avocado oil
- 1 red onion, sliced
- 1 cup bok choy, torn
- 2 tablespoons balsamic vinegar
- A pinch of salt and black pepper
- 1 tablespoon chives, chopped
- ½ cup beef stock

Directions:
Set your instant pot on Sauté mode, add the oil, heat it up, add the onion and the meat and brown for 5 minutes. Add the rest of the ingredients, put the lid on and cook on High for 25 minutes. Release the pressure naturally for 10 minutes, divide everything between plates and serve.

Nutrition: calories 200, fat 11, fiber 3, carbs 6, protein 15

Pork Chops with Chard

Preparation time: 10 minutes Cooking time: 25 minutes Servings: 4
Ingredients:
- 4 pork chops
- 2 tablespoons olive oil
- 2 cups red chard, torn
- 1 red onion, chopped
- 2 tablespoons lemon juice
- ½ cup tomato passata
- ½ cup beef stock
- A pinch of salt and black pepper
- 1 tablespoon cilantro, chopped

Directions:
Set your instant pot on Sauté mode, add the oil, heat it up, add the onion and the pork chops and brown for 5 minutes Add the rest of the ingredients, put the lid on and cook on High for 20 minutes. Release the pressure naturally for 10 minutes, divide everything between plates and serve.

Nutrition: calories 210, fat 5, fiber 3, carbs 8, protein 12

Pork and Herbed Sauce

Preparation time: 10 minutes Cooking time: 25 minutes Servings: 4
Ingredients:
- 4 pork chops
- 1 tablespoon cilantro, chopped
- 1 tablespoon parsley, chopped
- 1 tablespoon oregano, chopped
- Juice of 1 lime
- 2 tablespoons olive oil
- 2 teaspoons chili powder
- 1 cup coconut cream
- 2 garlic cloves, minced
- Salt and black pepper to the taste

Directions:
In a blender, combine cilantro with the parsley, oregano, lime juice, garlic and coconut cream and pulse well. Set the instant pot on Sauté mode, add the oil, heat it up, add the meat and brown for 5 minutes. Add the herbed sauce and the remaining ingredients, toss, put the lid on and cook on High for 20 minutes. Release the pressure naturally for 10 minutes, divide the mix between plates and serve.

Nutrition: calories 248, fat 11, fiber 3, carbs 6, protein 15

Paprika Pork Chops

Preparation time: *10 minutes* ***Cooking time:*** *25 minutes* ***Servings:*** *4*

Ingredients:
- 4 pork chops
- 1 cup beef stock
- 1 red onion, chopped
- ½ teaspoon chili powder
- 2 tablespoons olive oil
- ¼ cup tomato puree
- 4 teaspoons sweet paprika
- A pinch of salt and black pepper

Directions:
Set the instant pot on Sauté mode, add the oil, heat it up, add the onion and the pork chops and brown for 5 minutes. Add the rest of the ingredients, put the lid on and cook on High for 20 minutes. Release the pressure naturally for 10 minutes, divide everything between plates and serve.

Nutrition: calories 233, fat 9, fiber 3, carbs 7, protein 14

Pork with Watercress

Preparation time: *10 minutes* ***Cooking time:*** *25 minutes* ***Servings:*** *4*

Ingredients:
- 4 pork chops
- 1 bunch watercress
- 1 red onion, chopped
- 2 garlic cloves, minced
- 2 tablespoons olive oil
- A pinch of salt and black pepper
- 1 cup beef stock
- ¼ cup tomato sauce
- 1 tablespoon parsley, chopped

Directions:
Set your instant pot on Sauté mode, add the oil, heat it up, add the onion, garlic and the pork chops and brown for 5 minutes. Add the rest of the ingredients, put the lid on and cook on High for 20 minutes. Release the pressure naturally for 10 minutes, divide the mix between plates and serve.

Nutrition: calories 227, fat 14, fiber 4, carbs 6, protein 16

Chives Lamb Chops and Peas

*Preparation time: 10 minute **Cooking time:** 25 minute **Servings:** 4*

Ingredients:

- 4 lamb chops
- 1 tablespoon olive oil
- 2 scallions, chopped
- ½ cup chives, chopped
- 1 cup green peas
- 1 cup beef stock
- 1 teaspoon chili powder
- 1 teaspoon sweet paprika
- 1 cup tomato sauce

Directions:

Set your instant pot on Sauté mode, add the oil, heat it up, add the scallions, chili powder and the paprika and sauté for 5 minutes. Add the meat and brown for 5 minutes more. Add the rest of the ingredients, toss, put the lid on and cook on High for 15 minutes. Release the pressure naturally for 10 minutes, divide the mix between plates and serve.

Nutrition: calories 236, fat 12, fiber 2, carbs 7, protein 15

Pork with Lemony Sauce

*Preparation time: 10 minutes **Cooking time:** 30 minutes **Servings:** 4*

Ingredients:

- 1 pounds pork loin, cubed
- 1 cup beef stock
- 2 tablespoons lemon zest, grated
- 1 yellow onion, chopped
- 2 tablespoons lemon juice
- 2 tablespoons olive oil
- ¼ teaspoon garlic powder
- ½ teaspoon garam masala
- 1 tablespoon sweet paprika
- A pinch of salt and black pepper

Directions:

Set the instant pot on Sauté mode, add the oil, heat it up, add the onion, lemon juice, and lemon zest and sauté for 5 minutes. Add the meat and brown for 5 minutes more. Add the rest of the ingredients, put the lid on and cook on High for 20 minutes. Release the pressure naturally for 10 minutes, divide the mix between plates and serve.

Nutrition: 273, fat 12, fiber 4, carbs 7, protein 17

Pork Chops and Red Onion Mix

Preparation time: 10 minutes **Cooking time:** *25 minutes* **Servings:** *4*

Ingredients:
- 4 pork chops
- 2 tablespoons olive oil
- 2 red onions, sliced
- 1 tablespoon peppercorns, crushed
- ½ teaspoon coriander, ground
- 1 cup beef stock
- 2 tablespoons tomato sauce
- 1 teaspoon sweet paprika
- 4 garlic cloves, minced
- A pinch of salt and black pepper
- 1 tablespoon rosemary, chopped

Directions:
Set your instant pot on sauté mode, add the oil, heat it up, add the onions, peppercorns, coriander, paprika and the garlic and sauté for 5 minutes. Add the meat and brown for 5 minutes more. Add the rest of the ingredients, put the lid on and cook on High for 15 minutes. Release the pressure naturally for 10 minutes, divide the mix between plates and serve.

Nutrition: calories 244, fat 12, fiber 2, carbs 5, protein 16

Ground Pork Mix

Preparation time: 10 minutes **Cooking time:** *25 minutes* **Servings:** *4*

Ingredients:
- 2 pounds pork shoulder, ground
- 1 red onion, sliced
- 1 eggplant, cubed
- 1 cup green beans, trimmed and halved
- 2 tablespoons olive oil
- 1 carrot, peeled and sliced
- 1 and ½ cups beef stock
- 1 bunch rosemary, chopped
- A pinch of salt and black pepper

Directions:
Set the instant pot on Sauté mode, add the oil, heat it up, add the onion, carrotsand the meat and brown for 5 minutes. Add the rest of the ingredients, toss, put the lid on and cook on High for 20 minutes. Release the pressure naturally for 10 minutes, divide the mix between plates and serve.

Nutrition: calories 254, fat 14, fiber 3, carbs 6, protein 17

Chili Pork Ribs

Preparation time: 10 minutes Cooking time: 30 minutes Servings: 4

Ingredients:
- 2 pounds country style pork ribs
- 1 red chili, minced
- ½ teaspoon red pepper flakes, crushed
- 1 yellow onion, chopped
- 2 tablespoons olive oil
- A pinch of salt and black pepper
- 1 tablespoon smoked paprika
- 1 and ½ cups beef stock
- 1 tablespoon cilantro, chopped

Directions:
Set your instant pot on Sauté mode, add the oil, heat it up, add the chili, pepper flakes, the onion and the paprika and sauté for 5 minutes. Add the meat and brown for 5 minutes more. Add the rest of the ingredients, toss, put the lid on and cook on High for 20 minutes. Release the pressure naturally for 10 minutes, divide the ribs between plates and serve.

Nutrition: calories 263, fat 14, fiber 3, carbs 6, protein 20

Cayenne Pork Chops

Preparation time: 10 minutes Cooking time: 25 minutes Servings: 4

Ingredients:
- 4 pork chops
- 1 red onion, sliced
- 2 tablespoons avocado oil
- ½ cup beef stock
- A pinch of salt and black pepper
- 1 teaspoon onion powder
- ½ teaspoon sweet paprika
- 1 teaspoon cayenne pepper

Directions:
Set the instant pot on Sauté mode, add the oil, heat it up, add the onion, onion powder and the paprika and sauté for 5 minutes. Add the meat and brown for 5 minutes more. Add the rest of the ingredients, toss, put the lid on and cook on High for 15 minutes. Release the pressure naturally for 10 minutes, divide mix between plates and serve.

Nutrition: calories 283, fat 13, fiber 4, carbs 6, protein 16

Pork with Cabbage

Preparation time: *10 minutes* ***Cooking time:*** *30 minutes* ***Servings:*** *4*

Ingredients:
- 1 cup green cabbage, shredded
- 4 pork chops
- 2 tablespoons olive oil
- 1 red onion, chopped
- 3 garlic cloves, minced
- 1 tablespoon oregano, chopped
- 1 and ½ cups beef stock
- 2 tablespoons tomato sauce
- 1 tablespoon chives, chopped

Directions:

Set your instant pot on Sauté mode, add the oil, heat it up, add the onion, garlic and oregano and sauté for 5 minutes. Add the meat and brown for 5 minutes more. Add the rest of the ingredients, put the lid on and cook on High for 20 minutes. Release the pressure naturally for 10 minutes, divide the pork chops between plates and serve.

Nutrition: calories 253, fat 14, fiber 2, carbs 6, protein 18

Pork and Mustard Greens

Preparation time: *10 minutes* ***Cooking time:*** *25 minutes* ***Servings:*** *4*

Ingredients:
- 2 pounds pork loin, cubed
- 1 tablespoon olive oil
- 2 garlic cloves, minced
- 1 yellow onion, chopped
- A pinch of salt and black pepper
- ¼ cup tomato paste
- ½ pound mustard greens
- 1 tablespoon chives, chopped

Directions:

Set your instant pot on Sauté mode, add the oil, heat it up, add the onion, the garlic and the meat and brown for 5 minutes. Add the rest of the ingredients except the chives, toss, put the lid on and cook on High for 20 minutes. Release the pressure naturally for 10 minutes, divide everything between plates and serve with the chives sprinkled on top.

Nutrition: calories 264, fat 14, fiber 3, carbs 6, protein 17

Beef and Peppers

Preparation time: 10 minutes **Cooking time:** *35 minutes* **Servings:** *4*
Ingredients:
- 2 tablespoons olive oil
- 2 pounds beef stew meat, roughly cubed
- A pinch of salt and black pepper
- 1 red onion, chopped
- 1 red bell pepper, cut into strips
- 1 green bell pepper, cut into strips
- 1 orange bell pepper, cut into strips
- 3 garlic cloves, minced
- ½ cup tomato passata
- 2 cups beef stock
- 1 tablespoon coriander, chopped

Directions:
Set your instant pot on Sauté mode, add the oil, heat it up, add the onion, garlic and the meat and brown for 5 minutes. Add all the other ingredients, toss, put the lid on and cook on High for 30 minutes. Release the pressure naturally for 10 minutes, divide the mix into bowls and serve.

Nutrition: calories 273, fat 13, fiber 2, carbs 6, protein 15

Orange Pork and Pears

Preparation time: 10 minutes **Cooking time:** *35 minutes* **Servings:** *4*
Ingredients:
- 2 pounds pork stew meat, roughly cubed
- 2 tablespoons olive oil
- 1 red onion, sliced
- 3 garlic cloves, minced
- 1 tablespoon orange zest, grated
- Juice of 1 orange
- A pinch of salt and black pepper
- 1 tablespoon ginger, grated
- ½ cup beef stock

Directions:
Set the instant pot on Sauté mode, add the oil, heat it up, add the onion, garlic, orange zest and the meat and brown for 5 minutes. Add the rest of the ingredients, toss, put the lid on and cook on High for 30 minutes. Release the pressure naturally for 10 minutes, divide the mix between plates and serve.

Nutrition: calories 274, fat 14, fiber 2, carbs 6, protein 16

Pork and Corn

Preparation time: 10 minutes **Cooking time:** 35 minutes **Servings:** 4

Ingredients:
- 2 pounds pork shoulder, boneless and cubed
- 2 garlic cloves, minced
- 4 scallions, chopped
- A pinch of salt and black pepper
- 1 cup corn
- 1 cup beef stock
- 1 teaspoon rosemary, dried
- 1 tablespoon cilantro, chopped

Directions:
In your instant pot, combine the pork with the garlic, the scallions and the other ingredients, toss, put the lid on and cook on High for 35 minutes. Release the pressure naturally for 10 minutes, divide the mix between plates and serve.

Nutrition: calories 264, fat 14, fiber 2, carbs 8, protein 12

Cumin Pork

Preparation time: 10 minutes Cooking time: 30 minutes Servings: 4

Ingredients:
- 1 pound pork stew meat, roughly cubed
- 4 scallions, chopped
- A pinch of salt and black pepper
- 2 tablespoons hot sauce
- 1 cup beef stock
- 1 teaspoon cumin, ground
- 1 tablespoon parsley, chopped

Directions:
In your instant pot, combine the pork with the scallions and the rest of the ingredients, put the lid on and cook on High for 30 minutes. Release the pressure naturally for 10 minutes, divide the mix between plates and serve.

Nutrition: calories 200, fat 9, fiber 2, carbs 6, protein 12

Pork Shoulder Roast

Preparation time: 10 minutes **Cooking time:** 40 minutes **Servings:** 4

Ingredients:
- 2 pounds pork shoulder, boneless and sliced
- 2 tablespoons olive oil
- A pinch of salt and black pepper
- 2 tablespoons chili powder
- 4 garlic cloves, minced
- 2 cups beef stock

Directions:
In your instant pot, combine the pork roast with the oil and the other ingredients, put the lid on and cook on High for 40 minutes. Release the pressure naturally for 10 minutes, divide the roast between plates and serve with a side salad.

Nutrition: calories 234, fat 11, fiber 3, carbs 7, protein 15

Lamb, Brussels Sprouts and Kale

Preparation time: 10 minutes **Cooking time:** 30 minutes **Servings:** 4

Ingredients:
- 2 pounds lamb meat, cubed
- 1 cup beef stock
- 1 cup Brussels sprouts, trimmed and halved
- 1 cup kale, torn
- 2 tablespoons olive oil
- 1 tablespoon parsley, chopped

Directions:
In your instant pot, combine the lamb with the stock and the other ingredients, toss, put the lid on and cook on High for 30 minutes. Release the pressure naturally for 10 minutes, divide the mix between plates and serve.

Nutrition: calories 273, fat 14, fiber 2, carbs 6, protein 15

Balsamic Pork Chops

Preparation time: 10 minutes **Cooking time:** 30 minutes **Servings:** 4

Ingredients:
- 4 pork chops
- 1 tablespoon balsamic vinegar
- 2 tablespoons oregano, chopped
- 1 cup beef stock
- A pinch of salt and black pepper
- 1 tablespoon chives, chopped

Directions:
In your instant pot, combine the pork chops with the vinegar and the other ingredients, put the lid on and cook on High for 30 minutes. Release the pressure naturally for 10 minutes, divide everything between plates and serve.

Nutrition: calories 292, fat 12, fiber 3, carbs 7, protein 16

Pork with Corn and Cabbage

Preparation time: 10 minutes **Cooking time:** 30 minutes **Servings:** 4

Ingredients:
- 2 pounds pork stew meat, cubed
- 2 tablespoons olive oil
- 1 yellow onion, chopped
- 1 cup corn
- 1 cup red cabbage, shredded
- 2 tomatoes, cubed
- 1 and ½ cups beef stock
- A pinch of salt and black pepper

Directions:
Set the instant pot on Sauté mode, add the oil, heat it up, add the onion and the meat and brown for 3 minutes. Add the rest of the ingredients, put the lid on and cook on High for 25 minutes. Release the pressure naturally for 10 minutes, divide everything between plates and serve.

Nutrition: calories 277, fat 14, fiber 3, carbs 7, protein 17

Beef Meatloaf

Preparation time: 10 minutes *Cooking time:* 35 minutes *Servings:* 4

Ingredients:
- ½ cup almond milk
- ½ cup almond flour
- 1 yellow onion, minced
- A pinch of salt and black pepper
- 2 eggs, whisked
- 2 pounds beef stew meat, ground
- ½ cup tomato sauce
- 1 tablespoon parsley, chopped
- 2 cups water

Directions:
In a bowl, combine the beef with the almond milk, flour and with the rest of the ingredients except the water, stir well and shape a meatloaf and put it in a loaf pan that fits the instant pot. Add the water to your instant pot, add the steamer basket, put the pan inside, put the lid on and cook on High for 35 minutes. Release the pressure naturally for 10 minutes, cool the meatloaf down, slice and serve.

Nutrition: calories 274, fat 12, fiber 4, carbs 7, protein 16

Beef and Ginger Okra

Preparation time: 10 minutes *Cooking time:* 30 minutes *Servings:* 4

Ingredients:
- 2 pounds beef stew meat, cubed
- 1 tablespoon avocado oil
- 1 cup okra, sliced
- 2 scallions, chopped
- 1 tablespoon ginger, grated
- A pinch of salt and black pepper
- 1 and ½ cups beef stock
- 1 tablespoon oregano, chopped

Directions:
Set the instant pot on Sauté mode, add the oil, heat it up, add the scallions and the meat and brown for 5 minutes. Add the rest of the ingredients, put the lid on and cook on High for 25 minutes. Release the pressure naturally for 10 minutes, divide the mix between plates and serve.

Nutrition: calories 269, fat 12, fiber 3, carbs 5, protein 16

Paprika Lamb and Radishes

*Preparation time: 10 minutes **Cooking time:** 30 minutes **Servings:** 4*
Ingredients:
- 2 pounds lamb stew meat, cubed
- 2 tablespoons olive oil
- 1 red onion, chopped
- 1 cup radishes, halved
- 2 garlic cloves, minced
- A pinch of salt and black pepper
- 1 cup beef stock
- ½ teaspoon sweet paprika
- 2 tablespoons cilantro, chopped

Directions:
Set the instant pot on Sauté mode, add the oil, heat it up, add the onion and the garlic and sauté for 5 minutes. Add the meat and brown for 5 minutes more. Add the rest of the ingredients, put the lid on and cook on High for 20 minutes. Release the pressure naturally for 10 minutes, divide everything between plates and serve.

Nutrition: calories 293, fat 14, fiber 4, carbs 6, protein 18

Tarragon Lamb and Veggies

*Preparation time: 10 minutes **Cooking time:** 30 minutes **Servings:** 4*
Ingredients:
- 1 red onion, chopped
- 2 pounds lamb stew meat, cubed
- 1 tablespoon tarragon, chopped
- 1 cup beef stock
- 1 zucchini, sliced
- 1 carrot, peeled and sliced
- 1 tomato, cubed
- 1 eggplant, cubed
- A pinch of salt and black pepper
- 1 cup tomato puree
- 1 tablespoon cilantro, chopped

Directions:
Set the instant pot on Sauté mode, add the oil, heat it up, add the onion and the meat and brown for 5 minutes. Add the rest of the ingredients, put the lid on and cook on High for 25 minutes. Release the pressure naturally for 10 minutes, divide the mix between plates and serve.

Nutrition: calories 263, fat 12, fiber 3, carbs 6, protein 13

Instant Pot Fish and Seafood Recipes

Lemon Clams

Preparation time: 10 minutes *Cooking time:* 10 minutes *Servings:* 4

Ingredients:
- 1 pound clams, scrubbed
- ½ cup chicken stock
- 1 red onion, chopped
- Zest of 1 lemon, grated
- A pinch of salt and black pepper
- 1 tablespoon lemon juice

Directions:
In your instant pot, combine the clams with the stock and the other ingredients, put the lid on and cook on High for 10 minutes. Release the pressure naturally for 10 minutes, divide the mix into bowls and serve.

Nutrition: calories 198, fat 7, fiber 2, carbs 6, protein 7

Tarragon Cod

Preparation time: 10 minutes *Cooking time:* 10 minutes *Servings:* 4

Ingredients:
- 2 tablespoons olive oil
- 2 scallions, chopped
- 2 garlic cloves, minced
- 1 pound cod fillets, boneless and skinless
- ½ cup chicken stock
- A pinch of salt and black pepper
- ¼ cup tarragon, chopped

Directions:
Set your instant pot on Sauté mode, add the oil, heat it up, add the scallions and the garlic and sauté for 2 minutes. Add the fish and the rest of the ingredients, put the lid on and cook on High for 8 minutes. Release the pressure naturally for 10 minutes, divide the fish between plates and serve.

Nutrition: calories 221, fat 8, fiber 3, carbs 6, protein 7

Salmon and Shrimp Bowls

*Preparation time: 5 minutes **Cooking time:** 15 minutes **Servings:** 4*

Ingredients:
- 1 pounds salmon fillets, boneless, skinless and cubed
- 1 pound shrimp, peeled and deveined
- 1 tablespoon olive oil
- 1 red onion, chopped
- 3 garlic cloves, crushed
- 2 tablespoons chives, chopped
- 1 cup chicken stock
- A pinch of salt and black pepper

Directions:
Set the instant pot on Sauté mode, add the oil, heat it up, add the onion and the garlic and sauté for 5 minutes. Add the salmon, shrimp and the rest of the ingredients, put the lid on and cook on High for 10 minutes. Release the pressure fast for 5 minutes, divide the mix between plates and serve.

Nutrition: calories 235, fat 8, fiber 4, carbs 7, protein 9

Crab and Tomato Mix

*Preparation time: 10 minutes **Cooking time:** 12 minutes **Servings:** 4*

Ingredients:
- 1 tablespoon olive oil
- 1 pound crab meat
- 2 spring onions, chopped
- 1 cup cherry tomatoes, halved
- 1 cup chicken stock
- 1 teaspoon sweet paprika
- A pinch of salt and black pepper

Directions:
Set the instant pot on Sauté mode, add the oil, heat it up, add the onions and paprika and sauté for 2 minutes. Add the crab meat and the rest of the ingredients, put the lid on and cook on High for 10 minutes. Release the pressure naturally for 10 minutes, divide everything into bowls and serve.

Nutrition: calories 211, fat 8, fiber 4, carbs 8, protein 8

Crab and Kale Bowls

Preparation time: 10 minutes *Cooking time:* 10 minutes *Servings:* 4

Ingredients:
- 1 pound crab meat
- 1 cup veggie stock
- 1 cup kale, torn
- 2 tablespoons avocado oil
- 2 spring onions, chopped
- 1 tablespoon smoked paprika
- A pinch of salt and black pepper
- 2 garlic cloves, minced
- 1 tablespoon chives, chopped

Directions:
Set the instant pot on Sauté mode, add the oil, heat it up, add the spring onions, paprika and the garlic and sauté for 2 minutes. Add the crab and the rest of the ingredients, put the lid on and cook on High for 8 minutes. Release the pressure naturally for 10 minutes, transfer the mix to bowls and serve.

Nutrition: calories 193, fat 7, fiber 3, carbs 6, protein 6

Rosemary Salmon and Eggplant Mix

Preparation time: 5 minutes *Cooking time:* 12 minutes *Servings:* 4

Ingredients:
- 4 salmon fillets, skinless and boneless
- 1 eggplant, cubed
- 1 red onion, chopped
- 2 tablespoons olive oil
- Juice of 1 lime
- 4 garlic cloves, minced
- 1 tablespoon rosemary, chopped
- A pinch of salt and black pepper

Directions:
Set the instant pot on Sauté mode, add the oil, heat it up, add the onion and the garlic and sauté for 2 minutes. Add the salmon and the other ingredients, put the lid on and cook on High for 10 minutes. Release the pressure fast for 5 minutes, divide the salmon mix between plates and serve.

Nutrition: calories 200, fat 11, fiber 4, carbs 5, protein 12

Shrimp and Sweet Potatoes

*Preparation time: 10 minutes **Cooking time:** 8 minutes **Servings:** 4*

Ingredients:
- 1 pound shrimp, peeled and deveined
- 2 sweet potatoes, peeled and cubed
- 2 spring onions, chopped
- 1 cup chicken stock
- 1 tablespoon olive oil
- 1 tablespoon chives, chopped

Directions:
In your instant pot, combine the shrimp with the sweet potatoes and the other ingredients, toss, put the lid on and cook on High for 8 minutes. Release the pressure naturally for 10 minutes, divide the mix into bowls and serve.

Nutrition: calories 200, fat 12, fiber 3, carbs 7, protein 9

Creamy Mackerel and Zucchinis

*Preparation time: 5 minutes **Cooking time:** 15 minutes **Servings:** 4*

Ingredients:
- 1 pound mackerel fillets, boneless, skinless and cubed
- 1 tablespoon olive oil
- 2 zucchinis, cubed
- A pinch of salt and black pepper
- 1 cup heavy cream
- 4 garlic cloves, minced
- ¼ teaspoon coriander, ground
- 1 tablespoon cilantro, chopped

Directions:
Set the instant pot on Sauté mode, add the oil, heat it up, add the garlic and zucchinis and sauté for 3 minutes. Add the mackerel and the rest of the ingredients, put the lid on and cook on High for 12 minutes. Release the pressure fast for 5 minutes, divide the mix into bowls and serve.

Nutrition: calories 232, fat 10, fiber 4, carbs 6, protein 9

Shrimp, Corn and Peas

Preparation time: 6 minutes **Cooking time:** 10 minutes **Servings:** 4

Ingredients:
- 1 pound shrimp, peeled and deveined
- 1 cup corn
- 1 cup fresh peas
- 1 tablespoon olive oil
- 1 yellow onion, chopped
- 1 tablespoon olive oil
- ½ cup chicken stock
- 1 teaspoon sweet paprika
- Salt and black pepper to the taste

Directions:
Set your instant pot on Sauté mode, add the oil, heat it up, add the onion, stir and sauté for 2 minutes. Add the shrimp, corn and the rest of the ingredients, put the lid on and cook on High for 8 minutes. Release the pressure naturally for 10 minutes, divide the mix into bowls and serve.

Nutrition: calories 182, fat 7, fiber 3, carbs 6, protein 9

Coriander Cod and Peas

Preparation time: 10 minutes **Cooking time:** 15 minutes **Servings:** 4

Ingredients:
- 1 pound cod fillets, skinless, boneless and cubed
- 2 spring onions, chopped
- 1 cup fresh peas
- 2 green chilies, chopped
- ½ tablespoon lemon juice
- 1 tablespoon coriander, chopped
- A pinch of salt and black pepper
- 1 cup chicken stock

Directions:
In your instant pot, combine the cod fillets with the spring onions and the other ingredients, toss, put the lid on and cook on High for 15 minutes. Release the pressure naturally for 10 minutes, divide the mix between plates and serve.

Nutrition: calories 210, fat 8, fiber 3, carbs 6, protein 14

Shrimp and Sauce

Preparation time: 5 minutes **Cooking time:** *7 minutes* **Servings:** *4*

Ingredients:
- 1 pound shrimp, peeled and deveined
- 2 tablespoons avocado oil
- 4 spring onions, chopped
- 2 garlic cloves, minced
- 1 tablespoon ginger, grated
- Salt and black pepper to the taste
- Juice of 1 orange
- 1 tablespoon orange zest, grated
- 1 tablespoon chives, chopped

Directions:
Set the instant pot on sauté mode, add the oil, heat it up, add the garlic, spring onions and the ginger and sauté for 2 minutes. Add the shrimp and the rest of the ingredients, put the lid on and cook on High for 5 minutes. Release the pressure fast for 5 minutes, divide the mix into bowls and serve.

Nutrition: calories 200, fat 12, fiber 3, carbs 6, protein 11

Herbed Cod Mix

Preparation time: 5 minutes **Cooking time:** *12 minutes* **Servings:** *4*

Ingredients:
- 1 pound cod fillets, boneless, skinless and cubed
- 1 tablespoon olive oil
- 1 red onion, sliced
- 1 tablespoon chives, chopped
- 1 tablespoon cilantro, chopped
- 1 tablespoon basil, chopped
- 1 cup cherry tomatoes, halved
- 1 avocado, peeled, pitted and cubed
- 2 garlic cloves, minced
- Salt and black pepper to the taste

Directions:
Set the instant pot on Sauté mode, add the oil, heat it up, add the onion and garlic and sauté for 2 minutes. Add the fish and the rest of the ingredients, put the lid on and cook on High for 10 minutes. Release the pressure fast for 5 minutes, divide everything into bowls and serve.

Nutrition: calories 132, fat 9, fiber 2, carbs 5, protein 11

Salmon Curry

*Preparation time: 10 minutes **Cooking time:** 14 minutes **Servings:** 4*

Ingredients:
- 1 pound salmon fillets, boneless, skinless and cubed
- 1 red onion, chopped
- 2 tablespoons olive oil
- 1 cup fish stock
- ½ cup heavy cream
- 1 tablespoon yellow curry paste
- 2 garlic cloves, minced
- ½ teaspoon turmeric powder
- A pinch of salt and black pepper
- 2 tablespoons cilantro, chopped

Directions:
Set your instant pot on Sauté mode, add the oil, heat it up, add the onion, garlic , curry paste and turmeric and sauté for 4 minutes, Add the fish and the rest of the ingredients, put the lid on and cook on High for 10 minutes. Release the pressure naturally for 10 minutes, divide the mix into bowls and serve.

Nutrition: calories 200, fat 12, fiber 2, carbs 6, protein 11

Mustard Cod

*Preparation time: 10 minutes **Cooking time:** 12 minutes **Servings:** 4*

Ingredients:
- 4 cod fillets, boneless
- 1 yellow onion , chopped
- 2 tablespoons olive oil
- Juice of 1 lime
- 1 tablespoon mustard
- 1 teaspoon turmeric powder
- 2 garlic cloves, minced
- Salt and black pepper to the taste
- 1 tablespoon parsley, chopped

Directions:
Set the instant pot on Sauté mode, add the oil, heat it up, add the onion, lime juice, mustard, garlic and turmeric and sauté for 2 minutes. Add the fish and the rest of the ingredients, put the lid on and cook on High for 10 minutes. Release the pressure naturally for 10 minutes, divide the fish and sauce between plates and serve.

Nutrition: calories 200, fat 12, fiber 2, carbs 6, protein 9

Oregano Trout Mix

*Preparation time: 10 minutes **Cooking time:** 12 minutes **Servings:** 4*

Ingredients:
- 4 trout fillets, boneless
- 1 tablespoon olive oil
- 4 scallions, chopped
- ½ teaspoon chili powder
- ½ teaspoon sweet paprika
- 1 tablespoon oregano, chopped
- ½ cup fish stock
- A pinch of salt and black pepper

Directions:
Set the instant pot on Sauté mode, add the oil, heat it up, add the scallions, chili powder and the paprika and sauté for 2 minutes. Add the fish and the other ingredients, toss, put the lid on and cook on High for 10 minutes. Release the pressure naturally for 10 minutes, divide the mix between plates and serve.

Nutrition: calories 211, fat 13, fiber 2, carbs 7, protein 11

Lemon Shrimp

*Preparation time: 5 minutes **Cooking time:** 6 minutes **Servings:** 4*

Ingredients:
- 1 pound shrimp, peeled and deveined
- 1 tablespoon olive oil
- 2 scallions, chopped
- Zest of 1 lemon, grated
- Juice of 1 lemon
- ½ cup fish stock
- 2 tablespoons chives, chopped
- A pinch of salt and black pepper

Directions:
In your instant pot, combine the shrimp with the oil, scallions and the rest of the ingredients, put the lid on and cook on High for 5 minutes. Release the pressure fast for 5 minutes, divide the mix into bowls and serve.

Nutrition: calories 200, fat 12, fiber 4, carbs 6, protein 8

Tomato Shrimp

Preparation time: 5 minutes **Cooking time:** *5 minutes* **Servings:** *4*

Ingredients:
- 2 pounds shrimp, peeled and deveined
- ½ pound cherry tomatoes, halved
- ½ teaspoon rosemary, dried
- ½ teaspoon cumin, ground
- ½ cup chicken stock
- A pinch of salt and black pepper
- 1 tablespoon parsley, chopped
- 2 garlic cloves, minced

Directions:
In your instant pot, combine the shrimp with the cherry tomatoes, rosemary and the rest of the ingredients, put the lid on and cook on High for 5 minutes. Release the pressure fast for 5 minutes, divide the mix into bowls and serve.

Nutrition: calories 232, fat 7, fiber 3, carbs 7, protein 9

Salmon and Cauliflower Mix

Preparation time: 5 minutes **Cooking time:** *12 minutes* **Servings:** *4*

Ingredients:
- 2 pounds salmon fillets, boneless and roughly cubed
- 1 cup cauliflower florets
- 1 red onion, chopped
- 2 tablespoons olive oil
- ½ teaspoon garlic powder
- ½ teaspoon cumin , ground
- A pinch of salt and black pepper
- 1 cup chicken stock
- 2 tablespoons tomato puree
- 1 tablespoon cilantro, chopped

Directions:
Set the instant pot on Sauté mode, add the oil, heat it up, add the onion, garlic powder and the cumin and sauté for 2 minutes. Add the salmon and the other ingredients, put the lid on and cook on High for 10 minutes. Release the pressure fast for 5 minutes, divide the mix between plates and serve.

Nutrition: calories 232, fat 9, fiber 2, carbs 6, protein 8

Trout and Spinach

*Preparation time: 10 minutes **Cooking time:** 12 minutes **Servings:** 4*

Ingredients:
- 4 trout fillets, boneless
- 1 tablespoon olive oil
- 1 yellow onion, chopped
- ½ teaspoon sweet paprika
- ½ teaspoon chili powder
- ½ cup chicken stock
- 2 cups baby spinach
- 2 garlic cloves, minced
- A pinch of salt and black pepper
- 1 tablespoon cilantro, chopped

Directions:

Set the instant pot on Sauté mode, add the oil, heat it up, add the onion, chili powder, garlic and paprika and sauté for 2 minutes. Add the fish and the rest of the ingredients, put the lid on and cook on High for 10 minutes. Release the pressure naturally for 10 minutes, divide the mix between plates and serve.

Nutrition: calories 200, fat 13, fiber 3, carbs 6, protein 11

Spicy Mussels

*Preparation time: 5 minutes **Cooking time:** 8 minutes **Servings:** 4*

Ingredients:
- 1 pound mussels, debearded
- 1 tablespoon olive oil
- 1 red onion, sliced
- ½ teaspoon hot paprika
- 1 cup chicken stock
- 2 tablespoons chili pepper, minced
- Juice of 1 lime
- A pinch of salt and black pepper
- 1 tablespoon chives, chopped

Directions:

In your instant pot, combine the mussels with the oil, the onion and the other ingredients, toss, put the lid on and cook on High for 8 minutes. Release the pressure fast for 5 minutes, divide the mussels mix into bowls and serve.

Nutrition: calories 200, fat 12, fiber 2, carbs 6, protein 9

Sage Salmon

Preparation time: 10 minutes *Cooking time:* 12 minutes *Servings:* 4

Ingredients:
- 4 salmon fillets, boneless
- 1 tablespoon avocado oil
- 1 tablespoon sage, chopped
- 1 red onion, chopped
- 1 cup cherry tomatoes, halved
- A pinch of salt and black pepper
- 2 tablespoons chives, chopped

Directions:
Set the instant pot on Sauté mode, add the oil, heat it up, add the onion and sauté for 2 minutes Add the salmon and the rest of the ingredients, put the lid on and cook on High for 10 minutes. Release the pressure naturally for 10 minutes, divide the whole mix between plates and serve.

Nutrition: calories 200, fat 12, fiber 2, carbs 5, protein 6

Cod Meatballs Mix

Preparation time: 10 minutes *Cooking time:* 14 minutes *Servings:* 4

Ingredients:
- 1 tablespoon olive oil
- 1 egg, whisked
- 1 pound cod meat, minced
- 1 teaspoon lemon juice
- 1 tablespoon cilantro, chopped
- ½ teaspoon rosemary, dried
- ½ teaspoon chili powder
- A pinch of salt and black pepper
- 1 cup tomato sauce

Directions:
In a bowl, combine cod with the egg and the other ingredients except the tomato sauce and the oil, stir and shape medium meatballs out of this mix. Set the instant pot on Sauté mode, add the oil, heat it up, add the meatballs and cook them for 2 minutes on each side. Add the tomato sauce, put the lid on and cook on High for 10 minutes. Release the pressure naturally for 10 minutes, divide the mix between plates and serve.

Nutrition: calories 192, fat 9, fiber 2, carbs 8, protein 7

Creamy Cod

Preparation time: 10 minutes Cooking time: 12 minutes Servings: 4

Ingredients:
- 1 pound cod fillets, skinless, boneless and cubed
- 1 yellow onion, chopped
- 1 tablespoon olive oil
- 1 carrot, peeled and sliced
- ½ teaspoon turmeric powder
- ½ teaspoon chili powder
- 1 cup heavy cream
- A pinch of salt and black pepper
- 1 tablespoon chives, chopped

Directions:
Set the instant pot on Sauté mode, add the oil, heat it up, add the onion, chili powder and turmeric and sauté for 2 minutes. Add the fish and the other ingredients, toss , put the lid on and cook on High for 10 minutes. Release the pressure naturally for 10 minutes, divide the mix into bowls and serve.

Nutrition: calories 210, fat 9, fiber 2, carbs 6, protein 7

Salmon and Pesto Sauce

Preparation time: 5 minutes Cooking time: 15 minutes Servings: 4

Ingredients:
- 4 salmon fillets, boneless
- 2 scallions, chopped
- 2 tablespoons basil pesto
- Juice of 1 lime
- 2 tablespoons olive oil
- ½ teaspoon rosemary, dried
- 2 garlic cloves, minced
- 2 tablespoons parsley, chopped
- A pinch of salt and black pepper
- 2 tablespoons balsamic vinegar

Directions:
Set the instant pot on Sauté mode, add the oil, heat it up, add the scallions, pesto, lime juice and garlic and sauté for 5 minutes. Add the fish and the rest of the ingredients, toss, put the lid on and cook on High for 10 minutes. Release the pressure fast for 5 minutes, divide the mix between plates and serve.

Nutrition: calories 200, fat 10, fiber 2, carbs 5, protein 9

Garlic Sea Bass Mix

*Preparation time: 10 minutes **Cooking time:** 14 minutes **Servings:** 4*

Ingredients:
- 1 pound sea bass fillets, boneless and cubed
- 2 tablespoons olive oil
- 2 tablespoons garlic, minced
- 2 tablespoons lemon juice
- 1 teaspoon lemon zest, grated
- ½ cup tomato passata
- A pinch of salt and black pepper

Directions:
Set the instant pot on Sauté mode, add the oil, heat it up, add the garlic and sauté for 2 minutes. Add the sea bass and the remaining ingredients, put the lid on and cook on High for 12 minutes. Release the pressure naturally for 10 minutes, divide everything into bowls and serve.

Nutrition: calories 200, fat 13, fiber 3, carbs 6, protein 11

Shrimp and Roasted Peppers

*Preparation time: 5 minutes **Cooking time:** 10 minutes **Servings:** 4*

Ingredients:
- 3 ounces roasted red peppers, cut into strips
- 2 tablespoons avocado oil
- 4 scallions, chopped
- 1 pound shrimp, peeled and deveined
- 2 tablespoons garlic, chopped
- 1 tablespoon Creole seasoning
- 1 cup chicken stock
- 1 tablespoon cilantro, chopped

Directions:
Set your instant pot on Sauté mode, add the oil, heat it up, add the scallions and the garlic and sauté for 2 minutes. Add the shrimp and the rest of the ingredients except the cilantro, put the lid on and cook on High for 8 minutes. Release the pressure fast for 5 minutes, divide the mix between plates and serve with the cilantro sprinkled on top.

Nutrition: calories 211, fat 12, fiber 3, carbs 6, protein 7

Tuna and Green Beans

Preparation time: 10 minutes **Cooking time:** 12 minutes **Servings:** 4

Ingredients:
- 1 yellow onion, chopped
- 2 cups green beans, trimmed and halved
- ½ teaspoon chili powder
- ½ teaspoon garam masala
- 1 tablespoon olive oil
- A pinch of salt and black pepper
- 1 pound tuna fillets, boneless, skinless and cubed
- 1 tablespoon parsley, chopped

Directions:
Set your instant pot on Sauté mode, add the oil, heat it up, add the onion, chili powder and garam masala, stir and cook for 2 minutes. Add the tuna and the rest of the ingredients, toss, put the lid on and cook on High for 10 minutes. Release the pressure naturally for 10 minutes, divide the mix between plates and serve.

Nutrition: calories 200, fat 12, fiber 2, carbs 6, protein 13

Sea Bass with Endives and Olives

Preparation time: 5 minutes **Cooking time:** 12 minutes **Servings:** 4

Ingredients:
- 1 pound sea bass fillets, boneless
- 2 endives, shredded
- 2 tablespoons olive oil
- 4 scallions, chopped
- 1 cup black olives, pitted
- 1 cup tomato sauce
- A pinch of salt and black pepper
- 1 tablespoon cilantro, chopped

Directions:
In your instant pot, combine the sea bass with the endives, the oil and the other ingredients, put the lid on and cook on High for 12 minutes. Release the pressure fast for 5 minutes, divide the mix between plates and serve.

Nutrition: calories 200, fat 9, fiber 3, carbs 7, protein 10

Turmeric Salmon

Preparation time: 5 minutes *Cooking time:* 12 minutes *Servings:* 4

Ingredients:
- 4 salmon fillets, boneless
- 3 scallions, chopped
- ½ cup chicken stock
- 2 tablespoons olive oil
- 1 teaspoon turmeric powder
- 1 tablespoon ginger, grated
- 2 tablespoons chives, chopped

Directions:
Set the instant pot on Sauté mode, add the oil, heat it up, add the scallions and ginger and sauté for 2 minutes. Add the fish and the other ingredients, toss gently, put the lid on and cook on High for 10 minutes. Release the pressure fast for 5 minutes, divide the mix between plates and serve.

Nutrition: calories 211, fat 13, fiber 4, carbs 7, protein 10

Balsamic Tuna

Preparation time: 10 minutes *Cooking time:* 12 minutes *Servings:* 4

Ingredients:
1. 2 pounds tuna fillets, boneless, skinless and roughly cubed
2. 2 tablespoons olive oil
3. 2 tablespoons balsamic vinegar
4. 1 cup chicken stock
5. 2 garlic cloves, minced
6. 1 red onion, chopped
7. A pinch of salt and black pepper
8. 1 tablespoon parsley, chopped

Directions:
Set your instant pot on Sauté mode, add the onion and the garlic and sauté for 2 minutes. Add the tuna and the other ingredients, toss gently, put the lid on and cook on High for 10 minutes. Release the pressure naturally for 10 minutes, divide the mix into bowls and serve.

Nutrition: calories 220, fat 12, fiber 3, carbs 6, protein 13

Chives Shrimp Masala

Preparation time: *5 minutes* ***Cooking time:*** *5 minutes* ***Servings:*** *4*

Ingredients:
- 1 pound shrimp, peeled and deveined
- 2 scallions, chopped
- 1 tablespoon olive oil
- ½ cup chicken stock
- 2 tablespoons chives, chopped
- 1 tablespoon garam masala
- Juice of 1 lemon
- A pinch of salt and black pepper

Directions:
In your instant pot, combine the shrimp with the scallions and the other ingredients, toss, put the lid on and cook on High for 5 minutes. Release the pressure fast for 5 minutes, divide the mix into bowls and serve.

Nutrition: calories 200, fat 12, fiber 3, carbs 6, protein 11

Shrimp with Brussels Sprouts Mix

Preparation time: *5 minutes* ***Cooking time:*** *6 minutes* ***Servings:*** *4*

Ingredients:
- 2 pounds shrimp, peeled and deveined
- ½ cup Brussels sprouts, trimmed and halved
- 1 cup chicken stock
- 1 red onion, sliced
- 2 garlic cloves, minced
- 1 tablespoon dill, chopped

Directions:
In your instant pot, combine the shrimp with the sprouts and the other ingredients, toss gently, put the lid on and cook on High for 6 minutes. Release the pressure fast for 5 minutes, divide the mix into bowls and serve.

Nutrition: calories 182, fat 10, fiber 2, carbs 5, protein 6

Shrimp and Radish Mix

*Preparation time: 5 minutes **Cooking time:** 10 minutes **Servings:** 4*

Ingredients:
- 1 pound shrimp, peeled and deveined
- 2 scallions, chopped
- 2 chili peppers, chopped
- 2 tablespoons avocado oil
- 2 tablespoons balsamic vinegar
- 1 cup radishes, cubed
- A pinch of salt and black pepper
- ½ cup chives, chopped

Directions:
Set your instant pot on Sauté mode, add the oil, heat it up, add the scallions, chili pepper and the radishes, stir and cook for 5 minutes. Add the shrimp and the ingredients, put the lid on and cook on High for 5 minutes. Release the pressure fast for 5 minutes, divide the mix between plates and serve.

Nutrition: calories 192, fat 11, fiber 3, carbs 6, protein 9

Chili Trout Mix

*Preparation time: 10 minutes **Cooking time:** 13 minutes **Servings:** 4*

Ingredients:
- 1 pound trout fillets, boneless
- 4 scallions, chopped
- 1 red chili, minced
- 1 green chili, minced
- 2 tablespoons avocado oil
- ½ cup chicken stock
- ½ teaspoon red pepper flakes
- 2 tablespoons oregano, chopped

Directions:
Set your instant pot on Sauté mode, add the oil, heat it up, add the scallions and the chilies and sauté for 5 minutes. Add the trout and the rest of the ingredients, put the lid on and cook on High for 8 minutes. Release the pressure naturally for 10 minutes, divide the mix between plates and serve.

Nutrition: calories 132, fat 5, fiber 3, carbs 6, protein 6

Shrimp and Salsa

Preparation time: 5 minutes **Cooking time:** *6 minutes* **Servings:** *4*

Ingredients:
- 2 pounds shrimp, peeled and deveined
- 1 cup kalamata olives, pitted
- 1 cup cherry tomatoes, halved
- 1 tablespoon olive oil
- 2 scallions, chopped
- 1 tablespoon capers, drained
- 2 spring onions, chopped
- 1 tablespoon chives, chopped
- 1 tablespoon sweet paprika

Directions:
In your instant pot, combine the shrimp with the tomatoes, olives and the other ingredients, toss, put the lid on and cook on High for 6 minutes. Release the pressure fast for 5 minutes, divide everything into bowls and serve.

Nutrition: calories 162, fat 6, fiber 1, carbs 6, protein 8

Shrimp Salad

Preparation time: 5 minutes **Cooking time:** *8 minutes* **Servings:** *4*

Ingredients:
- 2 pounds big shrimp, peeled and deveined
- 2 red onions, sliced
- 1 cup baby spinach
- 1 cup cherry tomatoes, halved
- 1 cup radishes, halved
- 1 tablespoon olive oil
- ½ cup basil, chopped
- 1 cup chicken stock
- A pinch of salt and black pepper

Directions:
Set your instant pot on Sauté mode, add the oil, heat it up, add the onions and sauté for 2 minutes. Add the shrimp and the rest of the ingredients, put the lid on and cook on High for 6 minutes. Release the pressure fast for 5 minutes, divide the salad into bowls and serve warm.

Nutrition: calories 200, fat 14, fiber 3, carbs 8, protein 10

Flounder Fillets and Berries Mix

*Preparation time: 5 minutes **Cooking time:** 14 minutes **Servings:** 4*

Ingredients:
- 4 flounder fillets, boneless
- 2 tablespoons olive oil
- 1 cup blackberries
- ½ cup chicken stock
- 1 yellow onion, chopped
- 2 tablespoons parsley, chopped
- 1 tablespoon lemon juice

Directions:
Set your instant pot on Sauté mode, add the oil, heat it up, add the onion and sauté for 2 minutes. Add the flounder fillets and the rest of the ingredients, put the lid on and cook on High for 12 minutes. Release the pressure fast for 5 minutes, divide the mix between plates and serve.

Nutrition: calories 200, fat 12, fiber 3, carbs 7, protein 10

Tuna and Cucumber Mix

*Preparation time: 5 minutes **Cooking time:** 12 minutes **Servings:** 4*

Ingredients:
- 1 tablespoon olive oil
- 1 yellow onion, chopped
- 4 tuna fillets, boneless, skinless and cubed
- 1 cup cucumber, cubed
- 3 garlic cloves, minced
- ½ cup chicken stock
- ½ teaspoon chili powder
- ¼ cup parsley, chopped
- 1 tablespoon lime juice

Directions:
Set the instant pot on Sauté mode, add the oil, heat it up, add the onion and the garlic and sauté for 2 minutes. Add the fish and the rest of the ingredients, put the lid on and cook on High for 10 minutes. Release the pressure fast for 5 minutes, divide the mix into bowls and serve.

Nutrition: calories 199, fat 7, fiber 4, carbs 7, protein 12

Shrimp and Cabbage Mix

Preparation time: 5 minutes **Cooking time:** *12 minutes* **Servings:** *4*

Ingredients:
- 2 pounds shrimp, peeled and deveined
- 1 cup red cabbage, shredded
- 2 scallions, chopped
- 2 tablespoons olive oil
- 1 cup cherry tomatoes, halved
- 1 teaspoon sweet paprika
- ½ cup chicken stock
- 1 tablespoon chives, chopped

Directions:
Set the instant pot on Sauté mode, add the oil, heat it up, add the scallions and the paprika and sauté for 2 minutes. Add the cabbage and sauté for 5 minutes more. Add the shrimp and the remaining ingredients, toss, put the lid on and cook on High for 5 minutes. Release the pressure fast for 5 minutes, divide into bowls and serve.

Nutrition: calories 172, fat 11, fiber 4, carbs 7, protein 9

Tuna, Green Beans and Avocado Mix

Preparation time: 5 minutes **Cooking time:** *10 minutes* **Servings:** *4*

Ingredients:
- 2 pounds tuna fillets, boneless, skinless and cubed
- 1 avocado, peeled, pitted and roughly cubed
- 1 cup green beans, trimmed and halved
- 3 scallions, chopped
- 2 tablespoons olive oil
- 2 tablespoons parsley, chopped
- 4 garlic cloves, minced
- ½ cup chicken stock
- A pinch of salt and black pepper

Directions:
Set your instant pot on Sauté mode, add the oil, heat it up, add the scallions and the garlic and sauté for 2 minutes. Add the tuna and the rest of the ingredients, put the lid on and cook on High for 8 minutes. Release the pressure fast for 5 minutes, divide everything into bowls and serve.

Nutrition: calories 200, fat 12, fiber 2, carbs 6, protein 11

Cod and Cauliflower

*Preparation time: 10 minutes **Cooking time:** 12 minutes **Servings:** 4*

Ingredients:
- 1 pound cod fillets, boneless and skinless
- 1 cup tomato passata
- 1 tablespoon avocado oil
- 2 cups cauliflower florets
- 1 teaspoon chili powder
- ½ teaspoon cumin, ground
- A pinch of salt and black pepper
- 2 tablespoons basil, chopped
- 1 cup chicken stock

Directions:
In your instant pot, combine the cod with the tomato passata, the cauliflower and the rest of the ingredients, put the lid on and cook on High for 12 minutes. Release the pressure naturally for 10 minutes, divide everything between plates and serve.

Nutrition: calories 211, fat 14, fiber 3, fiber 6, carbs 11

Salmon with Radish and Corn

*Preparation time: 10 minutes **Cooking time:** 14 minutes **Servings:** 4*

Ingredients:
- 2 pounds salmon fillets, skinless, boneless and roughly cubed
- 1 cup corn
- 1 cup radishes, halved
- 4 scallions, chopped
- 1 tablespoon olive oil
- 1 cup chicken stock
- 1 tablespoon old bay seasoning
- A pinch of salt and black pepper
- 1 tablespoon chives, chopped

Directions:
Set the instant pot on Sauté mode, add the oil, heat it up, add the scallions and sauté for 4 minutes. Add the salmon and the other ingredients, put the lid on and cook on High for 10 minutes. Release the pressure naturally for 10 minutes, divide the mix between plates and serve.

Nutrition: calories 200, fat 11, fiber 2, carbs 6, protein 8

Cinnamon Shrimp

Preparation time: 5 minutes **Cooking time:** *12 minutes* **Servings:** *4*

Ingredients:
1. 1 pound shrimp, peeled and deveined
2. 1 tablespoon olive oil
3. 1 tablespoon cinnamon powder
4. 2 red onions, roughly cubed
5. 1 red chili, chopped
6. A pinch of salt and black pepper
7. ½ tablespoon chives, chopped

Directions:
Set the instant pot on Sauté mode, add the oil, heat it up, add the onions and chili and sauté for 5 minutes. Add the shrimp and the other ingredients, toss, put the lid on and cook on High for 7 minutes. Release the pressure fast for 5 minutes, divide the mix into bowls and serve.

Nutrition: calories 224, fat 13, fiber 3, carbs 7, protein 11

Cod Chili

Preparation time: 10 minutes **Cooking time:** *10 minutes* **Servings:** *4*

Ingredients:
- 1 pound cod fillets, boneless, skinless and cubed
- 1 cup tomato puree
- 1 teaspoon chili powder
- ½ teaspoon hot paprika
- 1 tablespoon lemon juice
- A pinch of salt and black pepper
- 1 yellow onion, chopped
- 2 tablespoons olive oil

Directions:
Set your instant pot on Sauté mode, add the oil, heat it up, add the onion, chili powder and the paprika and sauté for 2 minutes. Add the fish and the rest of the ingredients, put the lid on and cook on High for 8 minutes. Release the pressure naturally for 10 minutes, divide the mix into bowls and serve.

Nutrition: calories 221, fat 12, fiber 3, carbs 6, protein 8

Creamy Tilapia

*Preparation time: 10 minutes **Cooking time:** 12 minutes **Servings:** 4*

Ingredients:
- 1 pound tilapia, boneless, skinless and cubed
- 2 tablespoons olive oil
- 3 scallions, chopped
- 1 cup chicken stock
- ¾ cup heavy cream
- 1 tablespoon chives, chopped

Directions:
Set your instant pot on Sauté mode, add the oil, heat it up, add the scallions and sauté for 2 minutes. Add the fish and the rest of the ingredients, put the lid on and cook on High for 10 minutes. Release the pressure naturally for 10 minutes, divide the mix into bowls and serve.

Nutrition: calories 231, fat 11, fiber 3, carbs 6, protein 9

Coconut Shrimp and Bok Choy

*Preparation time: 5 minutes **Cooking time:** 12 minutes **Servings:** 4*

Ingredients:
- 2 pounds shrimp, peeled and deveined
- 1 cup bok choy, torn
- ½ cup chicken stock
- 1 red onion, chopped
- 1 tablespoon olive oil
- 1 cup chicken stock
- A pinch of salt and black pepper
- 1 teaspoon coriander powder
- 1 tablespoon cilantro, chopped

Directions:
Set the instant pot on Sauté mode, add the oil, heat it up, add the onion, bok choy and coriander powder and sauté for 5 minutes. Add the shrimp and the rest of the ingredients, put the lid on and cook on High for 7 minutes. Release the pressure fast for 5 minutes, divide the mix into bowls and serve.

Nutrition: calories 192, fat 9, fiber 4, carbs 7, protein 9

Chili Mackerel Mix

Preparation time: 6 minutes *Cooking time:* 12 minutes *Servings:* 4

Ingredients:
- 1 pound mackerel, skinless, boneless and cubed
- 1 red onion, chopped
- 1 tablespoon olive oil
- ½ cup fish stock
- 2 teaspoons chili powder
- 1 tablespoon balsamic vinegar
- 1 cup tomato sauce
- A pinch of salt and black pepper
- 2 tablespoons cilantro, chopped

Directions:
Set the pot on Sauté mode, add the oil, heat it up, add the onion and chili powder and sauté for 2 minutes. Add the mackerel and the rest of the ingredients, put the lid on and cook on High for 10 minutes. Release the pressure fast for 6 minutes, divide the mix into bowls and serve.

Nutrition: calories 232, fat 8, fiber 2, carbs 6, protein 11

Shrimp with Spinach and Mango

Preparation time: 5 minutes *Cooking time:* 6 minutes *Servings:* 4

Ingredients:
1. 1 pound shrimp, peeled and deveined
2. 1 cup baby spinach
3. 1 cup mango, peeled and cubed
4. 2 tablespoons olive oil
5. 2 spring onions, chopped
6. ½ cup tomatoes, cubed
7. 2 tablespoons balsamic vinegar
8. 1 cup chicken stock
9. 1 tablespoon chives, chopped

Directions:
Set the instant pot on Sauté mode, add the oil, heat it up, add the spring onions and tomatoes and sauté for 2 minutes Add the shrimp, spinach and the rest of the ingredients, put the lid on and cook on High for 4 minutes Release the pressure fast for 5 minutes, divide the mix into bowls and serve.

Nutrition: calories 232, fat 5, fiber 1, carbs 5, protein 8

Mustard Shrimp and Carrots

Preparation time: 5 minutes **Cooking time:** 8 minutes **Servings:** 4

Ingredients:
- 2 pounds shrimp, peeled and deveined
- 1 cup baby carrots, peeled
- 1 yellow onion, chopped
- A pinch of salt and black pepper
- 1 tablespoon mustard
- 1 tablespoon olive oil
- 1 teaspoon turmeric powder
- 1 tablespoon chives, chopped

Directions:
Set the instant pot on Sauté mode, add the oil, heat it up, add the onion, mustard and the turmeric and sauté for 2 minutes. Add the shrimp and the rest of the ingredients, toss, put the lid on and cook on High for 6 minutes. Release the pressure fast for 5 minutes, divide the mix into bowls and serve.

Nutrition: calories 222, fat 9, fiber 2, carbs 6, protein 7

Salmon and Zucchini Mix

Preparation time: 5 minutes Cooking time: 12 minutes Servings: 4

Ingredients:
1. 1 pound salmon fillets, boneless
2. 1 zucchini, roughly cubed
3. 1 yellow onion, chopped
4. 2 tablespoons olive oil
5. 1 garlic clove, minced
6. 10 ounces canned tomatoes, chopped
7. 1 tablespoon parsley, chopped

Directions:
Set your instant pot on Sauté mode, add the oil, heat it up, add the onion and the garlic and sauté for 2 minutes. Add the fish and the rest of the ingredients, put the lid on and cook on High for 10 minutes. Release the pressure fast for 5 minutes, divide the mix between plates and serve.

Nutrition: calories 200, fat 7, fiber 3, carbs 6, protein 8

Instant Pot Vegetable Recipes

Lime Green Beans

Preparation time: *5 minutes* *Cooking time:* *15 minutes* *Servings:* *4*

Ingredients:
1. 1 pound green beans, trimmed
2. 1 tablespoon lime zest, grated
3. 1 tablespoon water
4. Juice of 1 lime
5. 1 cup water
6. A pinch of salt and black pepper

Directions:
Put the water in your instant pot, add the steamer basket inside, and combine the green beans with the other ingredients into the basket Put the lid on, cook on High for 15 minutes, release the pressure fast for 5 minutes, divide everything between plates and serve.

Nutrition: calories 121, fat 2, fiber 1, carbs 5, protein 6

Balsamic Carrots

Preparation time: *5 minutes* *Cooking time:* *20 minutes* *Servings:* *4*

Ingredients:
- 1 pound baby carrots, peeled
- 2 tablespoons olive oil
- A pinch of salt and black pepper
- ¼ cup veggie stock
- 2 teaspoons balsamic vinegar
- 1 teaspoon Italian seasoning

Directions:
In your instant pot, combine the baby carrots with the oil, salt, pepper and the other ingredients, toss, put the lid on and cook on High for 20 minutes. Release the pressure fast for 5 minutes, divide the mix between plates and serve.

Nutrition: calories 120, fat 1, fiber 2, carbs 4, protein 2

Creamy Endives

Preparation time: 5 minutes **Cooking time:** *15 minutes* **Servings:** *4*

Ingredients:
- 2 endives, halved lengthwise
- ½ cup coconut cream
- 2 scallions, chopped
- 1 teaspoon turmeric powder
- 1 teaspoon basil, dried

Directions:
In your instant pot, combine the endives with the cream, scallions and the other ingredients, put the lid on and cook on High for 15 minutes. Release the pressure fast for 5 minutes, divide the endives between plates and serve.

Nutrition: calories 110, fat 2, fiber 2, carbs 4, protein 3

Parmesan Artichokes

Preparation time: 5 minutes **Cooking time:** *20 minutes* **Servings:** *4*

Ingredients:
- 4 artichokes, trimmed and halved
- 1 teaspoon chili powder
- ½ cup chicken stock
- 1 tablespoon coriander, ground
- 2 garlic cloves, chopped
- 1 cup parmesan, grated
- A pinch of salt and black pepper

Directions:
In your instant pot, combine the artichokes with the stock, chili powder and the other ingredients except the parmesan, toss, put the lid on and cook on High for 20 minutes. Release the pressure fast for 5 minutes, divide the artichokes between plates and serve with the parmesan sprinkled on top.

Nutrition: calories 140, fat 2, fiber 2, carbs 5, protein 2

Chives Fennel

Preparation time: 5 minutes **Cooking time:** *15 minutes* **Servings:** *4*

Ingredients:
- 2 fennel bulbs, sliced
- 1 red onion, chopped
- 1 tablespoon olive oil
- ½ cup chicken stock
- A pinch of salt and black pepper
- 1 tablespoon chives, chopped

Directions:
Set the instant pot on Sauté mode, add the oil, heat it up, add the onion and sauté for 2 minutes. Add the fennel and the other ingredients, toss, put the lid on and cook on High for 13 minutes. Release the pressure fast for 5 minutes, divide the fennel mix between plates and serve.

Nutrition: calories 120, fat 2, fiber 3, carbs 5, protein 6

Mustard Green Beans

Preparation time: 10 minutes **Cooking time:** *15 minutes* **Servings:** *4*

Ingredients:
- 1 tablespoon olive oil
- 2 scallions, chopped
- 2 garlic cloves, minced
- 1 pound green beans, trimmed
- 1 tablespoon mustard
- 1 tablespoon lime juice
- 1 cup veggie stock
- A pinch of salt and black pepper
- A pinch of red pepper flakes, crushed

Directions:
Set the instant pot on Sauté mode, add the oil, heat it up, add the scallions and the garlic and sauté for 2 minutes. Add the mustard, lime juice and the stock, stir and sauté for 3 minutes more. Add the green beans, salt, pepper and the pepper flakes, toss, put the lid on and cook on High for 10 minutes. Release the pressure naturally for 10 minutes, divide the mix between plates and serve.

Nutrition: calories 142, fat 2, fiber 2, carbs 4, protein 3

Dill Asparagus

Preparation time: *5 minutes* ***Cooking time:*** *8 minutes* ***Servings:*** *4*

Ingredients:
- 1 pounds asparagus spears, trimmed and halved
- 2 tablespoons avocado oil
- 2 tablespoons lemon juice
- A pinch of salt and black pepper
- 1 cup water
- 2 tablespoons dill, chopped

Directions:
Put the water in the instant pot, add the trivet inside and combine the asparagus with the other ingredients in the steamer basket. Put the lid on, cook on High for 8 minutes, release the pressure fast for 5 minutes, divide everything between plates and serve.

Nutrition: calories 120, fat 2, fiber 2, carbs 4, protein 2

Tomato and Goat Cheese Mix

Preparation time: *5 minutes* ***Cooking time:*** *15 minutes* ***Servings:*** *4*

Ingredients:
- 1 pound cherry tomatoes, halved
- 1 tablespoon olive oil
- 1 yellow onion, chopped
- A pinch of salt and black pepper
- 1 cup heavy cream
- 1 cup goat cheese, crumbled

Directions:
Set the instant pot on Sauté mode, add the oil, heat it up, add the onion and sauté for 3 minutes. Add the tomatoes and the other ingredients, toss, put the lid on and cook on High for 12 minutes. Release the pressure fast for 5 minutes, divide the mix between plates and serve.

Nutrition: calories 134, fat 2, fiber 3, carbs 4, protein 5

Asparagus and Radish Mix

*Preparation time: 5 minutes **Cooking time:** 8 minutes **Servings:** 4*

Ingredients:
- 1 pound asparagus, trimmed and halved
- 1 cup radishes, halved
- 2 tablespoons olive oil
- 2 scallions, chopped
- 2 teaspoons orange zest, grated
- 1 teaspoon chili powder
- A pinch of salt and black pepper

Directions:
In your instant pot, combine the asparagus with the radishes and the other ingredients, toss, put the lid on and cook on High for 8 minutes. Release the pressure fast for 5 minutes, divide the mix between plates and serve.

Nutrition: calories 121, fat 3, fiber 2, carbs 3, protein 3

Beets Sauté

*Preparation time: 10 minutes **Cooking time:** 20 minutes **Servings:** 4*

Ingredients:
- 1 cup chicken stock
- 4 beets, peeled and roughly cubed
- 1 red onion, sliced
- 2 tablespoons olive oil
- A pinch of salt and black pepper
- 1 tablespoon chives, chopped
- 1 tablespoon balsamic vinegar

Directions:
Set the instant pot on Sauté mode, add the oil, heat it up, add the onion and sauté for 2 minutes Add the beets and the rest of the ingredients, toss, put the lid on and cook on High for 18 minutes Release the pressure naturally for 10 minutes, divide everything between plates and serve.

Nutrition: calories 162, fat 3, fiber 1, carbs 4, protein 5

Creamy Brussels Sprouts

*Preparation time: 10 minutes **Cooking time:** 20 minutes **Servings:** 4*

Ingredients:
- 1 pound Brussels sprouts, trimmed
- 1 cup heavy cream
- 1 red onion, chopped
- 2 tablespoons olive oil
- 2 green onions, chopped
- 1 teaspoon rosemary, dried
- A pinch of salt and black pepper
- 1 tablespoon cilantro, chopped

Directions:
Set the instant pot on Sauté mode, add the oil, heat it up, add the onion, green onions and rosemary, stir and sauté for 5 minutes. Add the Brussels sprouts and the other ingredients, toss, put the lid on and cook on High for 15 minutes. Release the pressure naturally for 10 minutes, divide the mix between plates and serve.

Nutrition: calories 142, fat 2, fiber 1, carbs 3, protein 4

Cauliflower and Walnuts Mix

*Preparation time: 10 minutes **Cooking time:** 20 minutes **Servings:** 4*

Ingredients:
- 1 pound cauliflower florets
- 1 red onion, chopped
- 2 tablespoons olive oil
- 1 teaspoon turmeric powder
- 1 teaspoon fennel seeds
- ½ cup veggie stock
- 1 tablespoon chives, chopped
- 1 tablespoon walnuts, chopped

Directions:
Set the instant pot on Sauté mode, add the oil, heat it up, add the onion, turmeric and fennel, stir and sauté for 5 minutes. Add the cauliflower and the remaining ingredients, toss, put the lid on and cook on High for 15 minutes. Release the pressure naturally for 10 minutes, divide the mix between plates and serve.

Nutrition: calories 152, fat 2, fiber 2, carbs 4, protein 5

Garlic Tomato Mix

Preparation time: 10 minutes *Cooking time:* 15 minutes *Servings:* 4

Ingredients:
- 1 pound cherry tomatoes, halved
- 1 red onion, chopped
- 2 tablespoons avocado oil
- ½ cup veggie stock
- 4 garlic cloves, minced
- ½ teaspoon chili powder
- ½ teaspoon rosemary, dried
- A pinch of salt and black pepper
- 1 tablespoon cilantro, chopped

Directions:
Set the instant pot on Sauté mode, add the oil, heat it up, add the onion and garlic and sauté for 2 minutes. Add the tomatoes and the other ingredients, toss, put the lid on and cook on High for 13 minutes. Release the pressure naturally for 10 minutes, divide the mix between plates and serve.

Nutrition: calories 121, fat 2, fiber 2, carbs 4, protein 5

Radish and Nuts Mix

Preparation time: 5 minutes *Cooking time:* 15 minutes *Servings:* 4

Ingredients:
- 1 pound radishes, halved
- 2 tablespoons avocado oil
- 3 spring onions, chopped
- 1 tablespoon almonds, chopped
- 1 tablespoon walnuts, chopped
- 1 tablespoon pine nuts, chopped
- Juice of ½ lime
- 1 cup veggie stock

Directions:
In your instant pot, combine the radishes with the oil, spring onions and the rest of the ingredients, put the lid on and cook on High for 15 minutes. Release the pressure naturally for 10 minutes, divide the mix between plates and serve.

Nutrition: calories 110, fat 2, fiber 2, carbs 4, protein 4

Bell Peppers Sauté

Preparation time: 5 minutes **Cooking time:** *15 minutes* **Servings:** *4*

Ingredients:
- 1 pound mixed bell peppers, cut into strips
- A pinch of salt and black pepper
- ½ cup heavy cream
- 1 tablespoon lemon juice
- 1 tablespoon mustard
- 1 tablespoon chives, chopped

Directions:
In your instant pot, combine the bell peppers with the rest of the ingredients, put the lid on and cook on High for 15 minutes. Release the pressure naturally for 5 minutes, divide the mix between plates and serve.

Nutrition: calories 151, fat 2, fiber 3, carbs 5, protein 4

Chives Beets and Onions

Preparation time: 10 minutes **Cooking time:** *25 minutes* **Servings:** *4*

Ingredients:
- 1 pound beets, peeled and cubed
- 2 red onions, chopped
- 1 tablespoon olive oil
- Juice of 1 lime
- A pinch of salt and black pepper
- 1 cup chicken stock
- 3 tablespoons chives, chopped

Directions:
In your instant pot, combine the beets with the oil, the onions and the other ingredients, toss, put the lid on and cook on High for 25 minutes. Release the pressure naturally for 10 minutes, divide the beets between plates and serve.

Nutrition: calories 126, fat 1, fiber 2, carbs 4, protein 4

Dill Potatoes

Preparation time: 10 minutes *Cooking time:* 20 minutes *Servings:* 4

Ingredients:
- 2 pounds red potatoes, peeled and cut into wedges
- 1 cup heavy cream
- 1 teaspoon turmeric powder
- 1 cup beef stock
- A pinch of salt and black pepper
- 1 tablespoon dill, chopped

Directions:
In your instant pot, mix the potatoes with the cream, turmeric and the other ingredients, toss, put the lid on and cook on High for 20 minutes.Release the pressure naturally for 10 minutes, divide the mix between plate and serve.

Nutrition: calories 162, fat 8, fiber 2, carbs 4, protein 7

Parsley Avocado Mix

Preparation time: 5 minutes *Cooking time:* 5 minutes *Servings:* 4

Ingredients:
- 2 avocados, peeled, pitted and cut into wedges
- 1 tablespoon olive oil
- 2 tablespoons parsley, chopped
- 2 spring onions, chopped
- 1 cup Greek yogurt
- A pinch of salt and black pepper

Directions:
In your instant pot, combine the avocados with the oil, parsley and the other ingredients, toss, put the lid on and cook on High for 5 minutes. Release the pressure fast for 5 minutes, divide the mix between plates and serve.

Nutrition: calories 182, fat 4, fiber 2, carbs 4, protein 5

Garlic Leeks Mix

Preparation time: 10 minutes **Cooking time:** *15 minutes* **Servings:** *4*

Ingredients:
- 4 leeks, sliced
- 2 scallions, chopped
- 1 tablespoon avocado oil
- 4 garlic cloves, minced
- 1 cup chicken stock
- A pinch of salt and black pepper
- 1 tablespoon sweet paprika
- 1 tablespoon chives, chopped

Directions:
Set your instant pot on Sauté mode, add the oil, heat it up, add the scallions and the garlic and sauté for 2 minutes. Add the leeks and the rest of the ingredients, put the lid on and cook on High for 13 minutes more. Release the pressure naturally for 10 minutes, divide the mix between plates and serve.

Nutrition: calories 188, fat 2, fiber 2, carbs 4, protein 5

Turmeric Eggplant Mix

Preparation time: 10 minutes **Cooking time:** *15 minutes* **Servings:** *4*

Ingredients:
- 2 tablespoons olive oil
- 3 eggplants, roughly cubed
- 2 scallions, chopped
- 1 teaspoon turmeric powder
- A pinch of salt and black pepper
- 1 cup tomato passata
- 1 tablespoon cilantro, chopped

Directions:
In your instant pot, mix eggplants with the oil, turmeric and the other ingredients, toss, put the lid on and cook on High for 15 minutes. Release the pressure naturally for 10 minutes, divide the mix between plates and serve.

Nutrition: calories 162, fat 2, fiber 2, carbs 5, protein 6

Zucchinis Saute

Preparation time: 10 minutes Cooking time: 15 minutes Servings: 4

Ingredients:
- 4 zucchinis, sliced
- 2 garlic cloves, minced
- ¼ cup chicken stock
- 1 tablespoon chili powder
- A pinch of salt and black pepper
- ½ cup tomato passata
- ½ teaspoon red pepper flakes

Directions:
In your instant pot, mix the zucchinis with the garlic, the stock and the rest of the ingredients, put the lid on and cook on High for 15 minutes. Release the pressure naturally for 10 minutes, divide the mix between plates and serve.

Nutrition: calories 162, fat 4, fiber 3, carbs 5, protein 7

Celery and Tomato Sauce

Preparation time: 10 minutes Cooking time: 15 minutes Servings: 4

Ingredients:
- 4 celery stalks, roughly sliced
- ½ teaspoon chili powder
- ½ teaspoon cumin, ground
- ½ teaspoon fennel seeds, crushed
- A pinch of salt and black pepper
- 1 cup tomato sauce
- 1 tablespoon parsley, chopped

Directions:
In your instant pot, combine the celery with the chili powder and the rest of the ingredients, put the lid on and cook on High for 15 minutes. Release the pressure naturally for 10 minutes, divide the mix between plates and serve.

Nutrition: calories 121, fat 2, fiber 2, carbs 4, protein 2

Watercress and Spinach Mix

Preparation time: *5 minutes* **Cooking time:** *6 minutes* **Servings:** *4*

Ingredients:
- 2 cups watercress
- 1 cup baby spinach
- 2 scallions, chopped
- ½ cup veggie stock
- 1 tablespoon tomato sauce
- A pinch of salt and black pepper
- 1 tablespoon parsley, chopped

Directions:
In your instant pot, combine the watercress with the spinach and the other ingredients, put the lid on and cook on High for 6 minutes. Release the pressure fast for 5 minutes, divide the mix into bowls and serve.

Nutrition: calories 100, fat 1, fiber 2, carbs 2, protein 1

Creamy Okra

Preparation time: 10 minutes **Cooking time:** 12 minutes **Servings:** 4

Ingredients:
- 2 cups okra
- A pinch of salt and black pepper
- 1 cup heavy cream
- 1 teaspoon coriander, ground
- ½ teaspoon chili powder
- 2 tablespoon chives, chopped

Directions:
In your instant pot, mix the okra with the cream, coriander and the rest of the ingredients, put the lid on and cook on High for 12 minutes. Release the pressure naturally for 10 minutes, divide the mix between plates and serve.

Nutrition: calories 121, fat 2, fiber 2, carbs 4, protein 4

Balsamic Okra

Preparation time: 10 minutes *Cooking time:* 12 minutes *Servings:* 4

Ingredients:
- 2 cups okra
- 2 garlic cloves, minced
- 1 cup veggie stock
- 1 tablespoon olive oil
- 2 scallions, chopped
- A pinch of salt and black pepper
- 1 tablespoon balsamic vinegar
- 1 tablespoon dill, chopped

Directions:
In your instant pot, mix the okra with the garlic, the stock and the other ingredients, toss, put the lid on and cook on High for 12 minutes. Release the pressure naturally for 10 minutes, divide mix between plates and serve.

Nutrition: calories 123, fat 1, fiber 2, carbs 3, protein 2

Chives Collard Greens

Preparation time: 10 minutes *Cooking time:* 12 minutes *Servings:* 4

Ingredients:
- 1 pound collard greens, trimmed
- 1 red onion, sliced
- 1 cup veggie stock
- 1 tablespoon sweet paprika
- A pinch of salt and black pepper
- 1 tablespoon chives, chopped

Directions:
In your instant pot, combine the collard greens with the onion, the stock and the other ingredients, toss, put the lid on and cook on High for 12 minutes. Release the pressure naturally for 10 minutes, divide the mix between plates and serve.

Nutrition: calories 122, fat 2, fiber 2, carbs 5, protein 3

Okra and Peppers

*Preparation time: 10 minutes **Cooking time:** 15 minutes **Servings:** 4*

Ingredients:
- 1 cup okra
- 1 red bell pepper, cut into strips
- 1 green bell pepper, cut into strips
- ½ cup chicken stock
- 2 tablespoons tomato puree
- A pinch of salt and black pepper
- 1 tablespoon cilantro, chopped

Directions:
In your instant pot, combine the okra with the bell peppers and the other ingredients, toss, put the lid on and cook on High for 15 minutes. Release the pressure naturally for 10 minutes, divide the mix between plates and serve.

Nutrition: calories 130, fat 2, fiber 2, carbs 4, protein 6

Spinach and Berries Mix

*Preparation time: 5 minutes **Cooking time:** 6 minutes **Servings:** 4*

Ingredients:
- 2 spring onions, chopped
- 1 pound baby spinach
- 1 cup blackberries
- A pinch of salt and black pepper
- 1 cup chicken stock
- 1 tablespoon chives, chopped
- 1 tablespoon cilantro, chopped

Directions:
In your instant pot, combine the spinach with the berries and the other ingredients, toss, put the lid on and cook on High for 6 minutes. Release the pressure fast for 5 minutes, divide the mix between plates and serve.

Nutrition: calories 140, fat 2, fiber 2, carbs 5, protein 7

Endives and Radish Mix

Preparation time: 10 minutes **Cooking time:** *12 minutes* **Servings:** *4*

Ingredients:
- 2 endives, trimmed and shredded
- 1 cup radishes
- A pinch of salt and black pepper
- 1 cup chicken stock
- 1 tablespoon chives, chopped
- ½ teaspoon garam masala
- 1 tablespoon tomato sauce

Directions:
In your instant pot, mix the endives with the radishes, salt, pepper and the rest of the ingredients, put the lid on and cook on High for 12 minutes. Release the pressure naturally for 10 minutes, divide the mix between plates and serve.

Nutrition: calories 114, fat 2, fiber 2, carbs 4, protein 4

Nutmeg Potatoes and Apples

Preparation time: 10 minutes **Cooking time:** *25 minutes* **Servings:** *4*

Ingredients:
- 2 sweet potatoes, peeled and cut into wedges
- 2 green apples, peeled and cut into wedges
- A pinch of salt and black pepper
- ½ cup coconut milk
- ½ teaspoon nutmeg, ground

Directions:
In your instant pot, combine potatoes with the apples and the other ingredients, toss gently, put the lid on and cook on High for 25 minutes. Release the pressure naturally for 10 minutes, divide the mix between plates and serve.

Nutrition: calories 124, fat 2, fiber 1, carbs 3, protein 4

Greek Fennel

Preparation time: 10 minutes *Cooking time: 15 minutes* *Servings: 4*

Ingredients:
- 2 fennel bulbs, trimmed and sliced
- 1 cup Greek yogurt
- A pinch of salt and black pepper
- 1 tablespoon lemon juice
- ½ teaspoon garam masala
- ½ teaspoon coriander, ground
- 2 tablespoons parsley, chopped

Directions:
In your instant pot, mix the fennel with the yogurt, lemon juice and the rest of the ingredients, put the lid on and cook on High for 15 minutes. Release the pressure naturally for 10 minutes, divide the mix between plates and serve.

Nutrition: calories 121, fat 1, fiber 1, carbs 4, protein 5

Creamy Okra and Corn

Preparation time: 10 minutes *Cooking time: 15 minutes* *Servings: 4*

Ingredients:
- 2 cups corn
- 1 cup okra
- 2 spring onions, chopped
- 2 cups heavy cream
- 1 teaspoon turmeric powder
- A pinch of salt and black pepper
- 1 tablespoon dill, chopped

Directions:
In your instant pot, combine the corn with the okra, spring onions and the other ingredients, toss, put the lid on and cook on High for 15 minutes. Release the pressure naturally for 10 minutes, divide the mix into bowls and serve.

Nutrition: calories 200, fat 7, fiber 2, carbs 4, protein 6

Carrots and Parsnips Sauté

Preparation time: 5 minutes Cooking time: 15 minutes Servings: 4

Ingredients:
- 1 pound baby carrots, peeled
- 2 parsnips, peeled and cut into sticks
- 2 garlic cloves, minced
- A pinch of salt and black pepper
- 1 tablespoon sweet paprika
- 1 teaspoon rosemary, dried
- 1 cup heavy cream

Directions:
In your instant pot, mix the carrots with the parsnips and the other ingredients, toss, put the lid on and cook on High for 15 minutes Release the pressure fast for 5 minutes, divide the mix between plates and serve.

Nutrition: calories 124, fat 2, fiber 2, carbs 4, protein 5

Zucchinis and Olives

Preparation time: 10 minutes Cooking time: 15 minutes Servings: 4

Ingredients:
- 2 zucchinis, sliced
- 4 scallions, chopped
- 1 tablespoon olive oil
- 1 cup kalamata olives, pitted and sliced
- 1 cup black olives, pitted and sliced
- 1 teaspoon sweet paprika
- A pinch of salt and black pepper
- ½ cup chicken stock
- 1 tablespoon dill, chopped

Directions:
Set the instant pot on Sauté mode, add the oil, heat it up, add the scallions and paprika and sauté for 2 minutes Add the zucchinis, olives and the rest of the ingredients, put the lid on and cook on High for 13 minutes Release the pressure naturally for 10 minutes, divide the mix between plates and serve.

Nutrition: calories 135, fat 5, fiber 2, carbs 3, protein 4

Lime Eggplant Mix

*Preparation time: 10 minutes **Cooking time:** 14 minutes **Servings:** 4*

Ingredients:
- 1 pound eggplant, roughly cubed
- Juice of 1 lime
- Zest of 1 lime, grated
- 1 teaspoon chili powder
- 1 teaspoon coriander, ground
- A pinch of salt and black pepper
- ½ cup chicken stock
- 1 tablespoon chives, chopped

Directions:
In your instant pot, mix the eggplants with lime juice, lime zest and the rest of the ingredients, put the lid on and cook on High for 14 minutes. Release the pressure naturally for 10 minutes, divide the mix between plates and serve.

Nutrition: calories 128, fat 3, fiber 2, carbs 4, protein 5

Corn and Chard Mix

*Preparation time: 10 minutes **Cooking time:** 12 minutes **Servings:** 4*

Ingredients:
- 2 cups corn
- 1 cup red chard, torn
- 1 tablespoon lemon juice
- 2 tablespoons lemon zest, grated
- ½ cup chicken stock
- 1 tablespoon sweet paprika
- 1 tablespoon cilantro, chopped

Directions:
In your instant pot, combine the corn with the chard, lemon juice and the other ingredients, toss, put the lid on and cook on High for 12 minutes. Release the pressure naturally for 10 minutes, divide the mix into bowls and serve.

Nutrition: calories 146, fat 4, fiber 2, carbs 4, protein 6

Chili Corn

Preparation time: 10 minutes Cooking time: 12 minutes Servings: 4

Ingredients:
- 2 cups corn
- 1 red chili, minced
- ½ teaspoon hot paprika
- ½ teaspoon chili powder
- 2 garlic cloves, chopped
- ¾ cup veggie stock
- 1 tablespoon cilantro, chopped

Directions:
In your instant pot, combine the corn with the chili and the other ingredients, toss, put the lid on and cook on High for 12 minutes. Release the pressure naturally for 10 minutes, divide the mix into bowls and serve.

Nutrition: calories 146, fat 4, fiber 2, carbs 4, protein 7

Mango and Rice

Preparation time: 10 minutes Cooking time: 20 minutes Servings: 4

Ingredients:
- 2 cups wild rice
- 1 mango, peeled and cubed
- 1 red onion, chopped
- 2 cups chicken stock
- 1 tablespoon olive oil
- 1 teaspoon hot paprika
- 1 teaspoon turmeric powder
- A pinch of salt and black pepper
- ½ tablespoon cilantro, chopped

Directions:
Set your instant pot on Sauté mode, add the oil, heat it up, add the onion, paprika and turmeric and sauté for 2 minutes. Add the r rice and the rest of the ingredients, put the lid on and cook on High for 18 minutes. Release the pressure naturally for 10 minutes, divide the mix into bowls and serve.

Nutrition: calories 134, fat 2, fiber 2, carbs 5, protein 5

Kale Sauté

Preparation time: 5 minutes *Cooking time:* 12 minutes *Servings:* 4

Ingredients:
- 2 scallions, chopped
- 1 tablespoon avocado oil
- 1 pound kale, torn
- 1 tablespoon lime juice
- A pinch of salt and black pepper
- ½ cup tomato sauce

Directions:
Set the instant pot on Sauté mode, add the oil, heat it up, add the scallions and lime juice and sauté for 2 minutes. Add the kale and the rest of the ingredients, put the lid on and cook on High for 10 minutes. Release the pressure fast for 5 minutes, divide the mix into bowls and serve.

Nutrition: calories 129, fat 4, fiber 2, carbs 3, protein 2

Kale and Radishes

Preparation time: 10 minutes *Cooking time:* 14 minutes *Servings:* 4

Ingredients:
- 1 pound kale, chopped
- 1 cup radishes, halved
- 1 yellow onion, thinly sliced
- 1 cup veggie stock
- ½ cup cherry tomatoes, halved
- 1 tablespoon balsamic vinegar
- A pinch of salt and black pepper
- ¼ teaspoon rosemary, dried
- 1 tablespoon chives, chopped

Directions:
In your instant pot, combine the kale with radishes, the onion and the rest of the ingredients, put the lid on and cook on High for 14 minutes. Release the pressure naturally for 10 minutes, divide the mix into bowls and serve.

Nutrition: calories 119, fat 2, fiber 2, carbs 4, protein 5

Instant Pot Pasta Recipes

Creamy Pasta

Preparation time: 10 minutes *Cooking time:* 20 minutes *Servings:* 4

Ingredients:
- 2 cups whole wheat spaghetti
- Salt and black pepper to the taste
- 2 tablespoons ghee, melted
- 4 scallions, chopped
- 1 teaspoon Italian seasoning
- A pinch of cayenne pepper
- 2 cups heavy cream

Directions:
Set the instant pot on Sauté mode, add the ghee, heat it up, add the scallions and sauté for 5 minutes. Add the spaghetti and the other ingredients, toss, put the lid on and cook on High for 15 minutes. Release the pressure naturally for 10 minutes, divide everything between plates and serve.

Nutrition: calories 200, fat 2, fiber 1, carbs 5, protein 8

Chicken and Pasta Stroganoff

Preparation time: 10 minutes *Cooking time:* 30 minutes *Servings:* 4

Ingredients:
- 2 garlic cloves, minced
- 1 cup white mushrooms, roughly chopped
- ¼ teaspoon chili powder
- 2 cups heavy cream
- 1 yellow onion, chopped
- 1 pound chicken breasts, skinless, boneless and cubed
- ½ pound whole wheat spaghetti
- 2 tablespoons parsley, chopped
- Salt and black pepper to the taste

Directions:
Set the instant pot on Sauté mode, add the oil, heat it up, add the onion, garlic and the mushrooms and sauté for 5 minutes. Add the meat and brown for 5 minutes more. Add the rest of the ingredients, toss, put the lid on and cook on High for 20 minutes. Release the pressure naturally for 10 minutes, divide everything between plates and serve.

Nutrition: calories 364, fat 22, fiber 2, carbs 4, protein 24

Pork Pasta

Preparation time: *10 minutes* ***Cooking time:*** *30 minutes* ***Servings:*** *4*

Ingredients:

- 2 tablespoons olive oil
- 1 teaspoon garlic, minced
- 1 pound pork stew meat, cut into strips
- ¼ cup scallions, chopped
- ½ cup tomatoes, chopped
- ½ cup beef stock
- ¼ cup heavy cream
- ½ cup cheddar cheese, grated
- 1 ounce cream cheese
- ¼ cup cilantro, chopped
- 8 ounces favorite pasta
- Salt and black pepper to the taste

Directions:

Set the instant pot on Sauté mode, add the oil, heat it up, add the garlic, scallions and tomatoes and sauté for 5 minutes. Add the meat and brown for 5 minutes more. Add the rest of the ingredients, toss, put the lid on and cook on High for 20 minutes. Release the pressure naturally for 10 minutes, divide everything between plates and serve.

Nutrition: calories 345, fat 34, fiber 4, carbs 4, protein 39

Salmon Pasta

Preparation time: *10 minute* ***Cooking time:*** *14 minutes* ***Servings:*** *4*

Ingredients:

- 12 ounces angel hair noodles
- ¼ cup chicken stock
- 2 tablespoons avocado oil
- Salt and black pepper to the taste
- 1 pound salmon fillets, boneless, skinless and cubed
- Juice of 1 lime
- Zest of 1 lime
- ½ teaspoon paprika
- A handful basil, chopped

Directions:

Set the instant pot on Sauté mode, add the oil, heat it up, add the salmon and cook for 2 minutes on each side. Add the noodles and the other ingredients, toss, put the lid on and cook on High for 12 minutes. Release the pressure naturally for 10 minutes, divide the mix between plates and serve.

Nutrition: calories 300, fat 20, fiber 6, carbs 3, protein 12

Zucchini Pasta

Preparation time: 5 minutes *Cooking time:* 15 minutes *Servings:* 4

Ingredients:
- 1 zucchini, cubed
- 2 scallions, chopped
- Salt and black pepper to the taste
- 1 tablespoon olive oil
- ½ cup heavy cream
- 4 ounces mozzarella, shredded
- 2 tablespoons pine nuts, toasted
- 8 ounces spaghetti

Directions:
Set the instant pot on Sauté mode, add the oil, heat it up, add the scallions and the zucchini and sauté for 2 minutes. Add the pasta and the other ingredients, toss, put the lid on and cook on High for 13 minutes. Release the pressure naturally for 10 minutes, divide the mix between plates and serve.

Nutrition: calories 200, fat 8, fiber 2, carbs 4, protein 10

Simple Parmesan Spaghetti

Preparation time: 5 minutes *Cooking time:* 15 minutes *Servings:* 4

Ingredients:
- 12 ounces whole wheat spaghetti
- 2 cups almond milk
- Salt and black pepper to the taste
- 6 garlic cloves, minced
- ½ teaspoon red pepper flakes
- ½ teaspoon hot paprika
- 1 cup parmesan, grated
- ¼ cup chives, chopped

Directions:
In your instant pot, combine the spaghetti with the almond milk and the other ingredients, toss, put the lid on and cook on High for 15 minutes. Release the pressure fast for 5 minutes, divide everything between plates and serve.

Nutrition: calories 200, fat 6, fiber 3, carbs 4, protein 5

Mixed Cheese Pasta

Preparation time: 10 minutes *Cooking time:* 14 minutes *Servings:* 4

Ingredients:
- 2 cups spaghetti, cooked
- 1 cup heavy cream
- 3 spring onions, chopped
- ½ teaspoon garam masala
- 1 cup cheddar cheese, shredded
- 1 cup mozzarella cheese, shredded
- Salt and black pepper to the taste

Directions:
In your instant pot, combine the spaghetti with the cream and the other ingredients, toss, put the lid on and cook on High for 15 minutes. Release the pressure naturally for 10 minutes, divide the spaghetti between plates and serve.

Nutrition: calories 241, fat 12, fiber 5, carbs 16, protein 6

Ground Turkey Pasta

Preparation time: 10 minutes *Cooking time:* 20 minutes *Servings:* 4

Ingredients:
- 1 pound turkey meat, ground
- 12 ounces spaghetti
- 1 cup chicken stock
- 3 scallions, chopped
- 1 tablespoon olive oil
- 4 garlic cloves, minced
- 2 cups tomato puree
- 1 teaspoon sweet paprika
- Salt and black pepper to the taste

Directions:
Set the instant pot on Sauté mode, add the oil, heat it up, add the meat, scallions and garlic and sauté for 5 minutes. Add the rest of the ingredients, put the lid on and cook on High for 15 minutes. Release the pressure naturally for 10 minutes, divide everything into bowls and serve.

Nutrition: calories 200, fat 14, fiber 6, carbs 17, protein 8

Lemony Pasta

Preparation time: *5 minutes* ***Cooking time:*** *13 minutes* ***Servings:*** *4*

Ingredients:
- 1 cup heavy cream
- 1 cup chicken stock
- 4 scallions, chopped
- 16 ounces favorite pasta, cooked
- 1 tablespoon lemon juice
- 1 tablespoon lemon zest, grated
- 1 tablespoon chives, chopped
- 2 teaspoons olive oil
- Salt and black pepper to the taste

Directions:
Set the instant pot on Sauté mode, add the oil, heat it up, add the scallions, lemon juice and zest and sauté for 5 minutes. Add all the other ingredients, toss, put the lid on and cook on High for 8 minutes more. Release the pressure fast for 5 minutes, divide the pasta between plates and serve.

Nutrition: calories 242, fat 14, fiber 7, carbs 19, protein 6

Shrimp Pasta

Preparation time: *5 minutes* ***Cooking time:*** *10 minutes* ***Servings:*** *4*

Ingredients:
- 5 ounces spaghetti, cooked
- 1 pound shrimp, deveined and peeled
- Salt and black pepper to the taste
- 5 garlic cloves, minced
- 1 teaspoon chili powder
- 3 scallions, chopped
- ½ teaspoon coriander, ground
- ½ teaspoon rosemary, ground
- 2 tablespoons olive oil

Directions:
Set the instant pot on Sauté mode, add the oil, heat it up, add the garlic, scallions, coriander and the rosemary and sauté for 2 minutes Add the shrimp and the other ingredients, toss, put the lid on and cook on High for 8 minutes Release the pressure fast for 5 minutes, divide the mix between plates and serve.

Nutrition: calories 270, fat 7, fiber 4, carbs 12, protein 6

Spinach Ravioli

Preparation time: *5 minutes* ***Cooking time:*** *10 minutes* ***Servings:*** *4*

Ingredients:
- 12 ounces spinach ravioli
- 10 ounces marinara sauce
- ¼ cup cheddar cheese, grated
- A pinch of salt and black pepper
- ½ teaspoon oregano, dried

Directions:
In your instant pot, combine the ravioli with the marinara sauce and the other ingredients, toss, put the lid on and cook on High for 14 minutes. Release the pressure fast for 5 minutes, divide the ravioli between plates and serve.

Nutrition: calories 260, fat 12, fiber 4, carbs 14, protein 11

Oregano Spaghetti

Preparation time: *10 minutes* ***Cooking time:*** *14 minutes* ***Servings:*** *4*

Ingredients:
- 2 tablespoons olive oil
- 4 scallions, chopped
- ½ cup oregano, chopped
- 1 garlic clove, minced
- 10 ounces canned tomatoes, chopped
- 1 cup parmesan, grated
- 12 ounces spaghetti, cooked

Directions:
Set the instant pot on Sauté mode, add the oil, heat it up, add the scallions and garlic and sauté for 2 minutes. Add the tomatoes and cook the mix for 2 minutes more. Add the rest of the ingredients, toss, put the lid and cook on High for 10 minutes. Release the pressure naturally for 10 minutes, divide the mix between plates and serve.

Nutrition: calories 271, fat 12, fiber 4, carbs 14, protein 5

Spaghetti and Beef Sauce

Preparation time: 10 minutes Cooking time: 25 minutes Servings: 4

Ingredients:
- 1 pound beef, ground
- 1 red onion, chopped
- 2 tablespoons olive oil
- 2 garlic cloves, minced
- 14 ounces canned tomatoes, crushed
- 1 teaspoon Italian seasoning
- ¼ cup parmesan, shredded
- 12 ounces spaghetti, cooked

Directions:
Set the instant pot on Sauté mode, add the oil, heat it up, add the onion and garlic and sauté for 5 minutes. Add the meat and brown for 5 minutes more. Add the rest of the ingredients, toss, put the lid and cook on High for 15 minutes. Release the pressure naturally for 10 minutes, divide everything between plates and serve.

Nutrition: calories 231, fat 4, fiber 5, carbs 14, protein 9

Walnuts Spaghetti

Preparation time: 5 minutes Cooking time: 10 minutes Servings: 4

Ingredients:
- 1 tablespoon olive oil
- 1 red onion, chopped
- 4 zucchinis, cut with a spiralizer
- ½ cup cherry tomatoes, halved
- ¼ cup basil, chopped
- A pinch of salt and black pepper
- ½ cup walnuts, chopped
- 1 tablespoon chives, chopped

Directions:
Set the instant pot on Sauté mode, add the oil, heat it up, add the onion and sauté for 2 minutes. Add the zucchini spaghetti and the other ingredients, toss, put the lid on and cook on High for 8 minutes. Release the pressure fast for 5 minutes, divide everything into bowls and serve.

Nutrition: calories 150, fat 2, fiber 4, carbs 7, protein 10

Asparagus Pasta Mix

Preparation time: *10 minutes* ***Cooking time:*** *15 minutes* ***Servings:*** *4*

Ingredients:
- ½ pound whole wheat penne pasta, cooked
- 3 scallions, chopped
- 2 tablespoons olive oil
- 1 bunch asparagus, trimmed and cut into medium pieces
- 1 cup cherry tomatoes, halved
- A pinch of salt and black pepper
- 1 cup heavy cream
- 2 tablespoons parmesan, grated

Directions:
Set the instant pot on Sauté mode, add the oil, heat it up, add the scallions and sauté for 2 minutes. Add the pasta and the other ingredients, toss, put the lid on and cook on High for 13 minutes more. Release the pressure naturally for 10 minutes, divide between plates and serve.

Nutrition: calories 221, fat 4, fiber 4, carbs 15, protein 9

Tuna Pasta

Preparation time: *10 minutes* ***Cooking time:*** *10 minutes* ***Servings:*** *4*

Ingredients:
- 5 ounces canned tuna in water, drained and flaked
- 2 scallions, chopped
- 1 tablespoon olive oil
- ¼ cup heavy cream
- 2 cups baby spinach
- 1 tablespoon parmesan, grated
- A pinch of black pepper
- 4 ounces whole wheat pasta, cooked

Directions:
In your instant pot, combine the scallions with the tuna, pasta and the other ingredients, toss, put the lid on and cook on High for 10 minutes. Release the pressure naturally for 10 minutes, divide the mix between plates and serve.

Nutrition: calories 200, fat 4, fiber 4, carbs 14, protein 7

Broccoli Pasta

*Preparation time: 10 minutes **Cooking time:** 20 minutes **Servings:** 4*

Ingredients:
- 8 ounces whole wheat penne pasta, cooked
- 1 cup cherry tomatoes, halved
- 1 cup broccoli florets
- 1 cup coconut cream
- 1 egg, whisked
- 1 teaspoon garlic powder
- 1 teaspoon oregano, dried
- A pinch of salt and black pepper

Directions:
In your instant pot, combine the pasta with the broccoli, tomatoes and the other ingredients, toss, put the lid on and cook on High for 20 minutes. Release the pressure naturally for 10 minutes, divide the mix between plates and serve.

Nutrition: calories 247, fat 5, fiber 8, carbs 18, protein 7

Sage Spaghetti and Squash Mix

*Preparation time: 5 minutes **Cooking time:** 20 minutes **Servings:** 4*

Ingredients:
- 1 cup scallions, chopped
- 1 cup veggie stock
- 1 tablespoon olive oil
- 1 cup butternut squash, peeled and cubed
- 1 tablespoon sage, chopped
- 2 garlic cloves, minced
- ½ cup heavy cream
- 12 ounces whole wheat pasta, cooked
- A pinch of salt and black pepper

Directions:
Set the instant pot on Sauté mode, add the oil, heat it up, add the scallions, garlic and the squash and sauté for 5 minutes. Add the pasta and the other ingredients, toss, put the lid on and cook on High for 15 minutes. Release the pressure fast for 5 minutes, divide the mix into bowls and serve.

Nutrition: calories 200, fat 4, fiber 3, carbs 7, protein 12

Meatballs Spaghetti

*Preparation time: 10 minutes **Cooking time:** 20 minutes **Servings:** 4*
Ingredients:
- 1 yellow onion, chopped
- 1/3 cup mozzarella, shredded
- 1 egg, whisked
- ½ teaspoon basil, dried
- Salt and black pepper to the taste
- 1 pound pork meat, ground
- 1 tablespoon olive oil
- 2 cups tomato puree
- 10 ounces whole wheat spaghetti, cooked

Directions:
In a bowl, combine the meat with the egg, basil, onion, mozzarella, salt and pepper , stir and shape medium meatballs out of this mix. Set your instant pot on Sauté mode, add oil, heat it up, add the meatballs and brown for 5 minutes. Add the tomato puree and spaghetti, toss, put the lid on and cook on High for 15 minutes. Release the pressure naturally for 10 minutes, divide everything between plates and serve.

Nutrition: calories 200, fat 5, fiber 2, carbs 12, protein 8

Shrimp and Olives Pasta

*Preparation time: 6 minutes **Cooking time:** 10 minutes **Servings:** 4*
Ingredients:
- 1 pound shrimp, cooked, peeled and deveined
- 1 cup kalamata olives, pitted and sliced
- 2 tablespoons olive oil
- 1 red onion, chopped
- 1/3 cup tomato paste
- ¼ teaspoon oregano, dried
- 1 tablespoon parsley
- 12 ounces whole wheat pasta, cooked
- 1/3 cup chicken stock
- 1 cup parmesan, grated

Directions:
Set your instant pot on Sauté mode, add oil, heat it up, add the onion and sauté for 2 minutes. Add the shrimp, tomatoes, the pasta and the other ingredients, toss, put the lid on and cook on High for 8 minutes. Release the pressure fast for 6 minutes, divide the mix between plates and serve.

Nutrition: calories 266, fat 14, fiber 3, carbs 11, protein 7

Veggie Spaghetti

Preparation time: 10 minutes **Cooking time:** 15 minutes **Servings:** 4
Ingredients:
- 1 zucchini, cubed
- 1 eggplant, cubed
- 1 red onion, chopped
- 2 carrots, chopped
- 4 garlic cloves, minced
- 2 celery ribs, chopped
- 28 ounces canned tomatoes, crushed
- 1 tablespoon olive oil
- ½ teaspoon basil, dried
- ½ teaspoon oregano, dried
- 12 ounces whole wheat penne pasta, cooed
- 1 cup chicken stock

Directions:
Set your instant pot on Sauté mode, add the oil, heat it up, add the onion and garlic and sauté for 2 minutes. Add the pasta, zucchini and the other ingredients, toss, put the lid on and cook on High for 13 minutes. Release the pressure naturally for 10 minutes, divide the mix between plates and serve.

Nutrition: calorie 282, fat 12, fiber 4, carbs 20, protein 13

Spaghetti and Lentils Sauce

Preparation time: 10 minutes **Cooking time:** 20 minutes **Servings:** 4
Ingredients:
- 2 cups canned tomatoes, crushed
- 3 garlic cloves, minced
- 1 red onion, chopped
- ½ cup canned red lentils, drained and rinsed
- 12 ounces whole wheat spaghetti, cooked
- 2 tablespoons olive oil
- Salt and black pepper to the taste
- 1 and ½ cups chicken stock

Directions:
Set your instant pot on Sauté mode, add the oil, heat it up, add the onion and the garlic and sauté for 5 minutes. Add the spaghetti and the other ingredients, toss, put the lid on and cook on High for 15 minutes. Release the pressure naturally for 10 minutes, divide the mix between plates and serve.

Nutrition: calories 232, fat 12, fiber 4, carbs 13, protein 4

Spaghetti and Cauliflower Sauce

Preparation time: 10 minutes **Cooking time:** 15 minutes **Servings:** 4

Ingredients:
- 2 tablespoons butter
- 6 garlic cloves, minced
- 1 cup veggie stock
- ½ pound cauliflower florets
- Salt and black pepper to the taste
- ½ cup heavy cream
- 12 ounces whole wheat pasta, cooked

Directions:
Set your instant pot on Sauté mode, add the butter, melt it, add the garlic, stock, cauliflower and the cream, stir, cook for 10 minutes and blend using an immersion blender. Add the pasta, toss, put the lid on and cook on High for 5 minutes. Release the pressure naturally for 10 minutes, divide the spaghetti mix between plates and serve.

Nutrition: calories 200, fat 5, fiber 5, carbs 14, protein 6

Pasta and Zucchini Pesto

Preparation time: 10 minutes **Cooking time:** 12 minutes **Servings:** 4

Ingredients:
- 1 yellow onion, chopped
- 1 tablespoon avocado oil
- 2 zucchinis, chopped
- Juice of 1 lime
- 1 tablespoon pine nuts
- Salt and black pepper to the taste
- ½ cup Heavy cream
- 1 bunch basil, chopped
- 2 garlic cloves, minced
- 12 ounces whole wheat pasta, cooked

Directions:
Set your instant pot on Sauté mode, add oil, heat it up, add the onion, zucchinis, lime juice and the other ingredients except the pasta, stir, cook for 5 minutes and blend using an immersion blender. Add the pasta, toss, put the lid on and cook on High for 7 minutes. Release the pressure naturally for 10 minutes, divide everything between plates and serve.

Nutrition: calorie 241, fat 5, fiber 2, carbs 15, protein 6

Pasta and Beets Sauce

*Preparation time: 10 minutes **Cooking time:** 20 minutes **Servings:** 4*

Ingredients:
- 1 yellow onion, chopped
- 2 tablespoons olive oil
- 4 beets, peeled and grated
- 2 garlic cloves, minced
- 1 cup heavy cream
- ¼ cup lemon juice
- 1 bunch basil, chopped
- 12 ounces pasta, cooked
- Salt and black pepper to the taste

Directions:
Set your instant pot on Sauté mode, add oil, heat it up, add the onion and the garlic and sauté for 5 minutes. Add the rest of the ingredients, toss, put the lid on and cook on High for 15 minutes. Release the pressure naturally for 10 minutes, divide the mix between plates and serve.

Nutrition: calories 200, fat 11, fiber 5, carbs 12, protein 7

Chili, Sausage and Cheese Pasta

*Preparation time: 10 minutes **Cooking time:** 12 minutes **Servings:** 4*

Ingredients:
- 2 cups processed cheese, cut into chunks
- 1 cup Italian sausage, cooked and chopped
- 1 cup canned green chilies, chopped
- 12 ounces whole wheat pasta, cooked
- 1 cup heavy cream
- A pinch of salt and black pepper

Directions:
In your instant pot, combine the cheese with the sausage and the other ingredients, toss, put the lid on and cook on High for 12 minutes. Release the pressure naturally for 10 minutes, divide the mix between plates and serve.

Nutrition: calories 200, fat 12, fiber 5, carbs 12, protein 5

Pasta and Mushroom Sauce

Preparation time: *10 minutes* ***Cooking time:*** *20 minutes* ***Servings:*** *4*

Ingredients:
- 1 yellow onion, chopped
- 2 tablespoons olive oil
- Salt and black pepper to the taste
- 1 tablespoon rosemary, chopped
- 3 garlic cloves, minced
- 1 cup chicken stock
- ½ cup shiitake mushrooms, chopped
- 1 cup cremini mushrooms, chopped
- 1 cup Portobello mushrooms, chopped
- 12 ounces whole wheat pasta, cooked
- ½ cup heavy cream
- 1 tablespoons chives, chopped

Directions:
Set your instant pot on Sauté mode, add oil, heat it up, add the onion, garlic and the mushrooms and sauté for 5 minutes. Add the pasta and the other ingredients, toss, put the lid on and cook on High for 15 minutes. Release the pressure naturally for 10 minutes, divide the mix between plates and serve.

Nutrition: calories 245, fat 6, fiber 3, carbs 14, protein 6

Cinnamon Tomato Pasta

Preparation time: *10 minute* ***Cooking time:*** *15 minutes* ***Servings:*** *4*

Ingredients:
- 1 pound tomatoes, peeled and chopped
- 1 tablespoon olive oil
- 1 tablespoon balsamic vinegar
- 1 cup veggie stock
- 1 tablespoon ginger, grated
- 12 ounces whole wheat pasta, cooked
- 3 garlic cloves, minced
- 2 yellow onions, chopped
- ¾ teaspoon cinnamon, ground
- ¼ teaspoon cloves
- 1 teaspoon chili powder

Directions:
In a blender, combine the tomatoes with the oil, vinegar and the other ingredients except the pasta and pulse well In your instant pot, combine the pasta with the tomato mix, toss, put the lid on and cook on High for 15 minutes Release the pressure naturally for 10 minutes, divide everything between plates and serve.

Nutrition: calories 200, fat 12, fiber 5, carbs 12, protein 8

Dates and Tomato Pasta

Preparation time: 10 minutes **Cooking time:** *15 minutes* **Servings:** *4*

Ingredients:
- 1 pound tomatoes, peeled and chopped
- 2 scallions, chopped
- 2 tablespoons olive oil
- 1 yellow onion, chopped
- 1 cup dates, chopped
- Salt and black pepper to the taste
- ½ teaspoon allspice
- 1 tablespoon balsamic vinegar
- 2 tablespoons brown sugar
- 12 ounces whole wheat pasta, cooked

Directions:
In a blender, combine the tomatoes with the scallions, the oil and the other ingredients except the pasta and pulse well. In your instant pot, combine the tomato sauce with the pasta, toss, put the lid on and cook on High for 15 minutes. Release the pressure naturally for 10 minutes, divide the pasta between plates and serve.

Nutrition: calories 243, fat 13, fiber 5, carbs 17, protein 6

Ginger Green Tomato Spaghetti

Preparation time: 5 minutes **Cooking time:** *14 minutes* **Servings:** *4*

Ingredients:
- 1 pound green tomatoes, chopped
- 1 red onion, chopped
- 1 cup chicken stock
- 1 red chili pepper, chopped
- 2 tablespoons ginger, grated
- 2 tablespoons balsamic vinegar
- 12 ounces whole wheat pasta, cooked

Directions:
In your instant pot, mix combine the tomatoes with the red onion and the other ingredients, toss, put the lid on and cook on High for 14 minutes Divide the pasta between plates and serve.

Nutrition: calories 200, fat 12, fiber 5, carbs 12, protein 6

Instant Pot Dessert Recipes
Dates Cake
Preparation time: 10 minutes *Cooking time:* 35 minutes ***Servings:*** 6
Ingredients:

- 3 cups dates, chopped
- 1 cup coconut sugar
- 1 teaspoon almond extract
- 1 teaspoon vanilla extract
- 1 cup almond milk
- 2 eggs, whisked
- 2 cups almond flour
- 1 tablespoon baking powder
- Cooking spray
- 1 cup water

Directions:
In a bowl combine the dates with the sugar and the other ingredients except the water and the cooking spray and stir well. Grease a loaf pan that fits the instant pot with the cooking spray and pour the cake mix inside. Add the water to the instant pot, add the steamer basket, put the loaf pan inside, put the lid on and cook on High for 35 minutes. Release the pressure naturally for 10 minutes, cool the cake down, slice and serve.
Nutrition: calories 152, fat 5, fiber 2, carb 6, protein 3

Almond Apple Bread
Preparation time: 10 minutes *Cooking time:* 40 minutes ***Servings:*** 6
Ingredients:

- ¾ cup brown sugar
- 1/3 cup canola oil
- 1 teaspoon almond extract
- 2 eggs, whisked
- 2 cups apples, cored and grated
- 1 teaspoon baking soda
- 1 and ½ cups almond flour
- 1/3 cup almond milk
- 1 cups water
- Cooking spray

Directions:
In a bowl, mix the apples with the sugar, the oil and the rest of the ingredients except the water and the cooking spray and stir well. Grease a loaf pan that fits the instant pot with the cooking spray and pour the apples mix inside. Add the water to your instant pot, add the steamer basket, add the loaf pan inside, put the lid on and cook on High for 40 minutes. Release the pressure naturally for 10 minutes, cool the bread down, slice and serve.
Nutrition: calories 220, fat 4, fiber 2, carbs 4, protein 6

Berries Cake

Preparation time: 10 minutes *Cooking time:* 35 minutes *Servings:* 4

Ingredients:
- 2 egg, whisked
- ½ cup brown sugar
- 2 tablespoons avocado oil
- 1 cup coconut milk
- ¼ cup coconut cream
- 4 tablespoons almond flour
- 1 cup blackberries
- ½ teaspoon baking powder
- Cooking spray
- 1 cup water

Directions:
In a bowl, mix the eggs with the sugar, berries and the rest of the ingredients except the cooking spray and the water and stir well. Grease a cake pan with the cooking spray and pour the cake mix inside. Add the water to the pot, add steamer basket, add the cake pan inside, put the lid on and cook on High for 35 minutes. Release the pressure naturally for 10 minutes, cool the cake down, slice and serve.

Nutrition: calories 262, fat 7, fiber 2, carbs 5, protein 8

Vanilla Pears

Preparation time: 10 minutes *Cooking time:* 20 minutes *Servings:* 4

Ingredients:
- 2 teaspoons vanilla extract
- 4 pears, cored and cut into chunks
- 1 tablespoon brown sugar
- ½ cup heavy cream

Directions:
In your instant pot, mix the pears with the sugar, vanilla and the cream, toss, put the lid on and cook on High for 20 minutes. Release the pressure naturally for 10 minutes, divide the mix into bowls and serve.

Nutrition: calories 120, fat 2, fiber 2, carbs 4, protein 3

Apple and Berries Bowls

*Preparation time: 10 minutes **Cooking time:** 15 minutes **Servings:** 4*

Ingredients:
- 2 apples, cored and cut into wedges
- 1 cup blackberries
- 1 cup blueberries
- 1 cup heavy cream
- ¼ cup raisins
- ½ cup coconut sugar
- 1 teaspoon almond extract

Directions:
In your instant pot, combine the apples with the berries and the other ingredients, toss gently, put the lid on and cook on High for 15 minutes. Release the pressure naturally for 10 minutes, divide the mix into bowls and serve.

Nutrition: calories 162, fat 2, fiber 2, carbs 4, protein 5

Almond and Grapes Ramekins

*Preparation time: 5 minutes **Cooking time:** 10 minutes **Servings:** 4*

Ingredients:
- 2 cups heavy cream
- 1 cup almonds, chopped
- 1 cup grapes, halved
- 1 teaspoon coconut sugar
- 2 cups water

Directions:
In a blender, combine the cream with the other ingredients except the water, pulse and divide into 4 ramekins. Put the water in your instant pot, add the steamer basket, add the ramekins inside, put the lid on and cook on High for 10 minutes. Release the pressure fast for 5 minutes, and serve the ramekins cold.

Nutrition: calories 172, fat 2, fiber 3, carbs 4, protein 5

Strawberries Cocoa Cream

Preparation time: 10 minutes **Cooking time:** 20 minutes **Servings:** 4

Ingredients:
- 1 cup strawberries, chopped
- 2 cups water
- 2 cups heavy cream
- 1 cup coconut sugar
- 1 teaspoon ginger powder
- 1 tablespoon cocoa powder

Directions:
In a bowl, mix berries with the cream and the other ingredients except the water, whisk well and divide into 4 ramekins. Add the water to your instant pot, add the steamer basket, add the ramekins inside, put the lid on and cook on High for 20 minutes. Release the pressure naturally for 10 minutes, and serve the cream right away.

Nutrition: calories 200, fat 5, fiber 3, carbs 4, protein 5

Pumpkin Cream

Preparation time: 10 minutes **Cooking time:** 25 minutes **Serving:** 4

Ingredients:
- 1 pumpkin, peeled and flesh pureed
- 2 eggs, whisked
- 1 cups water
- 1 cup heavy cream
- 2 tablespoons brown sugar
- 1 teaspoon cinnamon powder
- Cooking spray

Directions:
In a bowl, mix pumpkin puree with the eggs and the rest of the ingredients except the water and the cooking spray and whisk well. Grease a big ramekin with the cooking spray and pour the pumpkin mix inside. Add the water to the instant pot, add the steamer basket, put the ramekin inside, put the lid on and cook on High for 25 minutes. Release the pressure naturally for 10 minutes, cool the cream down and serve.

Nutrition: calories 200, fat 5, fiber 2, carbs 5, protein 6

Rice and Quinoa Pudding

Preparation time: 10 minutes *Cooking time:* 20 minutes *Servings:* 4

Ingredients:
- 3 cups almond milk
- 1 cup white rice
- ¼ cup raisins
- ½ cup quinoa
- ½ cup coconut sugar
- 1 teaspoon cinnamon powder

Directions:
In your instant pot, mix the rice with the milk and the rest of the ingredients, stir, put the lid on and cook on High for 20 minutes Release the pressure naturally for 10 minutes, divide the pudding into bowls and serve.

Nutrition: calories 172, fat 4, fiber 2, carbs 4, protein 5

Avocado and Apples Cream Pudding

Preparation time: 10 minutes *Cooking time:* 10 minutes *Servings:* 4

Ingredients:
- 1 cup avocado, peeled, pitted and roughly cubed
- 1 cup apples, cored and roughly cubed
- 2 eggs, whisked
- 1 cup almond milk
- ¾ cup coconut sugar
- 1 teaspoon vanilla extract
- 1 cup apples, cored and cubed
- 1 cup water

Directions:
In a blender, combine the avocado with the apples and the other ingredients except the water, pulse well and divide into 4 ramekins. Put the water in the instant pot, add the steamer basket, put the ramekins in the pot, put the lid on and cook on Low for 10 minutes. Release the pressure naturally for 10 minutes and serve the mix cold.

Nutrition: calories 172, fat 2, fiber 2, carbs 4, protein 6

Grapes Cream

Preparation time: 10 minutes **Cooking time:** *15 minutes* **Servings:** *4*

Ingredients:
- 2 cups grapes, halved
- 1 cup heavy cream
- 1 tablespoon cinnamon powder
- 2 tablespoons brown sugar
- ½ teaspoon vanilla extract
- ½ teaspoon nutmeg, ground
- 1 cup water

Directions:
In a blender, mix the grapes with the rest of the ingredients except the water, pulse well and divide into 4 ramekins. Add the water to the instant pot, add the steamer basket, put the ramekins inside, put the lid on and cook on High for 15 minutes. Release the pressure naturally for 10 minutes and serve the cream cold.

Nutrition: calories 172, fat 3, fiber 2, carbs 6, protein 6

Lime Cream

Preparation time: 10 minutes **Cooking time:** *15 minutes* **Servings:** *4*

Ingredients:
- 2 cups heavy cream
- Juice of 1 lime
- Zest of 1 lime, grated
- 1 teaspoon vanilla extract
- 4 tablespoons brown sugar
- 1 tablespoon walnuts, chopped
- 1 cup water

Directions:
In a bowl, mix the cream with the lime juice, lime zest and the rest of the ingredients except the water, whisk and divide into 4 ramekins. Add the water to the instant pot, add the steamer basket, put the ramekins inside, put the lid on and cook on High for 15 minutes. Release the pressure naturally for 10 minutes and serve right away.

Nutrition: calories 162, fat 2, fiber 2, carbs 4, protein 6

Raisins and Nuts Pudding

Preparation time: 10 minutes *Cooking time:* 20 minutes *Servings:* 4

Ingredients:
- 4 eggs, whisked
- 1 teaspoon baking powder
- 2 cups heavy cream
- ½ teaspoon almond extract
- 2 tablespoons almonds, chopped
- 1 tablespoon walnuts, chopped
- 1 cup coconut sugar
- ½ cup raisins
- 1 cup water

Directions:
In a bowl mix the eggs with the cream, almond extract and the rest of the ingredients except the water, whisk well and divide into 4 ramekins. Add the water to the pot, add the steamer basket, add the ramekins inside, put the lid on and cook on High for 20 minutes. Release the pressure naturally for 10 minutes, and serve the pudding cold.

Nutrition: calories 200, fat 4, fiber 2, carbs 5, protein 4

Orange Stew

Preparation time: 10 minutes *Cooking time:* 10 minutes *Servings:* 4

Ingredients:
- 4 oranges, peeled and cut into segments
- 1 teaspoon vanilla extract
- 1 tablespoon nutmeg, ground
- 1 cup orange juice
- ½ cup water
- 2 tablespoons brown sugar

Directions:
In your instant pot, mix the oranges with the vanilla, nutmeg and the rest of the ingredients, put the lid on and cook on High for 10 minutes. Release the pressure naturally for 10 minutes, divide the mix into bowls and serve.

Nutrition: calories 182, fat 4, fiber 2, carbs 4, protein 6

Apples and Pears Bowls

Preparation time: 10 minutes **Cooking time:** *10 minutes* **Servings:** *4*

Ingredients:
- 4 pears, cored and cut into wedges
- 2 apples, cored and cut into wedges
- 1 tablespoon walnuts, chopped
- 1 cup apple juice
- ½ teaspoon vanilla extract

Directions:
In your instant pot, mix pears with the apples and the other ingredients, toss, put the lid on and cook on High for 10 minutes. Release the pressure naturally for 10 minutes, divide the mix into bowls and serve.

Nutrition: calories 162, fat 2, fiber 2, carbs 4, protein 6

Cauliflower Rice and Berries Pudding

Preparation time: 10 minutes **Cooking time:** *15 minutes* **Servings:** *4*

Ingredients:
- 2 cups cauliflower rice
- 1 cup blackberries
- 2 cups almond milk
- 1 cup heavy cream
- 3 tablespoon coconut sugar
- 1 teaspoon vanilla extract

Directions:
In your instant pot, mix the cauliflower with the berries and the other ingredients, toss, put the lid on and cook on High for 15 minutes. Release the pressure naturally for 10 minutes, divide the pudding into bowls and serve.

Nutrition: calories 172, fat 2, fiber 3, carbs 6, protein 6

Creamy Lemon Pudding

Preparation time: *10 minutes* ***Cooking time:*** *20 minutes* ***Servings:*** *4*

Ingredients:
- 2 cups cream cheese, soft
- 2 cups heavy cream
- ½ cup cauliflower rice
- 3 tablespoons brown sugar
- 4 eggs, whisked
- 1 teaspoon baking soda
- 1 teaspoon lemon zest, grated

Directions:
In your instant pot, combine the cream cheese with the cream and the other ingredients, toss, put the lid on and cook on High for 20 minutes Release the pressure naturally for 10 minutes and serve the puddings warm.

Nutrition: calories 200, fat 5, fiber 2, carbs 4, protein 6

Carrots Pudding

Preparation time: *10 minutes* ***Cooking time:*** *20 minutes* ***Servings:*** *4*

Ingredients:
- 1 cup carrots, peeled and grated
- 2 eggs, whisked
- 1 teaspoon baking powder
- ½ cup heavy cream
- 2 cups cashew milk
- 3 tablespoons brown sugar
- 1 teaspoon vanilla extract

Directions:
In the instant pot, combine the carrots with the eggs and the other ingredients, toss, put the lid on and cook on High for 20 minutes. Release the pressure naturally for 10 minutes, divide the mix into bowls and serve cold.

Nutrition: calories 162, fat 3, fiber 2, carbs 4, protein 3

Blueberries Cream

*Preparation time: 10 minutes **Cooking time:** 15 minutes **Servings:** 4*

Ingredients:
- 2 cups heavy cream
- 1 tablespoon lemon juice
- 2 eggs, whisked
- 1 teaspoon almond extract
- 1 cup blueberries
- 1 cup water

Directions:
In a bowl, mix the cream with the lemon juice and the rest of the ingredients except the water, whisk well and divide into ramekins. Put the water in the instant pot, add the steamer basket, put the ramekins inside, put the lid on and cook on High for 15 minutes. Release the pressure naturally for 10 minutes and serve.

Nutrition: calories 162, fat 2, fiber 2, carbs 4, protein 4

Plum Jam

*Preparation time: 10 minutes **Cooking time:** 40 minutes **Servings:** 6*

Ingredients:
- Juice of 1 lemon
- 1 tablespoon lemon zest, grated
- 2 cups brown sugar
- 1 pound plums, pitted and cubed
- 3 cups water

Directions:
In your instant pot, mix the plums with the sugar and the rest of the ingredients, put the lid on and cook on Low for 40 minutes. Release the pressure naturally for 10 minutes, blend the mix using an immersion blender, divide into jars and serve.

Nutrition: calories 162, fat 1, fiber 2, carbs 3, protein 6

Coconut Cream

Preparation time: 10 minutes Cooking time: 20 minutes Servings: 4

Ingredients:
- Zest of 1 lemon
- Juice of 1 lemon
- 2 cups coconut cream
- ½ cup coconut flakes
- 1 tablespoon cinnamon powder
- 1 teaspoon vanilla extract
- 1 cup water

Directions:
In a bowl, mix the lemon juice with the coconut cream and the rest of the ingredients except the water, whisk well and divide into 4 ramekins. Put the water in the instant pot, add the steamer basket, add the ramekins inside, put the lid on and cook on High for 20 minutes. Release the pressure naturally for 10 minutes and serve the cream cold.

Nutrition: calories 100, fat 1, fiber 2, carbs 4, protein 3

Cinnamon Cream

Preparation time: 10 minutes Cooking time: 20 minutes Servings: 4

Ingredients:
- 1 carrot, peeled and grated
- 1 apple, cored and grated
- 2 tablespoons lemon juice
- 1 cup coconut sugar
- 2 cups coconut cream
- 1 teaspoon cinnamon powder
- 2 cups water

Directions:
In a bowl, mix the carrot with the apples, cinnamon and the rest of the ingredients except the water, whisk well and divide into 4 ramekins. Put the water in the instant pot, add the steamer basket, put the ramekins inside, put the lid on and cook on High for 20 minutes. Release the pressure naturally for 10 minutes, and serve the cream cold.

Nutrition: calories 124, fat 2, fiber 2, carbs 4, protein 5

Grapes Stew

*Preparation time: 10 minutes **Cooking time:** 15 minutes **Servings:** 4*

Ingredients:
- 2 cups grapes, halved
- ¼ cup apple juice
- 1 cup water
- 3 tablespoons brown sugar
- 1 teaspoon vanilla extract

Directions:
In your instant pot, mix the grapes with the apples juice and the rest of the ingredients, put the lid on and cook on High for 15 minutes Release the pressure naturally for 10 minutes, divide the stew into bowls and serve.

Nutrition: calories 129, fat 2, fiber 2, carbs 4, protein 7

Ginger Cream

*Preparation time: 10 minutes **Cooking time:** 15 minutes **Servings:** 4*

Ingredients:
- 2 tablespoons coconut sugar
- 1 tablespoon ginger, grated
- 2 cups heavy cream
- 1 tablespoon almonds, chopped
- 1 teaspoon vanilla extract
- 1 cup water

Directions:
In a bowl, mix the ginger with the sugar and the rest of the ingredients except the water, whisk and divide into 4 ramekins. Put the water in the instant pot, add the steamer basket, put the ramekins inside, put the lid on and cook on High for 15 minutes. Release the pressure naturally for 10 minutes, and serve the cream cold.

Nutrition: calories 120, fat 1, fiber 1, carbs 4, protein 6

Strawberry Stew

Preparation time: 10 minutes **Cooking time:** 15 minutes **Servings:** 4

Ingredients:
- 12 ounces strawberries
- 2 tablespoons lime juice
- 2 tablespoons brown sugar
- 1 and ½ cups water
- 1 teaspoon vanilla extract

Directions:
In your instant pot, mix the strawberries with the lime juice and the rest of the ingredients, put the lid on and cook on High for 15 minutes. Release the pressure naturally for 10 minutes, divide the mix into bowls and serve.

Nutrition: calories 110, fat 2, fiber 2, carbs 4, protein 5

Pears Compote

Preparation time: 10 minutes **Cooking time:** 15 minutes **Servings:** 6

Ingredients:
- 3 cups pears, cored and cubed
- 2 tablespoons lemon juice
- 1 tablespoon lemon zest, grated
- 1 cup water
- ¾ cup coconut sugar
- 1 teaspoon almond extract

Directions:
In your instant pot, mix the pears with the lemon juice and the rest of the ingredients, put the lid on and cook on High for 15 minutes. Release the pressure naturally for 10 minutes, divide the compote into bowls and serve.

Nutrition: calories 152, fat 1, fiber 2, carbs 4, protein 5

Lime Compote

Preparation time: 10 minutes **Cooking time:** 15 minutes **Servings:** 6

Ingredients:
- 1 tablespoon lime zest, grated
- 2 tablespoons lime juice
- 2 cups apple juice
- 1 cup apples, cored and cubed
- 3 tablespoons brown sugar

Directions:
In your instant pot, mix the apples with the lime juice and the rest of the ingredients, put the lid on and cook on High for 15 minutes. Release the pressure naturally for 10 minutes, divide the mix into bowls and serve.

Nutrition: calories 110, fat 2, fiber 2, carbs 5, protein 5

Apricot Cream

Preparation time: 10 minutes **Cooking time:** 15 minutes **Servings:** 4

Ingredients:
- 2 cups apricots, cubed
- ¼ cup heavy cream
- ¼ cup coconut sugar
- 2 tablespoons ghee, melted
- 1 teaspoon vanilla extract

Directions:
In your instant pot, mix the apricots with the sugar and the rest of the ingredients, put the lid on and cook on High for 15 minutes. Release the pressure naturally for 10 minutes, blend the mix using an immersion blender, divide everything into bowls and serve.

Nutrition: calories 158, fat 4, fiber 1, carbs 5, protein 2

Vanilla Cream

Preparation time: 10 minutes Cooking time: 15 minutes Servings: 4

Ingredients:
- 1 cup coconut cream
- 1 cup heavy cream
- 1 teaspoon nutmeg, ground
- 4 tablespoons coconut sugar
- 1 teaspoon vanilla extract

Directions:
In your instant pot, mix the cream with the rest of the ingredients, put the lid on and cook on High for 15 minutes. Release the pressure naturally for 10 minutes, divide the cream into bowls and serve.

Nutrition: calories 152, fat 2, fiber 2, carbs 4, protein 4

Peach Bowls

Preparation time: 10 minutes Cooking time: 15 minutes Servings: 4

Ingredients:
- 4 peaches, cored and cut into chunks
- 1 cup coconut water
- ½ cup raisins
- 1 teaspoon cinnamon powder
- 1 teaspoon vanilla extract

Directions:
In your instant pot, mix the peaches with the coconut water and the rest of the ingredients, put the lid on and cook on High for 15 minutes. Release the pressure naturally for 10 minutes, divide the mix into bowls and serve.

Nutrition: calories 110, fat 1, fiber 2, carbs 4, protein 6

Yogurt Banana Mix

Preparation time: 10 minutes *Cooking time:* 10 minutes *Servings:* 4

Ingredients:
- ½ teaspoon vanilla extract
- 2 eggs, whisked
- 1 cup Greek yogurt
- 2 tablespoons brown sugar
- 1 tablespoon lime juice
- 3 bananas, peeled and mashed
- Cooking spray
- 2 cups water

Directions:
In a bowl, mix the yogurt with the bananas and the rest of the ingredients except the cooking spray and the water, and whisk really well. Grease a ramekin with the cooking spray and pour the banana mix inside. Add the water to the instant pot, add the steamer basket, put the ramekin inside, put the lid on and cook on High for 10 minutes. Release the pressure naturally for 10 minutes, and serve the mix cold.

Nutrition: calories 200, fat 6, fiber 2, carbs 5, protein 6

Zucchini Bread

Preparation time: 10 minutes *Cooking time:* 30 minutes *Servings:* 4

Ingredients:
- 1 cup coconut milk
- 3 zucchinis, grated
- 3 eggs, whisked
- 1 tablespoon vanilla extract
- 2 cups coconut sugar
- 2 cups almonds flour
- ¼ teaspoon baking powder
- 2 cups water
- Cooking spray

Directions:
In a bowl, combine the milk with the zucchinis and the rest of the ingredients except the cooking spray and the water and whisk well. Grease a loaf pan with the cooking spray and pour the bread mix in it. Add the water to the instant pot, add the steamer basket, put the loaf pan inside, put the lid on and cook on High for 30 minutes. Release the pressure naturally for 10 minutes, cool the bread down, slice and serve.

Nutrition: calories 200, fat 5, fiber 2, carbs 5, protein 6

Cream Cheese Strawberry Mix

Preparation time: *10 minutes* **Cooking time:** *20 minutes* **Servings:** *4*

Ingredients:
- 1 cup heavy cream
- 1 cup strawberries, chopped
- ½ cup coconut sugar
- 12 ounces cream cheese, soft
- 2 eggs, whisked
- Cooking spray
- 1 cup water

Directions:
Grease a ramekin with the cooking spray. In a bowl, mix the cream with the berries and the other ingredients except the water, whisk well and pour into the ramekin. Add the water to the instant pot, add the steamer basket, put the ramekin inside, put the lid on and cook on High for 20 minutes. Release the pressure naturally for 10 minutes, and serve the mix cold.

Nutrition: calories 200, fat 4, fiber 2, carbs 6, protein 6

Pineapple Pudding

Preparation time: *10 minutes* **Cooking time:** *20 minutes* **Servings:** *4*

Ingredients:
- 1 cup heavy cream
- ½ cup pineapple, peeled and cubed
- 2 eggs, whisked
- ½ cup coconut sugar
- ½ teaspoon vanilla extract

Directions:
In your instant pot, mix the cream with the pineapple and the other ingredients, whisk, put the lid on and cook on High for 20 minutes. Release the pressure naturally for 10 minutes, divide the pudding into bowls and serve.

Nutrition: calories 162, fat 3, fiber 2, carbs 5, protein 6

Coconut Mango Mix

Preparation time: 10 minutes **Cooking time:** *15 minutes* **Servings:** *4*

Ingredients:
- 3 eggs, whisked
- 2 cups coconut milk
- 1/3 cup brown sugar
- 2 mangoes, peeled and cubed
- ½ cup coconut cream
- 1 tablespoon cinnamon powder
- ½ cup coconut flakes
- 1 teaspoon vanilla extract

Directions:
In your instant pot, mix eggs with the mango and the other ingredients, whisk well, put the lid on and cook on High for 15 minutes. Release the pressure naturally for 10 minutes, divide the mix in bowls and serve.

Nutrition: calories 128, fat 5, fiber 1, carbs 2, protein 6

Cardamom Avocado Pudding

Preparation time: 10 minutes **Cooking time:** *20 minutes* **Servings:** *4*

Ingredients:
- 2 cups avocado, peeled and cubed
- 2 cups coconut cream
- 2 eggs, whisked
- 1/3 cup coconut sugar
- 2 teaspoons vanilla extract
- 2 cups water

Directions:
In a bowl, mix the avocado with the cream and the rest of the ingredients except the water, whisk well and divide the mix into 4 ramekins. Put the water in the instant pot, add the steamer basket, put the ramekins inside, put the lid on and cook on High for 20 minutes. Release the pressure naturally for 10 minutes, cool the mix down and serve.

Nutrition: calories 187, fat 4, fiber 2, carbs 4, protein 6

Cocoa Rice

Preparation time: 10 minutes **Cooking time:** *20 minutes* **Servings:** *4*

Ingredients:
- 2 cups almond milk
- 1 cup white rice
- 3 tablespoons brown sugar
- 1 tablespoon cocoa powder

Directions:
In your instant pot, mix the rice with the milk, sugar and the cocoa powder, whisk, put the lid on and cook on High for 20 minutes. Release the pressure naturally for 10 minutes, stir the pudding, divide into bowls and serve.

Nutrition: calories 200, fat 7, fiber 2, carbs 4, protein 6

Rhubarb and Grapes Stew

Preparation time: 10 minutes **Cooking time:** *15 minutes* **Servings:** *4*

Ingredients:
- 2 cups water
- 1 cup grapes, halved
- 2 cups rhubarb, chopped
- 3 tablespoon brown sugar
- 1 tablespoon lemon juice
- 1 teaspoon vanilla extract

Directions:
In your instant pot, combine the water with the grapes and the other ingredients, toss, put the lid on and cook on High for 15 minutes. Release the pressure naturally for 10 minutes, divide the mix into bowls and serve.

Nutrition: calories 142, fat 2, fiber 2, carbs 4, protein 6

Cashew Cake

Preparation time: 10 minutes **Cooking time:** *40 minutes* **Servings:** *4*

Ingredients:
- 1 cup cashews, chopped
- 1 cup heavy cream
- ¾ cup almond flour
- ½ cup cashew butter, soft
- 1 cup water
- 1 and ½ cups coconut sugar
- ½ teaspoon baking powder
- 3 eggs, whisked

Directions:
In a bowl, combine the cashews with the cream and the other ingredients except the water and whisk really well. Line a cake pan with parchment paper and pour the cake mix in it. Add the water to the instant pot, add the steamer basket, put the cake pan inside, put the lid on and cook on High for 40 minutes. Release the pressure naturally for 10 minutes, cool the cake down, slice and serve.

Nutrition: calories 182, fat 4, fiber 2, carbs 7, protein 5

Fruit Bowls

Preparation time: 10 minutes **Cooking time:** *10 minutes* **Servings:** *4*

Ingredients:
- 1 cup mango, peeled, and cubed
- 1 pineapple, peeled and cubed
- 1 avocado, peeled, pitted and cubed
- 1 cup grapes, halved
- 1 cup heavy cream

Directions:
In your instant pot, combine the mango with the pineapple and the other ingredients, toss, put the lid on and cook on High for 10 minutes. Release the pressure naturally for 10 minutes, cool the mix, divide into bowls and serve.

Nutrition: calories 200, fat 7, fiber 3, carbs 6, protein 7

Conclusion

Cooking with the instant pot is so much fun! This great kitchen tool allows you to cook some amazing dishes with minimum effort and time consumption. The instant pot has gained so much fans all over the world. More and more people decide to purchase and to use such a great appliance.
The cooking guide you discovered now brings to all of you rich, flavored and textured meals made in the instant pot.
The instant pot recipes collection brought to you today will allow you to learn that cooking in the instant pot is so much better than cooking using the traditional pans, pots and cooking methods.

So, let's embark in this great journey and enjoy cooking with the instant pot. Create delightful meals for all your loved ones using one simple and interesting appliance. Have fun cooking with the instant pot!

Made in the USA
San Bernardino, CA
17 March 2020